Acknowledgements

To Jenny, for your continued love and support. My rugby life is full of highs and lows but you remain the one constant.

To Sophie, I hope I can be an exceptional father.

To Mom, for your unconditional love and support throughout the years.

Eddie, I really respect you and aspire to be like you. To Eddie, Ultan and Emmet, for all the happy and fun memories of growing up together. You taught me great lessons that have stood to me in both rugby and life.

To Emer, you are so thoughtful and kind. I am blessed to have you as a sister and a friend.

I would like to thank every coach who has influenced my love for the game throughout my career at Highfield, Christians, Cork Con, Munster, Ireland and the Lions. With a special mention to my club Cork Con, who gave me the opportunity to succeed and progress.

To the strength and conditioning staff who I have worked with, for giving me the tools to apply my profession at the highest level and for always challenging me to improve. Especially Aidan O'Connell and Paul Darbyshire.

For all their help and advice and their friendship, my thanks go to Pat Geraghty and Mick Kearney.

To life-long friends Quaid, Bradley, Tommy, Whitey and Stan – thank you.

And to John Fogarty and Marcus Horan, who are so much more than team mates.

This book would not have been possible without Denis Walsh, who did an amazing job in putting my thoughts and feelings into words. You were a gentleman and a pleasure to work with, and made huge personal sacrifices. Thanks also to Eoin McHugh and the Transworld team for all your help and professionalism.

My thanks must also go to all my team mates throughout my career. The best and worst days of my rugby life have been shared with you. I have been lucky to play with not only gifted players but also great friends.

To all our supporters, who are always there encouraging us in good times and bad. You inspire us to perform beyond our limits. You really are the sixteenth man.

Donncha O'Callaghan was born in Cork in 1979. He began playing rugby at Highfield Rugby Club before going on to play for the Christian Brothers College Cork side, which won the Munster Schools Senior Cup in 1998. In the same year, he played on the Ireland U-19 World Championship winning side, which included other future stars such as Brian O'Driscoll and Paddy Wallace. First capped for Ireland in 2003, he has played more than seventy times for Ireland, forming a formidable second-row partnership with Paul O'Connell. He has won both the Heineken Cup and the Magners League twice with Munster, and has been on two tours with the British and Irish Lions, having the honour of captaining the Lions against the Southern Kings in South Africa in 2009.

Donncha became a UNICEF Ireland Ambassador in 2009. He married his long-time girlfriend, Jenny Harte, in December 2009, and their first child, Sophie, was born in July 2010.

Denis Walsh, who helped Donncha O'Callaghan in the writing of this book, is the chief sportswriter with the Irish edition of the *Sunday Times*. He is a former Sportswriter of the Year in Ireland and winner of the McNammee Award of Gaelic Games writing. His first book, *Hurling: The Revolution Years*, won the Boylesports Irish Sports Book of the Year in 2005, and the autobiography he wrote with Ronan O'Gara won the Irish Sports Book of the Year at the 2009 Irish Book Awards.

JOKING APART

MY AUTOBIOGRAPHY

DONNCHA O'CALLAGHAN

WITH DENIS WALSH

TRANSWORLD IRELAND

TRANSWORLD IRELAND
An imprint of The Random House Group Limited
20 Vauxhall Bridge Road, London SW1V 2SA
www.transworldireland.ie

JOKING APART
A TRANSWORLD IRELAND BOOK: 9781848270978

First published in Great Britain
in 2011 by Transworld Ireland
a division of Transworld Publishers
Transworld Ireland paperback edition published 2012

Addresses for Random House Group Ltd companies outside the UK
can be found at: www.randomhouse.co.uk
The Random House Group Ltd Reg. No. 954009

The Random House Group Limited supports The Forest Stewardship Council
(FSC®), the leading international forest-certification organization. Our books
carrying the FSC label are printed on FSC®-certified paper. FSC is the only
forest-certification scheme endorsed by the leading environmental
organizations, including Greenpeace. Our paper-procurement
policy can be found at www.randomhouse.co.uk/environment

Typeset in 12/15pt Minion by Falcon Oast Graphic Art Ltd.
Printed and bound by CPI Group (UK) Ltd, Croydon CR0 4YY.

2 4 6 8 10 9 7 5 3 1

To my dad

Contents

JOKING APART

Prologue

16 January 2011 – Toulon 32 Munster 16

Sometimes, this is my life.

It was nearly three o'clock in the morning when I turned the front door key and walked quietly into the hall. Jenny and our six-month-old daughter Sophie were sound asleep. For me, sleep was out of the question. In the afternoon our Heineken Cup campaign had come to an end in the south of France. For the first time in my career as a Munster player we had failed to qualify from our pool. Twelve years. Our reputation was built on winning must-win games, time after time. In those situations one team always breaks under pressure. Today, it was us.

I sat down to watch the match. I didn't want to put it off, I wanted to face it. Closing my eyes wasn't going to make the nightmare go away. After thirty-three minutes I was sin-binned. It looked worse on television than it seemed at the time. Their full-back, Rudi Wulf, was chasing a kick from a quick line-out, I blocked his run and caught him high. I couldn't get into position quickly enough to get into his path and make him go around me. Wulf was offside when the ball was kicked but he hadn't been whistled for that and his infringement wasn't going to spare me now. The home crowd were baying for my blood. I tried to argue my case with Dave Pearson, the referee. I pleaded that there was no malice in the hit. I asked him to take a minute. He consulted the touch judge. Yellow card.

I couldn't deny my stupidity. Indiscipline had been a problem for us in the first half of the season and we'd taken a lot of criticism on the issue. For the most part I'd kept my nose clean but in the pivotal game of our year I'd cocked up. In the sin-bin nobody came near me. Normally somebody would come over and say it was a harsh decision or some other fib. The gesture is always worth more than the words. They made me do without it.

I sat there with my thoughts, mortified. My right eye was black and swollen and nearly closed. I'd been hit with a swinging arm by one of their second rows and his thumb lodged in my eye. It felt like somebody had poured boiling water into it. My vision had been blurred for a few minutes, but sitting in the sin-bin everything was clear. Our Heineken Cup campaign was collapsing in plain view. We were ten points down when I left the field and twenty when I returned to the play.

I was replaced with about twenty minutes to go. That killed me. I was desperate to redeem myself. I had plenty left in the tank. I always feel that my fitness gives me an edge in the last ten minutes. I wanted to fight out every point and every minute. Instead I stood on the sideline, helpless. It was hell. The crowd was going crazy, we were being ripped apart, and I was a useless spectator.

In the dressing room afterwards Tony McGahan, our coach, went round to everyone. At half time he'd lost the rag a bit. It's not his style, but this wasn't a normal situation. At half time it hadn't felt like a Munster dressing room should. There was no buzz, no anger. On the field it hadn't felt like a Munster performance. That was our responsibility, the players. During the week we set the game up as something personal. Not just a professional challenge but a test of us as people. Our form hadn't been good so we went digging in our hearts for a performance. Our paranoia about not getting out of the pool had grown over the years. We kept putting ourselves in tight corners and fighting our way out of them, like Indiana Jones. In sport, though, you don't always get the Hollywood ending.

Tony has never let us down. In his time with Munster we've never taken the pitch under-prepared. He looks for perfection every day. In the minds of the players there are big games and smaller games but in his mind every game is an opportunity for perfection. His desire to win is off the scale and his standards make all of us stretch. His working day starts before most of us have opened our eyes and it finishes long after we've stopped thinking about it.

We let him down. A performance like that makes you feel like a fraud. When he came over to me, I apologised. Tony has a strong grip on his emotions but, after that match, there were tears in his eyes. He didn't say much to the group but he called it straight. The way we played, he said, we didn't deserve to get a result. Nobody else really spoke. That wasn't like us either.

Munster supporters had travelled in big numbers as usual. At the airport some of the die-hards came over to sympathise. Somebody said, 'Thanks for everything, we've had great years,' and you're thinking, 'It's not over! We're not finished!' We've been hearing that line too many times over the last while. Some supporters always travel on our chartered flight. I don't know when the tradition started but for years they've been applauding us on to the plane. Some days you don't feel worthy of their loyalty and affection. That day, there was no applause.

In the middle of the night I watched every minute of the match. When it was over I went upstairs to bed and stared at the ceiling. Monday was a day off. Some of the lads were meeting for coffee and a chat in Douglas, a suburb on the southside of Cork city, close to where I live. I couldn't face them. I didn't want to risk meeting a Munster supporter on the street. I'd felt embarrassed meeting them in the airport. After a big defeat, that feeling lasts for days.

Professional sports people all over the world will tell you what their jersey means to them. A lot of them are lying. Some of them will say it about a different jersey next year. With us, it's not like that. To us, the red jersey is like a second skin. Munster's biggest wins have been among the greatest days of our lives; Munster's biggest defeats have been scarring experiences. It only matters if you care. I sometimes think that we're bi-polar as a group. We can't separate our mood from our results.

On Tuesday morning I went to the gym before training. Sometimes I need to flog myself to get over a bad performance. It's part of the recovery process. When I got back to the car there was a missed call from Tony on my phone and a voicemail message. My blood ran cold. He said he wanted to talk to me about selection. I knew that could only mean one thing. I rang him back and he gave me the bad news. I was dropped. Mick O'Driscoll was going to be Paul O'Connell's partner in the second row for the final pool match against London Irish.

It took me years to make a breakthrough with Munster, but once I got in I was basically first choice. Over the course of a season there is a limit on the number of games Irish internationals can play for their provinces, but apart from that forced rotation I had been picked for every important Munster game since 2003. If I was fit I was in. I never took it for granted. I always trained and prepared like I was fighting for my place. That was the mentality that got me there in the first place and, in my mind, it was the only mentality that would keep me there. Playing for Munster was a huge part of my identity. It wasn't just my job, it was part of who I am.

Tony said we could talk about it later.

Before training there was a team meeting and a video session. At the team meeting Tony grabbed hold of us. Our first goal every season is to win the European Cup. That was gone now but the season was only half over and we owed it to everyone to make the second half of the season a success. He spoke about the Magners League and the Amlin Cup and Saturday's match against London Irish and he made it clear to everyone that we were starting again and driving on. There wasn't going to be any moping around or feeling sorry for ourselves. He said we were going to be slaughtered by criticism in the media and elsewhere but we had to be man enough to take it and move on.

Like all of our video review sessions it was frank and harsh. I was in the firing line. The message was clear: there are some penalties that the management were prepared to accept and some that they weren't. My penalty was unacceptable. I couldn't argue with that. In the dressing room after the game I didn't stand up and apologise to everyone for the sin-binning because, to me, 'sorry' didn't cut it. Telling them that I was gutted – what did that matter? My feelings about what happened were beyond words.

Being dropped felt like somebody had put their hand down my throat and ripped my heart out. The rule in Munster is that you can be sour about it for a day if you want but that's it. Not everyone follows that rule but I wasn't going to break it. I could suffer in my own time. I was determined not to go around with a long face. I was determined to train well that day, as if nothing had happened. I didn't want to be a drain on anybody.

My conversation with Tony was brief. He insisted that I hadn't been dropped for my yellow card. He said that against London Irish they needed other line-out options. I pushed him on a couple of points, but when you're dropped you never get any satisfaction from those conversations. At the end of it I wanted to let him know that I respected his call. 'If I play for eighty minutes on Saturday or eighty seconds,' I said, 'you'll get everything out of me.'

Micko and Paulie came up and had a word. Dougie Howlett gave me a high five and said nothing. Nobody knows what to say, people just know that you're hurting. I appreciated that. When I got back to my car after training there were texts on my phone from Marcus Horan and Jerry Flannery, two of my closest friends in rugby. I still have the text from Jerry on my phone. It started with a quote: '"The block of granite which was an obstacle in the pathway of the weak became a stepping stone in the pathway of the strong" – Thomas Carlyle. Honest hard work always wins through. Stay the course and be the best you can be. It always comes right.'

When I got home I let my emotions out. People might think that's strange behaviour for a grown man, and maybe it is, but you have to understand something about us. The success of Munster over the years was built on a lot of things but the most important thing was that people cared. It mattered. There was no other way for us to be a success. People talk about putting your body on the line but that's the least of it. When you give your heart and your soul to something, that's where the hurt comes from.

Training was in Cork that day and the Limerick players were staying over that night. Dinner was arranged for a place in town. Going out for a meal was the last thing I wanted to do but you can't wave the white flag. Marcus started the slagging, the bastard. 'Is it too soon?' he said in the restaurant, knowing that I'd have to put up with it. That's the other thing about us: the slagging is merciless and nothing is off limits.

For the third night in a row I didn't really sleep. Ronan O'Gara wanted to meet for a cup of tea the following day. We've been friends for years too and we're room mates in Ireland camp. I knew he meant well but I just wanted to park the issue until after the match. I didn't want to be the centre of anyone's attention or sympathy. I just wanted to do my work and do what I could to help us win.

On match day I carried on as normal in the dressing room. I didn't speak any less or any more. In the warm-up I didn't know what to do with myself. During the match I tried to be a little bit detached and a little bit involved but after half time the game started going against us and I couldn't sit quietly any longer. I asked Tony to put me on. I didn't really get a response, but two minutes later he called for changes. Shaun Payne, our manager, was doing the paperwork and they said something about waiting for the ball to get out of our half, but I just ignored them and sprinted on.

We were seven points down with ten minutes left and scored three tries to win it. We didn't play well but we kept going and we got away with it. What we did in the last ten minutes was more like us. It wasn't the kind of performance to turn our season around but we won a game that we'd looked like losing. We didn't disgrace the jersey.

Afterwards Tony thanked the bench for having a serious impact on the match. For the first time in my life I cried in a Munster dressing room. Some of our lads would lose it watching a Disney film but I'm not like that. I keep my emotions on an even keel and when you see an expression on my face it's usually a laugh. It wasn't a reaction to what Tony said either, it was a build-up of emotion from the week.

For me, all of this is personal. There's more to me

and my life than rugby, but at the same time all of me is in the jersey: the best of me and the worst of me. That week I felt doubted and distrusted. I couldn't just take off the jersey and walk around as a different person for the week. I can't make that separation.

This is the life I've made. This is the life I love.

1

Marie

I was five when Dad died. Hughie was only forty. It turned our world upside down. You live with the hole in your life without the hole ever being filled. As the youngest in the house my sister Emer and myself were shielded from the impact of Dad's death in the beginning, but there were consequences for all of us. It didn't take long for me to see that. More than anything else my childhood was shaped by Dad's absence, Mom's incredible strength and our togetherness as a family. For my two oldest brothers, Eddie and Ultan, it meant leaving school at fifteen and getting a job. There was no choice. Money was tight and we were a big family. They took on that responsibility. As a family we stuck together. Mom made sure of it.

20 March 1985 – I remember the day clearly. In the morning, after I woke, I went to my parents' bed. On a normal day they would have gotten up by then but the bed would still be warm and I'd snuggle into it for a few minutes. That morning it was cold, like it hadn't been slept in at all. I got up and went down to the kitchen. Aunt Angela was there. Even at that age you can pick up the feeling in a room when something bad has happened.

My dad was a plasterer. After years of working on the sites he had just started a new job with Cork Corporation a few weeks earlier. He was doing a foxer for a friend after work when he got the heart attack. They rushed him to hospital but they couldn't do anything for him. He was a smoker, which didn't help, I suppose. It must have been stressful, too, trying to earn a living in the building trade in the 1980s with five little mouths to feed at home, but I wasn't old enough to notice something like that and I don't ever remember Mom saying it. A job with the council was a bit of stability but he didn't live long enough to get the benefit of that. Mom didn't even get the pension because he needed to be in the job a bit longer.

He drove a Honda 50. Obviously that was a problem for family outings but we all used to take turns to have a day out with Dad on the motorbike. It might only be a spin to The Lough on a Sunday to feed the ducks and the swans but it was the attention, I suppose, the fact that you had Dad to yourself for a few hours. He'd pop in for a pint on the way home and I'd be sitting there with my orange and crisps.

For the summer we used to rent a house in Myrtleville, a seaside place a few miles outside the city. Dad would only have a couple of weeks' holidays but he'd come down every Friday after work to stay for the weekend. I still remember the excitement of him arriving. He always had sweets, and that was the slag: 'Are ye happy to see me or do ye just want the sweets?'

On the morning after he died Mom was very strong for all of us. She explained it to me completely and left me in no doubt that Dad wasn't coming back. I was at an age where they could have spun me a yarn. She understood straight away that this was the best way to handle it. There was no point in giving me false hope. 'Holy God needs your dad now.' The way she put it to me it was as if we were doing Holy God a favour. She left me in no doubt too that everything was going to be all right. I distinctly remember that feeling of reassurance.

Myself and Emer were kept away from the graveyard but we went to the funeral mass. At that age you don't really know what's going on. You don't understand grief. When I saw Mom and my older brothers crying, that's when I got upset. I've never forgotten the smell of incense from the church. Even now it gives me an empty, sickening feeling.

In the weeks that followed there was no shortage of callers to the house. Eventually, though, that stopped.

Then one day I saw Mom bawling her eyes out. It must have been about three months after the funeral and it was as if the whole thing had just hit her in the face. The sight of Mom in that state probably affected me as much as the funeral. It was the only time I saw her grief get on top of her. Whatever pain she was feeling she kept it hidden from us. Being strong for her children was the first thing on her mind.

We used to have these family meetings. Pow-wows, we called them. If somebody wasn't pulling their weight around the house they'd be told, straight out. At the first meeting Mom laid it out for us: 'We're on our own now so we've got to get really tight. Some people will have chips off you because you don't have a father and they'll think you're out of control. That's not going to be the case. We're going to look after each other.' Our behaviour was a big thing with Mom. She always felt that people would dread the thought of the O'Callaghan family arriving for a visit – four wild boys and Emer. The pressure was on us to be extra good.

We couldn't keep that up – not all the time. Stuff happened on the street, like it did with all kids. I remember one day Emmett and Ultan got into a serious scrape. Emmett was teasing a girl who lived a few doors down – calling her names or throwing stones or something stupid like that. She went in and told her dad, so he came out and grabbed Emmett. Ultan was playing ball on the green, saw the commotion, came steaming over and, bang, laid yer man out. Ultan was a big young fella but he was still only about fifteen and the guy he flattened was a grown man. Highly embarrassing for him.

Ultan went in and told Mom what had happened. She went out and tore strips off the neighbour. Then she ripped Ultan to pieces. That was the way it was. Mom would stand up for us against anybody but she wouldn't leave us to get away with anything. Nothing.

I don't know how she managed to keep the show on the road. Years later our next-door neighbour, Mr Mahony, told me what a nightmare we were to live beside. He took huge pride in his garden but we'd be hopping over the wall every two minutes to retrieve a ball, trampling over his plants and flowers. In Mom's house there are still dents in the walls from the rows we had as kids. We were big lads and we used to be hopping off each other.

Emmett probably got into more scrapes than any of us. I was too young to hang around with him but it didn't stop me trying. When he got to fourteen or fifteen I was only nine or ten and it was bad for his image to have a younger brother on the scene. In those days it was cool to wear a Parka jacket and smoke fags, and that's what Emmett did. One day I got thick with him for chasing me away and I showed Mom his secret cigarette stash. Mom went off and bought the strongest cigarettes she could find and made Emmett smoke them non-stop until he got sick. She thought that would cure him of the habit. Emmett, though, took the punishment in his stride, got sick, and smokes to this day.

I was no angel either. One day in primary school one of the lads brought in a deck of playing cards with pictures of naked women on the back. We were at an age where we probably didn't have a clue what we were looking at but we knew enough to know that it was bold. Anyway, we were caught looking at the cards behind one of the prefabs and I was singled out as the ringleader. In this case it was a massive miscarriage of justice but my reputation for devilment went before me. I was brought into the principal's office and Mom was called to the school. I was on the school Gaelic football team and we had a chance of playing in Páirc Uí Chaoimh – a big deal for us. For my punishment, I was dropped. To make things worse, Mom absolutely ate me when we got home. That's what she had to put up with.

Were we happy? Absolutely. I wouldn't want anyone to think that my childhood was hard. It wasn't. We didn't have much but it didn't matter. I know that's a cliché and it's the kind of thing our grandparents used to come out with, but it was true in our house. What we didn't have we did without. When you opened the cupboards in our kitchen you needed sunglasses for all the yellow pack stuff. It was always Flakes of Corn, it was never Cornflakes. If any of the boys in school had Milky Ways in their lunchbox we regarded them as posh. Going on school tours was out of the question. It wasn't even an issue. Our classmates went off on the bus to Fota, or wherever, and we went into a different class for the day. All of that was normal to me.

We didn't lose any privileges when Dad died because they weren't there in the first place. Dad worked very hard to make sure that we had what we needed but little extras didn't come easily. It was Emmett's eleventh birthday the day after he died and Mom gave Emmett a pair of adidas World Cup boots that Dad had bought for him. They were the cool boots at the time but they were expensive. Dad wouldn't have been able to buy them if he hadn't been saving for weeks.

When it came to Christmas time Eddie and Ultan kept myself and Emer under control. Just because we still believed in Santa didn't mean that we were getting away with murder. One Christmas I was looking for something ridiculous – whatever the in-toy was that year – and Eddie pulled me aside. 'You can't get that, it's far too expensive. Mom still has to pay Santa.' The following year I didn't ask for much at all. Mom took us to one of the Santas in town and he asked me what I was getting for Christmas. So I told him, and he said to me, 'Ah, you'll surely get more than that?' I remember thinking, 'I might be able to get a bit more if you'd lower your prices.'

When BMX bikes were the cool thing to have and all my friends were riding around on them, Emmett modified a clapped-out old bike to make it look like one. I knew it wasn't a BMX and my friends knew but I didn't care. We were brought up to appreciate what we had.

A bigger issue for Mom was keeping us fed on a tight budget. To save a few bob she used to do her grocery shopping in town. We'd meet her off the bus at the top of the park and her hands would be raw from carrying all the bags. To make things stretch she did a lot of baking at home but there was no feeding us. I remember once we gobbled up a week's worth of baking in a day: loaves of bread, apple tarts, the lot. Mom didn't get upset very often but she cried that day. She wasn't caught like that again. If she needed to keep a sliced pan to make our sandwiches for school she hid it. It was guerrilla warfare.

Meal times in our house were chaotic. When I first started going out with Jenny she couldn't get over it. Everything was put on the table at the same time – starters, main course, dessert – and you fought for what you could get. It was all elbows and the survival of the fittest. Mom would have worked out that it was the only way to do it.

She devised all kinds of strategies to keep us in check. On Sundays she taught swimming classes at a pool in Churchfield on the northside of the city. From our house in Bishopstown on the southside it was about a two-hour walk. We could have got a bus into town and another bus out to Churchfield but she wanted to wear us out. So she marched us up to the northside and marched us back again. We were in the pool for a couple of hours and on the way home we got a packet of Burger Bites as a treat. The alternative was a day spent playing on the road, tormenting people. Instead, we got home at tea-time flattened, only fit for bed.

I'd say it was the same thinking with our summer holidays in Myrtleville. The day we got out of school we were loaded up and packed off. Mom organised a lift with one of the neighbours and we took half the house with us – pots, pans, duvets, you name it. I used to get a hard time from the others for getting car sick. Myrtleville is only about ten miles away but we might have to pull over three times. I'd still be fine for a 99 when we stopped in Carrigaline though.

We rented a pokey little house from a local farmer. Two of my cousins used to come along so eight of us would be stuffed into it. There was no telly and we didn't miss it. We went out every morning in our shorts, whatever the weather. Mom wouldn't see us again until lunchtime when we'd wolf down a jam sandwich and head off out again, catching crabs or playing ball. The same families went there every year so we had our summer buddies. For young fellas it was paradise.

The United Beach Missions were active on Myrtleville beach but we abused their goodwill. They'd organise beach volleyball or beach soccer with cool nets but when the time came for the Bible stories we made ourselves scarce. They were really nice people but we had a busy schedule.

The one thing that didn't change from our normal

lives in town was my desire to hang around with Emmett. Sometimes he'd send me off to the shop to get me out of the way, and if he was in a good mood he'd let me keep the change. On other occasions he'd pick me up by one leg and dangle me over the wall above Myrtleville beach, threatening to drop me on to the rocks below if I didn't get out of his face. That worked.

Eventually I did fall on to the rocks, but it had nothing to do with Emmett. We were behind Bunny Connellan's pub one Sunday and I wanted the cartoon section from one of the papers. One of the lads wouldn't give it to me and he threw it over the wall. Like a fool I climbed down after it and slipped. I managed to climb back up and I lived with the pain for two days before I told Mom. I knew I shouldn't have been in behind Bunny Connellan's and I definitely knew I shouldn't have been chasing a cartoon supplement down the face of the cliffs. The pain was bad, but the thought of Mom's reaction convinced me to put up with it for a couple of days before I finally came clean.

After Mom chewed the head off me I was brought to hospital and was kept in for three months. I had thrown my hips out of line and I needed daily traction. For the rest of that summer I lay on a hospital bed with weights hanging off my legs. The funny thing is I don't remember being miserable. I was only seven or eight and they probably spun me a yarn that it was cool to be in hospital.

It's only when I look back that I can see how much of

a strain it must have been for Mom to raise five kids on her own. Even something like that – me in hospital in town, the other four kids below in Myrtleville, Mom trying to get up and down without a car in the family. Dealing with bits and pieces of hardship became a way of life for her.

We've all done well in our different careers but Mom is still fiercely independent and self-sufficient. I've been grocery shopping with her from time to time and she's still comparing prices and looking for bargains. Over the years she's loved travelling to Munster's big away matches in the Heineken Cup but she'll only do it if she has the money. If there was a big game coming up she'd take in students to raise a few bob and fund the trip that way. If she couldn't get the money together the last thing she'd want was for me or any of the others to pay for her. She never got anything soft and that's the only life she knows.

During the Celtic Tiger years I lost money in property deals that went sour. I feel angry about the money I lost but I feel more ashamed that I put myself in a position to lose it because we weren't brought up like that. I should have done more research into those projects but I accepted bad advice and pissed away money that I should have minded better. Mom couldn't afford to waste a bob.

Soccer was Dad's game, but he had a passion for all sports. Eddie is ten years older than me and he remembers Dad keeping himself and Ultan up late at night or getting them out of bed early in the morning to watch big sports events on telly. When John Treacy won a silver medal at the Los Angeles Olympics in 1984 the lads saw it live, regardless of the time difference. Emer didn't play much sport but all my brothers did. When he was alive Dad ferried the lads here, there and everywhere to training and matches. After he was gone Mom took up that role as much as she could. She wasn't a big sports fan but she knew how important it was to us and she always encouraged it. She liked the discipline of sport and I think she saw it as another way of trying to keep us on the straight and narrow.

Dad's absence always hit me on the big days in my career. I remember the hug that Brian O'Driscoll's dad Frank gave him after we won the U-19s World Cup, and I remember the embrace between Ryan Jones and his father in a hotel lobby in New Zealand when Ryan was a late call-up on the Lions tour. Ryan's dad was in tears. They wouldn't have shared many moments like that in their lives, but that opportunity was lost to us.

Bishopstown GAA Club and Highfield Rugby Club were close to where we lived. There were plenty of soccer teams around the place too but Emmett was the soccer player in our family. I tried my hand at Gaelic football until I was about fifteen and then I played basketball for a while with Blue Demons, a team on the northside of the city. Being honest, I played them both like a rugby second row. Awkward and dangerous.

I played corner-back in Gaelic football and my buddy Aodhán Bohan played in the other corner. We were ruthless. The ball would go up the field and by the time it came back down the corner forwards would be on the ground. We were so strong at that age we got away with murder.

In basketball it was much stricter. That didn't suit me. For a non-contact sport there's a lot of stuff goes on in basketball, but you have to be cute about it. My job was to win the rebounds and give the ball to Trevor, our best player. He was only about the size of Peter Stringer but he was a point-scoring machine and once he got enough of the ball we had a chance. Other teams, though, would try to rough him up, and there were days when I lost the head a bit. I didn't know the rules of basketball very well but that wasn't the reason why I was fouled out of so many games. I'd have a perplexed look on my face as I walked towards the bench, as if to say, 'What was that for?' The coach was a neighbour of ours from Bishopstown. He always had the answer: 'You punched him!'

The games were in the Parochial Hall, the old heart of Cork basketball. After matches we walked into town to catch a bus home but we got up to all sorts of desperate messing on our way down Shandon Street. The basketball was great craic, and it was good for me because I was quite a podgy teenager. Some of the physical training was savage. We did these things called suicide runs where you had to touch every line on the basketball court. For a big lad like me that was torturous.

I lost touch with the coach, Kieran Foley, but I bumped into him in town years later. He shouted at me across the street.

'I'm glad you made it at the rugby.'

'Thanks a million.'

'Because you were brutal at the basketball, boy.'

Typical Cork.

2

Four Play

Between our house and Highfield Rugby Club there was a short cut through the GAA fields. To get into the rugby grounds, though, you had to scale a high wall, and I couldn't manage it without Ultan hoisting me over. He was the biggest reason why I wanted to be there in the first place. When Ultan was only about seventeen he broke on to the Highfield senior team and they won the Munster Senior League, which was an important competition in those days. I remember the excitement of that match and I remember the thrill of being Ultan's younger brother.

I was born on Ultan's eighth birthday, which at the time wasn't a great thrill for him. Mom tells a story of

Ultan being brought into the hospital to see the new arrival.

'Look what we got you for your birthday, Ultan,' she said. 'A little brother.'

Ultan started bawling his eyes out. 'But I wanted Subbuteo!'

I always looked up to Ultan and as I got older I turned to him a lot for advice. In Dad's absence Ultan and Eddie became more than older brothers. You don't think of it like that at the time but that's how our relationships developed. When I started playing rugby I wanted to be like Ultan, right down to the last detail. Part of his pre-match routine was to clean his boots and get his gear bag ready on Friday nights before *The Late Late Show* came on telly at half nine, and that's what I did as soon as I started playing. I suppose I wanted to join him in his world.

I was big for my age, but I lacked aggression. In the beginning that was a problem. I was still a bit of a mommy's boy. Mom says that I was very clingy to her for a good while after Dad died and I was probably a bit soft by the time I started in Highfield. The coaches didn't give out to me about it until one day I lost the ball in contact in an U-12 match. Pat Morrissey was one of the guys in charge of the team and he said something to me that I'll never forget: 'When we give you the ball the least we expect is that we'll get it back.' That has stuck with me. I was the biggest young fella on the pitch and the other crowd had taken the ball off me. That must have driven the coaches demented. On the Munster and Ireland teams now there are more explosive ball-carriers than me, but the promise I make to myself and the team is that when I take it into contact it will come back on our side.

As young lads we were lucky with the coaches we had in Highfield. Pat Morrissey, Pat Halloran and Ted Stack had a fierce passion for rugby and they gave us that love for the game. They piled us into their cars for away matches and bought us stuff in the shop on the way home. Most of all they gave us their time.

We had a good team too. When Munster played Australia at Musgrave Park in 1992 there was a competition to find two teams for a mini-rugby exhibition at half time. We were beaten in the semi-final and it broke my heart. I still went to the match, and it's my first memory of watching Munster. Australia were the world champions, and on a miserable day Munster beat them with an injury-time drop goal from Jim Galvin. Nobody ever talks about the penalty try Munster scored when the pack pulverised them in the scrum at the Dolphin end of the ground, but I got a great kick out of that. The fancy stuff didn't interest me.

The first time I pulled on the red jersey I was sixteen, playing for the Munster Youths. Like all of my friends I went to the local secondary school, Bishopstown Community, where rugby wasn't played. The inter-provincial youths' championship was for the best club players not in the rugby schools system. Ultan and

Emmett had represented Munster at that level and following in their footsteps was my first big ambition as a rugby player.

Our first match against Ulster was also my debut in Thomond Park. There was only a tiny crowd and no atmosphere but none of that reduced its significance for me. The Heineken Cup had only just started around that time, in the mid-1990s, and the Munster phenomenon hadn't got going yet. The status of wearing the Munster jersey, though, existed long before the crowds and the hype. Being picked was an honour, and in all the years I've worn the jersey that feeling has stayed with me. I never took it for granted. That feeling for the jersey has always been a huge part of my performance.

I don't remember anybody telling me that I was a talented player with a future in the game. As a teenager that thought didn't occur to me – probably with good reason. But I must have done something to get noticed because after the Junior Cert I was approached by Christians and offered a rugby scholarship. The Christian Brothers College (CBC) and the Presentation Brothers College (PBC) are the two big rugby schools in Cork city. It was a fee-paying school so there was no chance I could have gone there unless I was invited. I was old enough to have the final call on a decision like that but I knew Mom wanted me to go and I didn't have to agonise much over what to do.

I spoke to Ultan, Eddie and Emmett about it too, and something Ultan said banished whatever tiny doubt was in my mind.

'Do you know who's coaching Christians?' he said.

'No.'

'Garrett Fitzgerald. Do you know who Garrett Fitzgerald is?'

'No.'

'He coached Munster to beat Australia.'

I knew I'd get a bit of stick from my friends. Around our estate anybody who went to Christians or Pres was labelled 'a posh kid'. For years I was one of the fellas dishing out the slagging. I could cope with that but I was worried about fitting in. I was happy in school, I loved Highfield, I had great friends around the estate, but going to Christians was going to impact on all of that. Were people going to look at me differently? What if it didn't work out? Would it be worse coming back and trying to pick up the pieces of the life I had before?

It seemed to me the only thing I'd have in common with the lads in Christians was rugby. But that was enough. More than enough. It was probably the first time that I realised I was really ambitious about rugby. I wanted to get better, and this was a challenging new environment where I could improve. Our house was only five minutes' walk from Bishopstown Community School but there were days when I was nearly the last boy arriving in class. To get to Christians I had to get up about an hour earlier, but I bounced out of bed every morning. I loved the place.

It was the start of pressure rugby for me. Christians hadn't won the Munster Senior Cup for nine years, which was an eternity for them. I had been signed up on a scholarship and I didn't need to be told that helping to win a Senior Cup was the purpose they had in mind for me. During one of my early matches the other school's supporters started chanting, 'What a waste of money!' The school had picked me out, but the pressure to justify their judgement fell on me.

The big thing in my mind was convincing the other lads in the squad that I was worth my place. At the first training session nobody went out of their way to make me feel welcome. I didn't feel like one of them. A few of them might have felt threatened by a new boy being parachuted into the team. I looked at them and saw a group of lads from a totally different social background. Were they looking at me and thinking the same thing? That thought might never have crossed their minds, but it didn't stop me thinking it.

A row broke the ice. We were doing a gym session one day and I turned on the radio. Dave Soden, one of the senior players on the team, came over and told me to turn it off. I refused, and he tore into me. 'I'm not losing any more Senior Cups over light-hearted bastards like you.' I remember thinking, 'How can he say that? He doesn't even know me.' I didn't back off in the argument and I gained a bit of respect in the dressing room for standing my ground. Dave ended up being my second-row partner in the Cup team that year, and we became good friends.

It didn't take long for them to see how serious I was about rugby. When I was in Bishopstown Community I'd dropped out of French class and at Christians I wasn't forced to take it up again. They said that I couldn't get into University College Cork without sitting a foreign language in my Leaving Cert, but tertiary education was never on my mind and they didn't push me. It meant I had a free forty-minute slot in my timetable that I filled with extra training.

I would go for runs around the Camp field near the school or do a fitness drill that I'd seen in a rugby magazine. The former All Black prop Graham Purvis had started coaching Highfield and Emmett gave me a training programme that Purvis had given them. It had the All Black crest at the top of the page and I thought it was the business. Ultan, though, was careful to manage my enthusiasm. He stopped me from doing weights until I could do fifty press-ups without stopping. I tried every night but it took weeks to reach that target. I was prepared to do anything to get fitter and stronger. Ultan told me once about a famous international player who did three minutes of wall squats three times a day. If he did three I had to do four. That was my outlook.

In Christians, Garrett Fitzgerald copped on fairly quickly that I was liable to do too much training and he tried to put a lid on it. He caught me doing extras a few times when I would have been better off doing less. My attitude back then, though, was the same one that has stayed with me throughout my professional career. I never felt I could depend on whatever ability I had. To survive, I believed I had to work harder and do more. Doing extra sessions gave me a certain amount of reassurance that I was ready. I needed that.

Fitzy's training was so savage, though, that nobody needed to do any more. When we were building up for the Cup campaign he brought us in for Sunday morning sessions and we trained during the Christmas holidays. The school grounds were called Lansdowne, a huge open area, high above the city centre, where there was no shelter from the wind and rain. It was at the top of Patrick's Hill, a climb that wouldn't have been out of place on the Alpine stages of the Tour de France. Fitzy used it for stamina runs. We might have to run up Patrick's Hill twelve times in a session. Fellas would be in a heap, getting sick all over the place. But nobody questioned Fitzy and everybody was afraid to stop.

A great friend of mine, Cian Bradley, was one of our props. He came in one day and informed Fitzy that he had been diagnosed with shin splints and couldn't do the running part of the session. Fitzy wasn't having any of it. 'Shin splints?' He turned to the rest of us. 'Who told Cian Bradley that he had shin splints?' He turned back to Cian. 'Bradley, you're a prop, you can't get shin splints. You have to be fast to get shin splints.' He basically convinced Cian that he was all right and he did the session that day as normal.

I remember talking to him afterwards. 'Cian,' I said, 'the physio told you that you've got shin splints.'

His answer was, 'Garrett told me that I didn't have them.'

If anybody cocked up in training the punishment was a lap of Lansdowne. It happened to me one day. Like every other team we had set plays to get the ball out of our 22. We were practising the drill and the ball came to me instead of Brian O'Mahony, our out-half. Basically, I got in the way. I should have set it up for a quick recycle but instead I panicked and booted the ball away. Fitzy stopped the session and nailed me. All I heard was his bellowing voice: 'What the fuck!'

He sent me for a lap. It was such a big area that a lap normally took five or six minutes but I was so pissed off with myself that I sprinted round. I nearly made myself sick. I was white when I got back to Fitzy.

He looked at me. 'Are you back already? Take another lap.'

The training was tough, but it was brilliant. In schools rugby you're only allowed to gain a metre by putting on a shove in the scrum, but the way we used to hit the scrummaging machines it was like we were preparing to buckle Australia at the Dolphin end like Munster did under Fitzy. Somebody pointed out to him one day that we didn't need to push so hard to gain a metre. That thinking wouldn't have entered his head.

'We'll make sure we get the metre every fecking time.'

He used to be a teacher in Christians but he had left to take a job in the bank by the time I arrived in the school. In the professional era he became involved with Munster again, first as a coach then as the team manager; now he's the chief executive. In later years I had good fun with him, and sometimes at his expense. With Munster nobody was immune from slagging and that gave me a licence to take the piss out of Fitzy that I didn't have in Christians. Obviously we did a bit of unlicensed mickey-taking behind his back in school but we were always petrified that he'd turn round and catch us.

Fitzy was good for me. He lived not far from us in Bishopstown and sometimes he'd give me a lift home after training. From my perspective those journeys were tense. I didn't know what to talk to him about. Small talk wasn't Fitzy's strong suit and I was afraid to say the wrong thing. There were two questions he always asked: 'How's school?' 'Are you improving?' If one of the teachers wanted me to buck up on a subject they'd have a word with Fitzy and he'd raise it with me.

He wasn't the kind of coach that would put his arm around your shoulder. It wasn't in his nature. The Munster Schools team was picked in the first half of the season and I didn't make it. I was devastated. I started to question if I had made the right decision to come to Christians, sacrificing my place with the Munster Youths and the chance of playing for Ireland Youths.

Fitzy called me aside one day to talk about it. I thought we were going to have a heart-to-heart. He asked me was I disappointed, and I said I was. Next thing he killed the subject stone dead. 'It's gone,' he said. 'You have to move on.' The next focus was the Senior Cup, and if that went well I might still get a call-up for Irish Schools. That was it. He wasn't going to let me wallow in self-pity. At the time I thought his approach was insensitive and harsh, but he was right.

Declan Kidney had a say in picking the Munster Schools squad and he told me years later that he was against my selection. He said that I needed more time working with Fitzy. When I heard this my first reaction was fury. I thought to myself, 'Have you any idea how much pain that caused me?' I didn't say it to him but I was hopping mad. When I thought more about it again though, he was probably right.

After a few games I settled into the Christians team and I lost the feeling of being an outsider. Some of the lads on the team became my best friends in school. We trained together in the afternoons and at lunchtime we played pool in a place called the Victoria Sporting Club. There were days when I spent my bus fare in the Vic and walked home after school. Mom would never have known about that. At one stage she suggested getting me a weekly bus ticket to save a few bob but I was dead against it and I persuaded her to leave things as they were. The bus fare was my only discretionary income. It was my entertainment budget.

We weren't supposed to be in the Vic and teachers sometimes raided the place. Normally we'd hide the second we saw them coming but in the couple of weeks before a Cup match we'd brazen it out. It's the same in every rugby school – members of the Senior Cup team have unwritten privileges. It was grand to be in the Vic feeling untouchable.

Around Christmas time a drinking ban was put in place. Half of the team would have been under the legal drinking age, but that didn't mean we were a crowd of teetotallers. The ban was proposed by senior members of the team like Brian O'Mahony and Andrew Mullins and they policed it at weekends, showing up in night-clubs where the lads used to hang out.

It wasn't a problem for me because I didn't drink. I never have. I don't remember having to think about this issue and make a conscious decision. Eddie and Ultan didn't drink; Emmett, though, loved his pints, and see-ing the state of him the morning after a heavy night out probably influenced my outlook. The other thing was that I didn't need a drink to let myself go and have a good time. Other fellas needed it to relax or release their inhibitions. I wasn't like that. I was outgoing by nature and when the messing started I was in the thick of it. I probably started it.

When you don't take a drink you're always open to peer pressure. I was slagged about it in school and the pressure still comes on from time to time. On the night we won the Heineken Cup in 2006 Denis Leamy was on my case. With Munster and Ireland there'll be occasional blow-outs during the season when fellas can let their hair down and somebody will bring it up – 'Go on, have one.'

I promised John Fogarty that if I ever got pissed he'd be there to witness it, but since I made that promise he seems to think it's actually going to happen. In his days as a Munster player – before he finished his career with Leinster – we'd be coming home from somewhere and he'd say to me, 'We can stop off in that off-licence, get a few cans, go back to my place, get pissed and nobody will ever know about it.'

'I've no interest, John.'

'Look, I'm just throwing it out there. Just letting you know, whatever you do I'll be there for you . . .'

The biggest problem for me in my late teens was getting into nightclubs. Even though I was tall and broad I had a babyish face. It wrecked my head because it would ruin your night. I suppose I didn't help myself either because I'd be messing in the queue and the bouncers would think I was locked. I don't know how many times a bouncer told me to go off for a coffee and sober up. The other lads used to get a great kick out of that. None of them ever stayed with me out of sympathy. They carried on, and I made my way home.

During our Cup run after Christmas we changed our Friday night routine because nobody was drinking. We'd go to the cinema and then to an ice-cream parlour in town. That's how serious it was. As that 1996/97 season went on the pressure on me to perform continued to grow, at least in my mind. Nobody said anything but the feeling that I had been signed to deliver the Cup was always there and as far as I was concerned any other outcome would be a personal failure. Part of me knew that was a crazy way to look at it. I was thinking, 'I'm not an out-half, I'm only a second row.' I wasn't even the best player on the team. I didn't contribute to team talks. I wasn't a leader really. I just tried to do my job. I worried, though, that just doing my job wouldn't be enough.

I didn't sleep properly for days before the final against St Munchin's. Everybody was so nervous that Fitzy took us to the beach in Youghal the day before the match, hoping that the sea breeze would relax us. One lad was late for the bus and he was dropped from the squad. It was ruthless, but it wasn't his first offence and those were the standards that had been set for us. Christians were desperate to win and we all felt that pressure.

The match was a panic. Jeremy Staunton, who had a long career as a professional later on, was their star player and he nearly won it on his own for them. We went from 18–0 in front to 20–18 behind and it was the first time that we had trailed in a Cup match that season. I can still remember walking behind the posts after one of their tries and hearing abuse from Pres boys on the terrace who had come to support Munchin's. We got away with it in the end and the relief was unreal.

Jerry Flannery played for Munchin's in that match too, and I knew him by then. Earlier in the season, when they held trial weekends for the Munster Schools team, Cork boys stayed with Limerick families and vice versa. Fla stayed with us and we got on great. In Munster squads over the years he has been a hugely positive influence and his work ethic set a standard for everyone. Even back then you could see that attitude.

During the game, though, I made a ham-fisted attempt at sledging him. I can't even remember what I said but I felt bad about it afterwards and I made a point of apologising to him. I needn't have bothered. Jerry said he couldn't understand a word I was saying. All he could see was my over-sized gum shield moving up and down and foam coming out of my mouth. I never mastered sledging.

The good Cup run with Christians opened the door for me with the Irish Schools team – as Fitzy had said it would. The final trial was at Blackrock in Dublin and I was picked on the Possibles team. The Munster lads travelled together, including Fla. He was so worried about one of the other hookers that he nearly talked himself out of it. He was climbing the walls.

Trials are nerve-racking, though, and everyone has their own troubles. On the train to Dublin Matt Foley from Christians suggested that I should jump at two rather than four. Matt was the person who approached me about going to the school in the first place and I respected his opinion. The four jumper on the

Probables team was a 6ft 8in giant from Terenure who was a good player by all accounts. But I'd never jumped at two in my life. As soon as we got to Dublin I rang Ultan to ask him what I should do. He convinced me on the spot that I could do it.

It might not seem like a big call, but it was a turning point for me. Jumping at two was where I made my career later on, but just as important to me was knowing that I was versatile. If I had to jump elsewhere in the line I could do it. In the scrum I've always been able to swap sides. When I was trying to make my breakthrough with Munster years later, and they were stuck, I played at blindside flanker. All that has stood to me.

Jumping at the front of the line-out went well for me that day. In a trial everybody is watching his own back so when I caught a few balls the hooker started throwing more to me. Every ball I won made him look good too. After a while I was switched to the Probables team and everything was going smoothly until I nearly blew it with a moment of madness.

We were awarded a penalty and their out-half wouldn't give me the ball. Trial games are all quick-taps and trying to look good with the ball in hand but he was stopping us from taking a fast penalty so I hit him a dig, flush on the jaw. The penalty was reversed, which was bad enough, but the full lunacy of what I did wasn't made clear to me until later on. The guy I hit was the son of the coach, Keith Patton. I was in the horrors for days afterwards.

In the end it didn't count against me. I was picked for the opening game against England and the coach's son was left out.

That match was one of the greatest days of my career. I was desperate to make that team. At the time I might not have realised just how desperate. In Munster over the years we have often talked about the value of bitterness and having a chip on our shoulders. I always bought into that outlook and there was a bit of it in my mentality that season. I felt like an outsider in Christians and I overcame that. I always felt that I was less talented than other players and in the Irish trial that was another obstacle I had to cross. I was bitter about not being picked for the Munster Schools team at the start of the season and that drove me on for the rest of the year.

There was a fierce sense of privilege about being involved in the Irish Schools squad. It was the first time that I got a big stash of gear, and every piece of Irish kit was like a status symbol. In the professional game you take something like that for granted but back then it was a massive buzz. It was like a fashion show in my room, trying everything on. You'd wear the tracksuit on the train home after a match or training, hoping that somebody would notice. Over the years I've given away half of my gear because you don't need all of it, but my Irish Schools gear is stored safely in Mom's house.

That first international at Lansdowne Road in April 1997 was a huge occasion for our family. I had this feeling of doing something useful, of giving something back instead of taking all the time. At home I knew I was spoilt. Ultan used to slag me about the dinner arrangements in our house. For the Cup campaign in school they'd brought in a nutritionist and we were all given a diet sheet. I brought it home to Mom and she made me chicken and pasta on demand. At that stage Ultan was playing for Cork Con in the boom period for the All-Ireland League. He might have been facing a match against Shannon at the weekend in front of twelve thousand but he still got a bowl of stew or whatever the others were having while I was eating the meal our nutritionist had recommended.

England brought a huge team to Dublin and they beat us that day. Jonny Wilkinson was playing, and Steve Borthwick and Andrew Sheridan and a few others who went on to represent the senior England side. We had Brian O'Driscoll before he was a superstar. He was a good player and you were glad to have him but he didn't have the same reputation as Ciaran Scally, our scrum-half. Everybody was already talking about him as a future Ireland international and he was capped within a couple of years. It took a little longer for Brian O'Driscoll to turn into Drico. Paddy Wallace was in the squad too. Fla was on the bench.

It's funny the things that stick out in your memory. I couldn't tell you much about the match except that about twenty English schoolboys stripped off and ran bare-arsed across the pitch. The crowd thought it was hilarious and I can think of plenty of situations where that sight would have made me laugh, but that match was such a big deal for me that I could have taken their heads off.

We beat Wales and Scotland in the away games but there was a bit of commotion on one of the trips. One of the lads had a few pints in the team hotel and charged it to his room which meant the IRFU would be picking up the tab. Needless to say, he wasn't going to get away with that. While the investigation was going on it was grand to sit back and watch the drama unfold, completely innocent – for once.

For my last year in Christians I was too old to play in the Senior Cup. That should have given me time to prepare properly for the Leaving Cert, but I didn't see it like that. I never let school get in the way of rugby. Mom did her best to keep on top of it but I managed to get around her more often than not. I ended up failing one subject and passing the rest. I appealed the paper that I failed and the mark was upgraded but I ended up with exactly the kind of results my preparation deserved. As my older brothers had all left school early after Dad died I was the first in our house to sit the Leaving Cert. Straight away the pressure went on to my sister, Emer, who was two years younger than me. 'Look at the mess this ghoul made of his exams! Don't you make the same mistake!'

After schools rugby anybody who's serious about the

game goes back into the club system, and that involved a decision for me. Most of the lads on the Senior Cup team went to Dolphin, but I had no connections there. Highfield wanted me back and that would have been the easy option. Emmett was still playing there and it's where I'd started as a young fella. I knew a lot of people in the club. To make the decision even easier they offered me a signing-on fee. The All-Ireland League was flying at the time and there was some money sloshing around but it was still a crazy offer. Madness. I was only a teenager, still in school. Money was always tight at home so obviously it was very tempting but I had to look beyond the money and think about the future.

The other club that approached me were Cork Con. They were the biggest club in Cork and one of the biggest in the country. By then Ultan was an established member of their team, having transferred from Highfield a couple of years earlier. He wasn't far off being club captain at that stage.

I spoke to Fitzy about it and he cut through all the bullshit. The first thing he said was, forget about the money. 'Where will you develop as a player?' For the following season the Con U-20s were being coached by Michael Bradley and Paul McCarthy, two former inter-nationals. That swung it for me.

During my first year with Con I was called up to sit on the bench for a few All-Ireland League matches. I was too young for it really. A bit innocent. For some of the away games we'd travel on Friday evening for a

Saturday game. I'd arrive at the train station straight from school, still in my uniform and carrying my school bag. The unexpected bonus was that the lads started helping me with my homework. It turned into a bit of craic on the train. Fellas like Conor O'Mahony would help me with my Business Studies homework and after a while I was passing it around. 'Who's handy at Physics?'

On my first away trip I was rooming with Philip Soden. I'd played second row with his brother Dave in school and I knew Philip from calling to the house, but it was still a shock when they didn't put me in with Ultan. Philip was a lot older than me, married with kids. I was a schoolboy. What the hell was I going to talk to him about? So, when we got the keys I went to our room and got straight into bed. It was only about eight o'clock in the evening but I didn't care. I didn't want to be awake when Philip came in. Like a fool I told Ultan all this and he slaughtered me in front of the others. Slagged to death. The Con dressing room was a man's world and it didn't matter that I was a boy.

The big goals for me that year were getting an Academy contract and making the Ireland squad for the U-19s World Cup. I had a fitness test in Dublin for the Academy the day our Leaving Cert results came out. The Leaving Cert wasn't even on my mind. I wasn't concerned about my grades, I was worried about the beep test.

I'd applied for Electrical Engineering in the Cork

Institute of Technology but I didn't have enough points to get in. Looking through the list of courses available to me I could have done Fish Farming in Mayo. I guess that didn't suit. In the end I opted for a Marketing course in the School of Commerce.

But the only thing in my head was rugby. In April of that year, 1998, I'd made the Ireland U-19s World Cup squad while I was still in Christians. Declan Kidney was the coach. It was the start of a relationship that was going to shape my career in many different ways.

3

Raw

I didn't know Declan Kidney back then the way I know him now. I didn't know what to expect. None of us did. That gave Deccie an advantage he wasn't going to waste. As a talented group of teenagers, Deccie's first priority was to put us on the back foot. He probably knew how good we were and I suppose we had a fair idea. As far as Deccie was concerned, though, that's as much as we needed to know.

It had all started at the end of February 1998 with a warm-up match against Spain. We won 63–0 and left the field full of ourselves. In the dressing room Deccie ate the head off us. All he talked about was dropped chances. I left the dressing room thinking that we had played desperate. Exactly what he wanted.

The tournament was in France about six weeks later and our opening game was against the USA. Before the team was announced he told a few of us privately that we weren't in the starting fifteen. I was one, Brian O'Driscoll was another, and there were more – a handful of players who thought they were guaranteed their place. He broke the news in a way that didn't make you feel you were being rested for bigger challenges ahead. It was deadpan: 'I haven't got a place for you in this game.'

Many years later he employed the same tactic before the 2008 Heineken Cup final with Munster when myself, Denis Leamy and Marcus Horan were in the firing line. When Ireland won the Grand Slam in the following year he dropped four players for our second last match against Scotland. None of them deserved to be left out but Deccie was working on the same principle: insecurity creates an edge.

When he did it to me as an established Munster player I was furious, upset, confused, driven to distraction. As an Ireland U-19, though, I went on to the training field fighting for my life. That's what he wanted.

For the tournament we stayed in a one-horse town in the south of France that seemed to be miles from anywhere. The only places to visit in the town centre were a Champion Sports shop and a big furniture place. In those circumstances we were forced to make our own fun. We turned the furniture shop into a playground where we had games of hide and seek. There would be a dozen of us in there, hiding behind sofas, standing in wardrobes. The woman who ran the place used to be freaking. She'd hunt us out of there but we kept going back.

Cooped up in camp, we started behaving like big children. On most of our trips to the town centre all we bought were sweets, but one day we decided to buy a team pet. A rabbit. In the sit-com *Father Ted* there was a famous scene where Father Dougal bought a rabbit and called him Sampras. That was our inspiration. To be honest, though, we didn't think it through. We forgot to buy a cage or food. I guess we weren't ready to foster a little furry animal. When we brought Sampras on to the team bus Deccie lost the head completely. Anybody who had been in contact with the rabbit had to report to the team doctor in case we needed an injection and we were ordered to bring him back to the shop. So we swapped him for a goldfish. That worked out a lot better. We kept our fish in a jug and brought him everywhere with us, like a mascot.

When I think back, we really tested Deccie's patience. After we arrived in France the forwards decided that we'd get our heads shaved. I suppose you'd call it a bonding thing. I'll never forget the look of horror on Deccie's face when we turned up for training the next morning. 'Why did ye do this?' One of the lads said we thought it would be cool. That was probably the wrong answer, but in this situation I don't think there was a right answer. Deccie was disgusted at the sight of us. I'd say he thought we looked like a crowd of gougers. It was so hot, too, that I think he was worried about us getting sun burn on our exposed heads.

But if he was concerned about that he wasn't long getting over it. At the end of training the forwards were kept back for thirty minutes of extra running in the baking heat. Torture. Deccie was roaring at us: 'Who are the hard men now?' He was really pissed off. What we did was daft but it did bring us closer together. We had made a statement by shaving our heads and it got us into trouble. After all that we had to back it up on the pitch.

My chance came against South Africa in the quarter-final. All the players who were shocked to be left out against the USA were back in the team. For the first half, though, it didn't seem as if it was going to make any difference. South Africa went 17–0 in front and at half time Deccie let rip. It was a great speech. We were showing them far too much respect just because they were the Springboks and Ireland teams didn't beat the Springboks. We went out in the second half and tore into them. It finished 17–17 and after that it went to a penalty shoot-out. In rugby, it's a ridiculous way to decide a match. The penalties are taken from directly in front of the posts, 22 metres out, and it looks like the easiest thing in the world but more than half the players on a rugby team never kick the ball in a match and only one or two ever kick it off the pitch.

Drico was our place kicker and in the shoot-out he missed. Like a soccer team we lined up on the halfway line with our arms around each other's shoulders in a display of solidarity. It was a fake. When Drico missed we slaughtered him. The slagging started immediately. The opportunity was too good to pass up. 'Drico, what the fuck? You were right in front of the posts!'

When it looked like the shoot-out was going to end in stalemate Deccie started looking for volunteers for the sudden-death kicks. Myself and the other second row Damien Broughal both volunteered and he ignored us. He asked the question again. 'Who'll take a penalty if it goes to sudden death?' We volunteered again; he ignored us again. He was probably right, I probably would have hit the corner flag, but that prospect didn't put me off. I was one of the ghouls who thought it looked easy.

Anyway, we lost. We weren't going home straight away because there were play-offs to determine exactly where each team finished in the competition. It was something to do with seedings for the next World Cup. A day or two after the match, though, we heard that the IRFU were lodging an appeal. The South Africans had used their reserve out-half in the shoot-out even though he hadn't appeared in the match. The appeal was upheld and we were awarded the game. Deccie came into the team room to tell us the good news and warned us not to celebrate or lose the run of ourselves. As soon as he walked out we were jumping around the place.

We destroyed Argentina in the next game, 18–3, and qualified to meet France in the final. All of a sudden we started to get a bit of attention. Photographers showed up for our final training session, stuff we wouldn't have been used to. For some reason New Zealand, Australia and England didn't take part, which obviously devalued the competition, but around that time there was nothing much going on in Irish rugby and we were a good-news story. Toulouse was a brilliant venue for the final, a big stadium where France played some of their Test matches, and it was live on French TV. For all of us this was the biggest game of our lives.

There were only four days between the semi-final and the final and a good few of the parents arrived. Mom travelled too. We'd only been away for a couple of weeks but fellas were already missing the little comforts of home. The moms were arriving with bars of Cadbury's chocolate and bottles of Chef tomato sauce. We were so thrilled you'd swear we'd been marooned on a desert island.

France were hot favourites and one of the local papers didn't spare us in their preview. We had a team meeting on the morning of the final and Deccie produced a cutting from the newspaper with an English translation written in the space between the lines. We were sitting in a circle in the team room and each of us was given a copy of the article. The headline was something like 'France Guaranteed Victory'. Kieran Campbell was our scrum-half, a really good player who was with London Irish at the time and played for Ulster later on. He took one look at it, rolled it up into a ball and threw it on the ground in the middle of the circle. None of us said anything but we were all thinking the same thing: 'He's dead for doing that.'

'Kieran, I want you to read that,' Deccie said to him.

'It's bullshit, Deccie. I'm not looking at it.'

Silently, all of us were cheering. Playing in front of a strong scrum-half is really important for any pack but especially at that age. On the pitch he bossed us around, and we needed that. Kieran's reaction to the article fired us up more than anything that had appeared in print. We went out and blew them away, 18–0.

We came home to a hero's welcome. In Dublin airport we were greeted by television cameras and supporters; we were on the front pages of the newspapers; Deccie read out a letter of congratulations from President Mary McAleese. Back home in Cork I did my first interviews in the local media. I was still in school, a few weeks away from doing my Leaving Cert. It was mad. For a couple of days we felt like mini-celebrities.

For me, that feeling lasted until I met my great friend John Fogarty: 'No New Zealand, no Australia, no England. Christ, boy, you'd want to put away that medal, don't be embarrassing yourself.'

Welcome home.

Leaving school is a crossroads in everyone's life. I knew I wanted to be a professional rugby player. What I also knew was that I didn't want to work on building sites. Emmett was a plasterer, just like Dad had been. He worked for himself, and from about the age of fourteen I worked for him during the summer holidays. It was hellish.

The hours were seven in the morning to seven in the evening for £40 a week, including Saturdays. Being the boss's brother only made things harder for me. At one stage I earned enough money to buy a new bike. Emmett tried to claim that he'd bought me the bike because he paid my wages. I wasn't going to allow him to take the credit for that. I earned the money, it was my money, I bought the bike. His answer was to make me cycle to the building sites from then on. We were living in the same house but I had to leave for work half an hour before him. He'd pass me in the van, beeping the horn as he went by.

There were plenty of laughs, but what I remember most is the hardship. It was all little things. Emmett was going out with a girl one of those summers and we were doing a job for her dad. At lunchtime Emmett's girl-friend would arrive with sandwiches. There was enough to feed an army, but as far as Emmett was concerned that was his lunch and if he was going to provide lunch as well as work for me it would have to come out of my wages.

On another job he screwed me in a different way on the eating arrangements. A few lads who had worked with Dad years earlier were on the site too and Emmett roped them in on the act. The line was that labourers never ate with tradesmen. That was the case in my father's time, they told me, and it should never be allowed. So, I was asked to leave their company during lunch break. I was so naive I did what I was told every day for as long as we were on that job. When I tried to take the paper with me they stopped that as well.

When I think back, it was good preparation for a life in the Munster dressing room because every weakness was exploited. It was ruthless. When I let it slip that I was afraid of heights they had me running up ladders day and night. There was no relief. If I had nothing to do, Emmett would make something up. One day he told me to carry bags of cement downstairs. I tried to tell him that there was no need to move the cement but I was never going to win that argument. As soon as I shifted the cement he was laughing his head off. I ended up having to lug them back upstairs.

The other job that broke my heart was doing the shop run. As the boy on site I had no choice. On the shopping list were packets of cigarettes, newspapers, pies, sweets, you name it. Everybody knew how much they gave me and, more importantly, they knew exactly how much change they were owed. Keeping track of all that was a nightmare.

I laugh about those days now, looking back, but I hated it at the time. There were days when I absolutely hated Emmett and I wouldn't talk to him. But he'd get a kick out of that as well. I couldn't win.

You'd think my summer experiences with Emmett would have made me work harder in school and, I suppose, that would have been the sensible thing to do. Of all the jobs on the sites, electrician was the only trade that appealed to me a little bit. It was clean and there was no heavy lifting. But apart from that Electrical Engineering application to CIT I never did anything about it. I had no interest in the Marketing course I enrolled on after Christians at the School of Commerce but I had to be seen to be doing something. The reality is that I did nothing. I never went to class and at the end of the year I didn't sit my exams.

I was, however, accepted into the IRFU's Academy, and the fitness programme we were given was my curriculum for the year. John Fogarty was in a similar position to me. He was on a development contract with Munster which gave him time to study if he wanted to. Instead, we became training partners. We went to the gym together and then we'd cycle out to Cork Con to do ball work. We'd pick up drills from various sources and copy what the Munster players were doing.

The Academy contract was only worth about three grand a year. Even for a student living at home it was tight, but in my mind I had made a leap into full-time rugby. Nowadays the provinces have their own academies and the players are closely supervised in their training, but back then you were given a programme and expected to follow it. We only met up about four times a year when we were assessed and given coaching clinics. Nobody needed to stand over me though. I did everything they asked and more.

The only thing I requested of them was a Swiss ball. I had poor shoulder flexibility and a physio recommended that I needed to do special exercises. I asked Steve Aboud, who was head of the Academy, and he put me through the ringer before he agreed to get me one. I was nearly begging in the end. When I finally got the Swiss ball I nearly wore it out.

I wouldn't turn twenty until March of that 1998/99 season, but by then I had already been given a sniff of the big time. In the summer of 1998 Munster had a short summer tour of Wales and I was picked to go with them. For me it represented a week of full-time training and I loved the thought of that. Ultan had been on these pre-season camps before where they absolutely slaughtered them. Because they were professionals now the feeling was that they should be made to train like lunatics. They were trying to do in a day what the current Munster squad would do in a week. There was no rest built into the programme. It was all about quantity rather than quality.

I was so mad for training, though, that I was thrilled to be in the camp. We stayed in a hotel near the Millennium Stadium in Cardiff and we had to jog about two miles along the river to the training field. Nowadays we'd be up in arms, wondering why there wasn't a bus to take us there, but I thought this was brilliant.

Ultan was an established Munster player at the time and the prospect of playing with him was a big deal for me. A friendly against Llanelli was the main focus of the trip but we also played a mid-week game against a small Cardiff club called Rumney. It didn't count as an official Munster cap but that was my first appearance for the senior team. We beat them 57–0, but I treated it like a World Cup final.

A few weeks later, at the end of August, I won my first Munster cap in a friendly against Edinburgh Reivers at Musgrave Park. My biggest memory of the game is being cleaned out at a re-start and rolling around on the ground like a soccer player. The guy had taken my legs but I wasn't that badly hurt. Ultan came on as a sub in the second half, lined yer man up and nailed him. Once he got hold of him he drove him back and gave him a few clips into the bargain. Flattering myself, I believed he had done this to take revenge for what had been done to his kid brother. When I said it to Ultan afterwards he blew me out of the water. He said the thought never crossed his mind.

In any case, I thought I was bulletproof. I loved the status that I thought I'd been given. A Munster player at nineteen. A gang of my friends came to the match in Musgrave Park, we won, and I played for the full eighty minutes. In my mind I was on my way.

The next match was a mid-week game against Ulster in Ravenhill where we hadn't won for twenty years. The Christians' Graduation Ball was on that Monday night but all the Munster forwards had to report for a session in Limerick on Tuesday morning. I could have travelled first thing in the morning. I wasn't going to be hung over and I definitely wouldn't have stayed up all night. But Deccie insisted that I stay with our forwards coach Niall O'Donovan in Limerick on Monday night. He allowed me to show my face at the Grads but I had to be gone by a certain time, like Cinderella. I didn't have a girlfriend but a lovely girl called Hazel O'Callaghan agreed to be my escort. I had to explain to her that I wouldn't be able to hang around. It must have been weird for her but she was incredibly sound about it. At the appointed time our hooker Frankie Sheahan pulled up at the Silversprings Hotel in his Micra and carted me off to Limerick. It was probably a little test from Deccie too: 'You're a professional now, you need to start acting like a professional.'

Behaving like professionals at all times, though, was something that Munster players were still coming to terms with. Ulster won the match and we stayed over in Belfast that night. The lads went on the tear and started acting the maggot. One of the things that the players had requested was a carbohydrate supplement for their drinks. It came in powder form, and a supply of it was left in the team room at the hotel. Once the lads got drunk, though, the supplement was thrown all over the place. Our out-half Mick Lynch went to bed before some of the others and when he woke up the following morning he was plastered in the stuff. We were all given dress shirts that had a little fabric hook stitched to the back and that became the other party game that night, trying to flick off the hooks without wrecking the shirt. The odds of doing it sober were slim enough; drunk, it was impossible. The shirts were destroyed.

Jerry Holland was the Munster manager at the time and the following morning he tore strips off us. This was a million miles from the attitude and the standards that made us successful in later years, but in those days some elements of the amateur game were still part of our mentality. After a match you went on the tear because that's the way it always was. In the early years of the professional era Wednesday was usually a day off, which presented another opportunity for a drinking session. Munster didn't have that many games in a season which meant that you played for your club in the All-Ireland League at every reasonable opportunity but an AIL game on a Saturday didn't stop the lads from letting their hair down on a Wednesday. As a new boy on the scene I went along. For me it was part of fitting in. I enjoyed it for what it was. Some of the lads were better fun when they were drunk. When they got messy, I went home.

I had my own run-in with Jerry early that season. When I left school I bleached my hair. Silver. I loved it. My mother hated it. She gave me a belt as soon as I got in the door and then she wanted to know if any of the neighbours had seen me. Once I'd ridden out that storm, though, I thought I was in the clear. It was the week of a Munster A match and I was still new on the scene. I showed up for the game and straight away Jerry nailed me.

'What are you doing here?'

'Mr Kidney told me to come down for the A match?'

'That's fair enough, but not with that hair.'

I laughed, a bit nervously, thinking and hoping that it was a joke. It wasn't.

'John Hayes has clippers upstairs. Go and get rid of it.'

So I did. I shaved off my hair on the spot. He probably thought I looked like a punk, and for a Munster rugby player that image wasn't encouraged. I fell back into line.

The Ulster match in Belfast turned out to be another part of my education. I came on as a sub and got involved in a bit of shoeing. The Clohessy brothers, Peter and Dessie, led the charge and I followed them in. An Ulster player was lying on the wrong side and they were tearing the shirt off his back. A couple of days later Deccie called me over to his house. He had a video of the match and he highlighted the shoeing incident. He put it to me straight: 'As long as I'm coaching you I never want to see you doing something like that again.' It didn't matter that I was following the example of a couple of senior players – Peter Clohessy was an international and one of Munster's biggest names. From Deccie's point of view I needed to set my own standards. For a teenager it was a brilliant lesson. He probably knew he couldn't change the others at that stage of their careers, but I was only starting off.

The next lesson, though, was delivered in public and was much harder to take. Early in October Munster played Perpignan away in the Heineken Cup and I was picked in the squad. Six minutes before half time I came on as a sub for Mick O'Driscoll, who had picked up a knock. Twenty minutes into the second half Deccie took me off. The embarrassment nearly killed me.

They murdered us 41–24 and scored six tries in the process. I was creamed for one of them. Their big number eight was running towards our line and I launched myself at him, thinking I was going to blow him into the crowd. I landed in a heap and yer man didn't even know he'd been hit. He went right over the top of me. If I was faced with the same tackle now I'd be hopeful of cutting him in two, but then, in terms of my physique, I was massively underdeveloped.

We gathered under the posts for the conversion and I tried to think like a professional. 'There's nothing you can do about it now,' I said to myself. 'Forget about it and carry on.' Deccie, though, had a different view. He probably thought my head would be fried by what happened. When my number flashed up on the board I had to look twice. 'It can't be number eighteen . . .'

Deccie knew straight away that it was a rough call on a young player. As soon as I came off he apologised. 'What do you mean?' I said. His only answer was to apologise again.

When the game was over, Deccie called myself and Mick O'Driscoll over to the side of the pitch. Micko was only six months older than me and this was just his second appearance in the Heineken Cup. Being substituted before half time was easier for him to handle because he got injured. Deccie made us look around the ground. 'Don't let this happen to you again,' he said to both of us. He wasn't really making sense because in my head I was thinking, 'You're the one that took me off and made me look like a ghoul. There was no shame in the tackle, there was shame in being taken off.' Then he said, 'Now you know what you've got to do.'

And to be honest, I didn't. The game was barely over, my head was still spinning, I was pissed off and confused. I hadn't analysed the whole thing and worked out what it meant for me. I needed Deccie to spell it out.

'What are you on about, Deccie?' I said.

'You need to work on your upper body.'

It was an obvious thing to say, and he was dead right. When I look at pictures of me from around that time I had no chest. I was nearly inverted. It would take me nearly two minutes to recover properly from a full-on scrum. There were a lot of other things that I needed to do but I hung on those words from Deccie for the rest of the season. That was my mission. I went from being able to bench-press 105kg to over 130kg in the space of a few months. It was a simplistic solution but at least it gave me a focus. The reality is that I wasn't ready for that level of rugby. I wasn't strong enough and I was also raw and green. Micko would have been the most mature twenty-year-old you ever met but I had a fair bit of growing up to do.

Munster reached the quarter-final of the Heineken Cup for the first time that season but I was out of the picture after Perpignan. It would be nearly a year before I played for Munster again.

I spent most of that season with Cork Con. I wasn't a regular in the first team but I was given my share of game time. The All-Ireland League was strong in those days and coping at that level was a more realistic stretch for me than playing for Munster. There was also a few bob flying around and I needed whatever money I could get my hands on because, basically, I was broke.

I tried to pull a scam with the club raffle. I'd take a book of tickets from behind the counter in the clubhouse bar and start selling them. The people buying the tickets thought they were putting money into the club's coffers. The reality was that I was pocketing half the money and giving out the other half as first prize. I pulled in about £30 a week for a month until I was rumbled. For my punishment I was forced to sell a book of club raffle tickets, above board, for the rest of the season. After home games on a Saturday I had to go around the clubhouse to make sure that everyone was in the draw. Murder.

I was taught another lesson in Con that season that has probably stood to me for life. Money was the issue starting out, but it wasn't really about that in the end. In Con the senior players were paid £200 if they won and nothing if they lost. At the start of the season I didn't think I would be in the senior squad every week and I definitely wasn't sure we would win every match. I needed a more secure income, so Ultan said I should speak to the manager, Bobby Kahn, and see if we could come to an arrangement. The deal we reached was that he would give me £50 after training every Thursday night regardless of whether I was in the squad for the weekend but I'd forfeit the £200 if we won.

I was happy with the arrangement, and I thought I was the smartest boy in Cork when Con made a bad start to the season and we were losing more games than we were winning. The lads were getting nothing and I was picking up £50 every Thursday night. Another defeat against Garryowen in Dooradoyle, though, was the turning point in our year. I remember David Corkery going around the dressing room afterwards saying that this was the last game we were going to lose and we were going to win the league from here.

His words came true. We went on a massive winning run and all of a sudden I was badly out of pocket. On Ultan's advice I tried to renegotiate the deal. Bobby's a nice man and I appealed to his better nature.

'Bobby,' I said, 'I got it wrong. Any chance I could go back on the win bonus?'

'Donncha,' he said, 'I'm going to teach you a valuable lesson today. Always back your ability and always back your team mates.'

I was stuck with the original deal.

In some ways I was making good strides for a teenager, in other ways my behaviour was daft. As well as being a regular in the Munster squad, Ultan was the captain in Con and he looked out for me in every way he could. I had unbelievable respect for him but I didn't always show it. Training in Con was hard and competitive. There were mini-games between the forwards where Packie Derham was the referee and he would leave an awful lot go. It was primitive-man stuff. The ball would be thrown up between the senior pack and the junior pack and we had to fight for it in a small area marked out by four cones. I could go in offside and cause havoc without Packie blowing the whistle. Ultan would pull me up afterwards, trying to help me. Discipline was an issue in my game and he felt I needed to know when I had committed a penalty. In the heat of the moment, and being a competitive bastard, I might tell him to fuck off. It was the wrong reaction but Ultan used to cut me a fair bit of slack.

One night, though, I went too far and I hopped the ball off his head. I knew straight away that I had cocked up. I looked around at all the other forwards and their faces had dropped. In those mini-games we used to knock lumps out of each other but I had crossed a different line. I had been disrespectful to the captain.

Being Ultan's younger brother bought me a bit of credit in Con but suddenly all bets were off. When the game resumed they kicked the shit out of me.

I also overstepped the mark in a match against Lansdowne. Liam Toland was playing for them and at one stage I tried to split him in two. Tempers flared and I lost the run of myself. Toland had started his inter-provincial career with Munster and had played with Ultan in the back row but he had changed his allegiance and he was a Leinster player at this stage. Ultan and Liam were friends, but I put that to one side. I started mouthing at Liam, telling him that he should have stayed with Munster and fought for his place. I may as well have told him that he'd run away from the challenge. Same thing. Ultan was mortified. In the club-house afterwards Ultan made me apologise. It was one of the most embarrassing things I ever had to do, but Liam was brilliant about it. Ultan was dead right and I was dead wrong.

Just like with Munster there was a lively social scene with Con. After matches there was a circuit of pubs we used to visit. We always ended up in The Office, which was owned by Micko's brother Johno, a legend in Con and an incredible clubman. The craic in there was out-rageous at times. One night we were stage-diving off the bar top, like a heavy metal band. The lads would catch you, pass you along overhead and spin you out at the end. It had run its course, though, by the time one of the back-room lads climbed up on the bar. He hadn't read the signs. When he jumped nobody caught him. All we heard was a splat as he landed face down on the floor. The messing that goes on in rugby can be cruel. We all really liked this guy but nobody showed him an ounce of sympathy. He crawled out the door, hailed a taxi and went to the hospital to get stitched. It was indefensible behaviour. Did we feel guilty at the time? Not a chance.

The All-Ireland League final that season, against Garryowen, was played in Lansdowne Road and I came on with fifteen minutes left. The match finished in a draw and went to extra time. The lads were out on their feet. I was delighted. More game time. At least I gave them value for their £50.

4
Mad Young Fella

Over the years people have often asked me about Mick Galwey – Gaillimh. Most of the time I told them what they wanted to hear. Most of it was true. When I first joined the Munster squad and for a couple of years afterwards he was our captain. There was no shortage of leaders in our dressing room but he was an inspirational figure. Before big matches his speeches always worked. If you put the same words in another player's mouth they wouldn't have had the same effect. Nothing that Gaillimh said ever sounded false. He would get emotional because he had a genuine feeling for the jersey and the team. Everyone respected that and could connect with it. On the field he backed it up. When it came to Munster, he had an X factor.

In lots of ways he was typical of us. He had been given a raw deal by different Ireland managements over the years and that struck a chord with other players in our dressing room who had been dropped or overlooked by the national set-up at various times. He had a chip on his shoulder, too, which we all believed was the best Munster mentality. He was also at the centre of the craic. Like many others in that dressing room his career had started in the amateur days of play hard and party hard. When the game turned professional Gaillimh didn't leave the amateur game behind completely. In that line of thinking he wasn't short of support.

In every respect Peter Clohessy – the Claw – was his closest ally. I remember one pre-season bonding weekend when I was included in a group with Gaillimh and Claw. We were sent off orienteering and had to find various clues in the woods, one clue leading to the next one. Halfway through this exercise Claw and Gaillimh got sick of it. 'Who thought we'd enjoy this shit?' was their attitude. So they took us down to the pub. While the rest of the squad were chasing around the woods the boys were having a couple of pints. I didn't know what to do. I was only a young fella and I was new to this scene. I was afraid that we'd be killed when we got back to base but I was even more afraid of walking out on Claw and Gaillimh. In the end we basically got away with it. Because of their status nobody was going to hammer Gaillimh and Claw for ducking out of the orienteering.

People assumed that because he was the Munster number four before me I learned my trade from Gaillimh. It wasn't like that. I respected him, I liked him and I learned a certain amount from watching him, but he didn't go out of his way to look after me or bring me along. At training sessions I'd be dying to get in for some of the line-outs and scrums and run-throughs but he basically shut me out. I'd ask and he'd say, 'Next one.' It was always the next one. Marcus Horan was trying to break through around the same time and it was the complete opposite with him. Marcus did most of the training and then Claw would rock up and play the matches.

It probably meant that I didn't have the same relationship with Gaillimh as many of the others. Apart from the fact that I was much younger and I wasn't a drinker, Gaillimh was wearing the jersey that I desperately wanted. I was champing at the bit to get on and he was standing in my way. I couldn't pretend to be his best mate or his biggest admirer when there were days when I wanted to put him through the wall. I wouldn't be false like that with anybody. The competitive streak in me dictated my relationship with Gaillimh to a certain extent.

A few years ago I said some of this stuff in an interview with the *Sunday Times*. Anthony Foley called me to say that Gaillimh was upset and that I should give him a call. So I rang him and we had a chat about it. We never spoke about it while it was going on, although he must have known that I was frustrated. I was sorry that he was upset and people were probably thinking, 'Why has he bothered to say it in public?' Gaillimh is regarded as a Munster legend and people were used to hearing only good things about him. But everything I said in that interview was true. Gaillimh wasn't trying to bring me along, he was trying to hang on to the jersey.

In the end, it was the biggest lesson he taught me. I have the same attitude now. At Munster training there are young lads who are desperate to be tagged in for line-outs but I make them wait and suffer – exactly as I had to do. The Munster jersey is a precious thing. You have to earn it and you have to prove yourself. And keep proving yourself. When they get their chance they'll carry a certain bitterness about the way they were treated and, as Munster players, that bitterness will stand to them.

Ken Murphy, our other second row in Con, was the guy who helped me most when I was trying to get on. My nuts-and-bolts education in second-row play came from him. He would stay on after a training session and show me different binds for scrums or go through a pattern or show me how to 'chew the top off a ball' – a vital technique for jumping at the front. He didn't need to do any of that but he was a generous fella and I never forgot the kindness he showed me.

I think he also knew that I was mad keen to learn. I was always looking out for new training drills and I'd run them past him. The Australian John Eales was the best second row in the world at the time and I remember hearing that he used to practise jumping with weights tied to his ankles. So I bought the weights and began doing the drills. The physios would probably tell you now that something like that is bad for your back and your knees, but at the time I was looking for any edge I could find.

For the 1999/2000 season there was a direct Australian influence in the Munster second row. John Langford arrived from the ACT Brumbies and brought a lot of good things with him. He had different calls and different movement and he basically ran our line-out. His impact was so strong that a lot of Langford's calls were used for years after he left. What he brought most of all was professionalism. We were still trying to learn good habits that had been common practice in Australia for years. It was a whole load of little things that we wouldn't think twice about now but were impressive at the time. Like, Langford used to apply ice to his ankles after every match. They would get a little swollen during a game and he had a routine to manage the problem. Something like that wouldn't have occurred to the rest of us.

He was a serious athlete too. One of the things we used to do in pre-season was a 3km run. I would have fancied myself to record one of the better times, especially among the forwards, but he blew me away. I busted a gut to run eleven minutes something and he did it in a little over ten minutes.

In theory, the arrival of a top-class second row reduced my chances of getting a game, but in reality it had more of an effect on Micko. If they were only going to name one specialist second row on the bench there was more chance of Langford lasting eighty minutes than Gaillimh and I was the natural cover for Gaillimh at the front of the line-out. I can't imagine that Micko welcomed Langford's arrival, but for those couple of years in his first spell at Munster I hung on his every word.

I don't know what he thought of us. Straight away he would have seen that our gym work was loose and haphazard. Not everyone followed the programme and not everyone was nailed about that failure. During the previous season the IRFU did fitness tests on every contracted player in the system and a lot of the Munster players fared badly. The results leaked out and were published in April 1999, six months before the World Cup. There was a lot of bitterness around the place when some Munster players were left out of the Ireland squad, but those fitness results definitely harmed their chances. The impression of us was that we weren't putting in the work.

When I first started training seriously with Munster I remember thinking that my gym programme from the IRFU Academy was better than Munster's. On top of that the messing that went on in the gym was crazy.

Just like now, that work was done in your local training centre, either Cork or Limerick. In the beginning Deccie was in charge of the Cork gym sessions at the Cork Institute of Technology but in fairness to him he had no expertise in this area. He did his best to control the situation but he couldn't be there all the time, and anyway, as professionals, nobody should have had to stand over us. That attitude, though, didn't really exist. Ken O'Connell was an unbelievable character in the squad and if Ken started telling one of his epic stories in the gym the whole place stopped and gathered around until he got to the punch line. He'd have the place in stitches, but fellas were listening to him when they should have been doing their work.

If it was a Thursday morning gym session a few lads would come in still hung over or even half-cut after the Wednesday piss-up. You could be setting up your maximum lift on the bench press and get a lash of a Swiss ball in the gob.

After a while specialists were hired, especially for fitness work. Mark McManus was appointed to supervise the gym work in Cork and he did his best too, but he was dealing with some tough cookies who were used to doing whatever they wanted, more or less. Mark would write up the day's gym programme on a whiteboard and then the arguing would start: 'We're not doing that, we want less of that . . .'

In Limerick, the lads didn't really expect to see Claw in the gym. There was a big laugh when he arrived early one morning and sat up on the exercise bike. Apparently, he'd been tipped off that the IRFU's head of fitness, Liam Hennessy, was paying a surprise visit. Claw's attitude, though, would have been that fitness results weren't going to impact on his performance on the pitch one way or another. He knew that he would do his job and everybody else knew that they could depend on him. Around the Munster dressing room that attitude would have been shared by a good few of the lads. Training was important, but doing it on the day was even more important. The link between the two wasn't established in the way that it would be later on.

This was the culture that John Langford had walked into. His first eye-opener came on the training field. He had just arrived in Ireland and, still jet-lagged, he was watching the session rather than taking part. We were running through line-outs and it was Denis Leamy's first time training with the senior squad. The first-choice pack were jumping against what used to be known as the Muppets. Alan Quinlan was acting the maggot, interfering with the lifters, and Dessie Clohessy's patience was running out. He told Quinny that if he did it again he'd get a flake. It was the kind of thing that was often said but never done. Leamy, though, didn't know any better and took Dessie at his word. So Quinny crossed the line again and Leamy gave him a flake.

All hell broke loose. In a flash everyone got stuck in

– sixteen of us, team mates taking lumps out of each other. At one stage Quinny's head popped up and I gave him a flake. It was a sneaky one because Quinny couldn't defend himself. Claw saw me do it and gave me an awful hiding. He marched me in a headlock from the middle of the field down to the 22 belting me in the face, non-stop. He was an incredibly strong bastard. I'm a lot stronger now than I was ten years ago but I still wouldn't fancy myself against Claw in that mood. This was Claw's way of marking my card, and he was right. I shouldn't have hit Quinny like that.

I spoke to Langford afterwards and he was stunned. He thought he had landed in a zoo. Fights are rare at Munster training now and if one flared up other lads would be in like a shot to break it up. The bad feeling isn't allowed to fester either. The rule is that the lads have to make up by kissing on the lips in front of the squad, either in the team room or on the bus. Back when I started, though, fights happened every now and then and the rest of us would just let them at it. If the lads were sour with each other for a few days afterwards, so be it. It was almost like a schoolyard situation. The lads would be rolling around on the ground and we'd be standing over them in a circle, almost egging them on. The belief we had in those days was that it showed we were up for the match and ready to roll if fellas were knocking lumps out of each other on a Thursday. It took us a few years to realise how stupid that was.

We got better at team meetings as the years went on too, but when I started the most important lessons were always delivered on the training field. In some respects I was a slow learner. It took me a long time to realise, for example, that there was a difference between match intensity and training intensity. When it came to tackling drills that difference was particularly important. In my anxiety to train hard and get noticed I didn't have enough respect for that difference.

John Hayes did his best to teach me very early on. He was holding a tackle bag for a drill and I flew at him. It was a good hit and I didn't think twice about it. The next time, though, Hayes turned his hip into me at the last second and I was flattened. It was my first ever 'stinger'. I thought I was paralysed. I was lying on the ground in a desperate condition. I thought it was all over. I was looking at my hand but I had no feeling in it. All I had was a burning sensation going down through my body and out through my feet. The physio came over, tried to explain what a stinger was and told me I'd be all right in a few minutes. At that moment, I didn't believe him. I'd never felt anything like it.

For years afterwards Hayes wouldn't allow me into his group for tackling drills. You'd see him with fellas like Claw, Gaillimh, Keith Wood and maybe Langford, doing the drills at a reasonable level without killing each other. Then you had fellas like myself, Colm McMahon, David Wallace, Marcus Horan and Paul O'Connell and there'd be skin and hair flying. I learned the value of moderation years later, but even now, if my contact work isn't at the level it needs to be in the week of a match I'll look for the mad young fellas.

I was given my first Munster contract for that season, 1999/2000. It was classic Deccie. He gave me a deal with no money and made me feel as if I'd won the lottery. I was still on an IRFU Academy contract worth three grand a year and the only difference with the Munster contract was that I was entitled to match fees if I was in the squad and win bonuses if we won. But there was no basic wage. Nothing.

Deccie also made me cop on about my education. My brother Eddie had been giving me grief at home as well. If I failed to make it as a professional rugby player I had no trade or qualification to fall back on. Eddie thought Cork Con should have sorted me out with a job. I didn't want a job. I wanted to train full-time. The only thing in my mind was making it as a rugby player. This was a concern to everybody else except me.

On Deccie's advice I enrolled in a Recreation and Leisure course at CIT. It took me eleven years to finish the three-year course and I never would have made a start if Deccie hadn't pushed me. In the beginning, though, there were complications. Part of the course was step aerobics and these classes took place in a hall with a viewing balcony. Most of the class was made up of women, dressed appropriately in leotards. I was there in my rugby shirt and shorts with the Munster lads whistling and shouting from the balcony. It was hard enough to get them to do weights; they were never going to stay in the gym when I was providing priceless entertainment in a nearby location. They slaughtered me.

In terms of win bonuses, though, I hit the jackpot. The year of my no-income contract coincided with the most successful season in Munster's history. We reached the final of the Heineken Cup for the first time and I was a regular in the match-day squad. In terms of game time I made three appearances in the campaign for a total of four minutes, including two minutes at the end of the semi-final against Toulouse. By the end of the season my income had been more than doubled to about £7,000.

I loved everything about the build-up to the final against Northampton. Because I wasn't in the starting fifteen I wasn't shattered by nerves. As professionals you're told to play the match and not the occasion. Step away from the hype. For that match, I was playing the occasion. The thought of a massive crowd, the thought of running out at Twickenham for the first time – I couldn't wait.

A lot has been said over the years about our team meeting the night before the game. As everyone knows by now, it was over the top. Far too much was said about what it would mean to win. Far too much emotion was spent before a ball was kicked. We were sitting around in a circle and everybody was expected to make a contribution.

Speaking in team meetings has never been my thing over the years, and as a twenty-one-year-old sitting in that room the thought of having to speak was daunting. I couldn't think of anything inspirational. I just said they should go out and enjoy it. At the time that would have been my general outlook before matches. I suffer a lot with nerves now and have done for years, but when I was younger that wasn't the case. Some of the lads started laughing. By this stage a lot of them had shed tears and my contribution was completely at odds with the mood in the room. It might have relieved the tension a bit, but that wasn't my intention.

I had it in my mind that I would get a run in the final even though I had no evidence for thinking that. The only game I had started that season was against Connacht and the only appearances I'd made in the Heineken Cup were in the dying minutes after a game had been decided. Looking in from the outside you would have said that they didn't trust me, but I wasn't burdened by that thought. It might sound mad, but I had a fearless attitude. In my head I was saying, 'Fuck it, I can make a difference here.'

When Gaillimh was sin-binned late in the second half, though, any chance I had of getting on disappeared. Being selfish, I was frustrated about that. The game went down to the wire and we lost by a point. At that stage of my Munster career they weren't going to put me into a game like that unless they were badly stuck. Simple as that.

* * *

Outside Munster my other big focus was the Ireland U-21s. We had nine games that season, starting with a World Cup in Argentina in the summer of 1999. For us, it was a disaster. All the big nations showed up and we finished eighth out of eight. Last.

It was a miserable tour. No fun. Joyless. Buenos Aires was a brilliant place to visit and we stayed in a five-star hotel, but it was like a prison. We weren't allowed to do anything. England were staying in the same hotel and they had permission to go out for a few drinks after matches. We went to the team room to play red-arse. It's one of those juvenile games that you only get in rugby. It involves a group of lads and two rugby balls. Each ball is thrown in a different direction until one is dropped. The player that drops the ball must drop his pants and all the others fire a rugby ball at his bare behind. It doesn't sound great when you put it into words, but that was our entertainment until the final week when the management asked us if we had enjoyed the tour. We told them 'No' straight out so they organised go-karting, two days in a row. There wasn't much craic in that either but it was probably too late to please us at that stage.

We were allocated a terrible training pitch too, and the conspiracy theory was that it was a present from our hosts, Argentina, who were in the same group as us. Every day before our session we had to go around the field and pick up broken glass. The management tried to turn it into a virtue: 'Get on with it – you've got to be hard.' They beasted us at times on that trip and we were probably over-trained. For one of our games we had an hour-long journey and fellas were dozing off on the bus.

We beat Argentina in the first game and then lost to New Zealand. They had a good team with guys like Chris Jack and Jerry Collins but too many of our guys were beaten before they went out. Beaten by the jersey. That's what annoyed me. The senior Ireland team had never beaten the All Blacks, but why should we have had any hang-ups? We didn't know who they were and they didn't know us.

Losing to them put us into a play-off with Argentina, which they won. We ended up in a play-off for seventh and eighth, which we lost. With the team we had we should have done a lot better. Our pack was massive, for a start. Bob Casey and Mick O'Driscoll were in the second row, and Leo Cullen and myself played in the back row with Aidan Kearney. Jeremy Staunton was the out-half with Kiaran Campbell at number nine and Shane Horgan in the backs. If you look at the team photos we were a monstrous size. There was no excuse for flopping the way we did.

The only good thing was that the Ireland coach Warren Gatland made the trip. He took some of the sessions and watched everything we did. Socially he kept his distance, but if he wasn't up for a game of red-arse there wasn't much point hanging around with us. From little remarks that he passed I could tell that I had impressed him. He picked me out in training a few times as an example to the others. Listening to him, I grew a foot taller.

I played at blindside flanker at that tournament. It wasn't my natural position but we were well stocked with second rows. I had the work rate to play there but probably not the pace or the explosiveness to be really effective at a higher level. I saw myself as a second row with a flanker's work rate which was something that not all second rows had. In Argentina, Gatty said that he thought number six was an option for me long term. I wasn't convinced, and I didn't think much more about it.

Later that season, he sat down with myself, John Fogarty, Paul O'Connell and Jerry Flannery. He wanted us to consider joining Connacht, where he had been the coach before he took over the Ireland job. Steph Nel was in charge there now and the IRFU saw it as a place to blood emerging players and give them game time. I remember him saying, 'Look at the Munster set-up. Realistically, none of you are going to break into the team for a while.'

He was right about that. Ultan had played for Connacht for a while after he finished with Munster. He wasn't against the idea completely and he wasn't knocking Connacht. He just said it was different. Not better. I knew he felt it was too soon for me to make a move like that. In his view I wasn't doing too badly where I was. I was young, I had time on my side. I spoke to Deccie as

Above left: Marie and Hughie, my mom and dad, at a Saturday-night dance in City Hall.

Above right: Mom and Dad at my Christening.

Left: First day in Scoil an Spioraid Naoimh, September 1983.

Below left: Me and my sister, Emer, at home.

Below right: Visiting Santa with Dad. Emer is on Santa's lap and Ultan is to the front, Christmas 1980.

Left: Confirmation day with Nan.

Centre left: All the family on my First Communion day. (*Back left to right*): Ultan, Emmett, Mom, Eddie. (*Front*): me and Emer.

Bottom left: On Myrtleville beach with Emer and cousins Brian and Colin.

Above: On site, working with Emmett in summer 1995.

Below: Highfield U-14 South Munster League champions, 1992.

Above: Mom, Ultan and me (with cap!). Ultan played for the Irish Colleges vs Japan in Derry.

Left: Celebrating CBC's Munster Schools Senior Cup win with coach Garrett Fitzgerald.

Below: 'Rallying the troops' during CBC's successful Munster Schools Senior Cup run in 1996/7.

Above: Holding the
U-19 World Cup trophy
in France with Mom,
1998.

Right: First game in
Thomond for Munster
Youths vs Ulster, 1996.
With Ultan and Eddie.

Below: Shaved heads
at the U-19 World
Championship in
France, 1998.

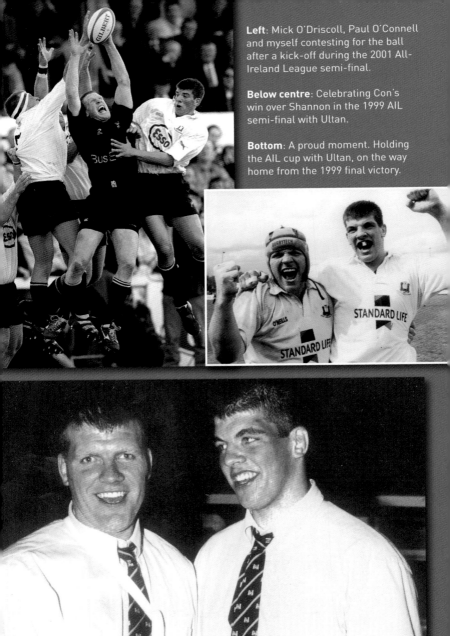

Left: Mick O'Driscoll, Paul O'Connell and myself contesting for the ball after a kick-off during the 2001 All-Ireland League semi-final.

Below centre: Celebrating Con's win over Shannon in the 1999 AIL semi-final with Ultan.

Bottom: A proud moment. Holding the AIL cup with Ultan, on the way home from the 1999 final victory.

Above: On the day of my first cap for Ireland, standing to face a Stephen Jones penalty with Marcus Horan and John Hayes.

Below: Having a bit of fun during the Irish rugby squad photo session before the departure to South Africa in June 2004.

well and he was quick to turn it back on me. Was I not learning from the Munster sessions? He was the coach. There was only one answer to that question. I took the opportunity to tell him that I needed to be involved more in the sessions, but he didn't give me any concrete guarantees about that. As far as he was concerned I was serving my apprenticeship. If I moved on, somebody else would step into that role. It was my decision. The way he put it made me feel like I would be foolish to leave.

The other thing that Gatty said, though, frightened the life out of me: 'Donncha, I only see you as a six.' I was still only twenty at the time so clearly it wasn't too late to change but I really didn't see a future for myself as a flanker. I could see the value in being flexible, but I was convinced I could make it as a second row. I really believed I could be a good second row, and at the time I needed that conviction.

I guess the easy thing would have been to take the advice of the national coach. I didn't. I stuck to my guns.

5

Skittles

Warren Gatland was still the Ireland coach when I was first invited to join the senior squad. The phone call came from Brian O'Brien, who had taken over as the Ireland manager from Donal Lenihan for the summer tour in 2000. I knew Brian from the Munster scene where he had been the manager too. Strictly speaking it wasn't a call-up. Brian chose his words carefully.

'We need you to come up and give us a hand with training,' he said.

'Yeah, brilliant! Jesus, I'd love it, Brian. Thanks very much.'

In those days the Ireland squad stayed in the Glenview Hotel in County Wicklow, not far from

Dublin. I arrived not knowing what to expect but thrilled to be there. Guy Easterby, Simon's brother, was one of the first people I met and he was really friendly and chatty. In conversation, though, he referred to me as a 'skittle'. I didn't know what that meant and I didn't want to look like a ghoul for asking.

The following day at training I found out. There were eight 'skittles' and our function was to be knocked down and run over by the rest of the squad. Basically, our job was to have the shit kicked out of us. We became known as the Glenview Eight: myself, Marcus Horan, Gavin Duffy, Simon Keogh, Des Dillon, Dave Quinlan, Aidan McCullough and Peter Bracken. Over time, others came and went. We were all young enough and ambitious enough to believe that this experience would be good for us. We were sharing a hotel and a training pitch with the Ireland squad and there was a chance to get noticed. We weren't sharing a room with any of the proper squad members and we were excluded from team meetings, but we didn't take offence. In our role you couldn't afford to be sensitive.

It gave me fierce confidence. In terms of power and physique I still had ground to make up but those Ireland sessions showed me that I was making progress. I was hopping off big fellas like Victor Costello and Gary Longwell and coming through in one piece. On the first day I was clobbered by Girvan Dempsey and it caught me by surprise because he didn't look that big to me. But he was further down the road of physical development and he had excellent technique. It put me on guard that I couldn't take any of these fellas for granted.

Occasionally you'd get your hands on the ball and make a shape, but these sessions weren't designed for our benefit. We weren't there to look good. In theory, we were getting our chance with the Ireland A squad. In reality, we were too exhausted to make any impression. I remember one week heading north for an A international in Belfast when myself and Marcus could barely stand we were so flogged. We considered pulling over in the car and going for a nap. We hadn't even had time to eat, and when we joined the A squad they had a match organised against Bangor, a club team. One of the props and one of the second rows obviously didn't fancy it so myself and Marcus were thrown in from the start. We spent the morning having lumps kicked out of us by the senior squad and we spent the evening playing a match where the emphasis was on contact.

I didn't like the A squad. It didn't feel like a team. Nobody really wanted to be there and everyone was looking out for themselves. Everybody's priority was making themselves look good. The second rows would complain about the lifts they were getting from the props in the line-out and the props would complain that the second rows weren't pushing with everything they had in the scrum. And these issues weren't thrashed out, like they would be in a normal team environment. I suppose everybody knew the rules. In the A squad everybody believed they were only passing through so nobody was going to waste their energy making somebody else look good.

It was during my time with the A squad that I first heard the phrase 'train like Tarzan, play like Jane'. Some of these guys would be unbelievable in the squad sessions and flop in the matches. You could see them a mile away. I suppose the A games served a purpose in exposing those guys.

The problem for me and the other members of the Glenview Eight is that we were training like lunatics and getting very little game time. During the Six Nations we'd spend most of the week with the senior squad and then be given a place on the bench for the A team. You might only get a few minutes at the end, but because that was a Friday-night fixture and it might be away from home you weren't always available for your club in the All-Ireland League. Cork Con didn't see me at all those weeks so I'd be named on the bench for them too.

I went through a period of training with Ireland and playing for Cork Con's minors – which was their third team – purely because I needed game time and their matches were on a Sunday morning, when I was definitely available. It was ridiculous when you think about it. I remember one match against Dolphin's thirds, a group of mostly old lads who had been in the pub on Saturday night. The smell of drink in the scrums was sickening. The Con third team was basically a gang of young fellas, and in that match Dolphin blew us over for a push-over try from miles out. It was embarrassing, but it was the only chance they had to dominate us. Once we had the ball in hand we ran rings around them.

I got over for a try, and on the way out I tried to take the conversion with a drop goal, like in sevens, and fluffed it completely. I thought it was a bit of a laugh but it was hugely disrespectful to the Dolphin lads and in the next two plays they absolutely hammered me. Chewed me up and spat me out. When Ultan got to hear about it he gave out yards to me as well.

I'd say I spent two years making occasional appearances for the thirds. The only purpose it served was to let me run off some steam after a week of training, but part of me felt that I was serving my time too. I hadn't grown up in Con and I didn't come from a Con family. I was new in the place and lining out for the thirds was one way of showing that I had the club at heart.

I've always said that long after I finish in professional rugby I'm going to end up playing for the Con minors. At the time, though, it showed how far I still had to travel.

Progress with Munster was slow that season. In fact, I probably went backwards. Mick O'Driscoll had overtaken me on the bench as the reserve second row for Heineken Cup matches and I was reduced to a handful of substitute appearances in the inter-provincial games.

The Magners League didn't exist so the only chance to make an impression was in the All-Ireland League.

Every chance I got with Con I broke my back to play well. Interest in the All-Ireland League, though, was starting to fall off. The crowds weren't as big as before and neither was the coverage. I came to the conclusion that the only way to get noticed was to score tries. That might have been a paranoid reaction on my part but I went bald-headed for the try line every chance I got, and going into the last match of that season I was Con's leading try scorer. Were Munster paying any attention to the All-Ireland League? I'm not sure they were.

As a rule, my morale is good. I'm not the sort of person that gets down about things – or at least I don't show it. But that 2000/01 season I was really frustrated. For the previous season I had been in the match-day twenty-two for all the big games and now I'd lost that status. My form was good, I was getting stronger, I was knocking around with the Ireland squad, but with Munster I was surplus to requirements.

One of Deccie's skills is making everybody feel valuable and included. He always makes a point of talking about the lads who are not in the team or not in the twenty-two. You could be number twenty-five but he'd try to make you believe that you were the guy making the whole operation tick. He tried that with me, but I needed something more concrete. I needed work. I needed a plan that could take me from where I was to where I wanted to be. I needed Deccie to tell me exactly where I needed to improve and how I could achieve it.

In those days I was more standoffish with coaches and people in authority. You wouldn't think I was shy by the way I carried on around the other players, but approaching Deccie and looking for that kind of feedback was a big deal for me. I wouldn't have done it unless I was starting to get desperate. The first time I asked I didn't really get much of an answer, but he asked me to come back to him again. The next time wasn't much of an improvement on the first visit. Then he called me into his office one day and gave me a tennis ball. He said I needed to work on my hand–eye co-ordination. Bounce the tennis ball off a wall and catch it. When I went to him looking for drills I didn't have something like this in mind, but Deccie could be full of surprises. When the lads saw me with a tennis ball the slagging was savage.

My opportunity that season came out of the blue. Alan Quinlan broke his thumb and he wasn't going to be fit in time for the semi-final of the Heineken Cup against Stade Français. I was on the bus coming home from a Con match when one of the lads heard the news. Half messing, they said I might get a game at blindside. I don't think any of them believed it even though I had played some games for Con at six that season.

Anthony Foley – Axel – and David Wallace were also carrying knocks so we weren't overflowing with options in the back row. In those days, though, you could sign new players for the knock-out stages of the Heineken Cup and Munster had gone for Dion O'Cuinneagain. He had captained Ireland in the 1999 World Cup but his international career was over now and he was back living in South Africa. He was a specialist back-row player, though, and that wasn't great news for me.

The other complication in the spring of 2001 was foot and mouth. Ireland played only two of their Six Nations matches before they were forced to stop and the All-Ireland League was put on hold for weeks. The only match Munster played in the build-up was a friendly game against a Rest of Ireland selection at Thomond Park eight days before the semi-final. Dion flew into Shannon only four hours before kick-off so I was given my first start of the season. I nailed it. I was so pumped up that I accidentally broke Victor Costello's arm in a tackle. I was running around like a fella with my hair on fire, as Eddie O'Sullivan used to say. Dion came on for the last twenty minutes but I knew I'd done enough to make them think seriously about me for the semi-final.

Deccie didn't tell me until the night before the game that I was starting even though I pretty much knew by then. In every play that was run in training that week I was at number six. Maybe he thought he was shielding me from the pressure by not telling me sooner, but I'd have preferred to know.

Was I out of my depth? I didn't think so. I was fit enough to cope with the pace of the game and I wasn't overawed by the occasion. In my mind, this was a freebie. I was a young player being pitched into a big game in an unfamiliar position. Nobody was expecting anything. They couldn't have been. I knew the nuts and bolts of playing number six. What I lacked was a back row's instincts. As a second row you arrive at a ruck and you melt into it. As a back row you have an instant decision to make. Can I get an off-load here? Is there something on?

In terms of scrum defence, I was learning it on the hoof. In training they would have drilled it into me but I could have done with more repetitions and more game time. I was lucky that I was playing alongside David Wallace because he wasn't the kind of fella who would give out. He was one of the soundest fellas in our dressing room and an incredible player. I cocked up on one scrum when I should have been covering their eight while he pushed out on the nine. I was scorched and, calmly, Wally just explained the situation again. He was such an athlete that he could nearly always fix a mistake he made before it hurt the team; I didn't have that capacity.

Stade Français had three internationals in their back row: Christophe Moni, Richard Pool-Jones and Christophe Juillet, their captain. Against quality like that I should have been exposed, but I thought I was all right. I was replaced by Dion with ten minutes to go but if I'd been a disaster I would have been dragged long before that. Other people, though, didn't share that opinion. In some of the post-match comments from the Munster camp our 'inexperienced' back row was mentioned in passing as part of the reason why we lost. That annoyed me. Whatever was said behind closed doors or whatever they really thought about my performance I was entitled to a bit of protection in public.

I knew I didn't play great, but one of the papers gave me a rating of three out of ten. Ronan O'Gara and Frankie Sheahan spotted it and slaughtered me. You must have a thick skin for the Munster dressing room, and over the years I've been well able to dish out slagging, but I found that very hard to take. I was really upset by it. It drove me fucking mad. I was mortified that people thought I'd played as badly as that. I'd waited all season for my chance and it had turned into a nightmare. We'd lost by a point after John O'Neill's perfectly good try was ruled out and my performance was regarded as a failure. It hurt me for ages. Around the squad I felt like I was carrying the shame of that performance.

After a game like that you want to get back on the pitch the following week and put the record straight but our season was over and I didn't know when I would start another significant match for Munster. For the following season, 2001/02, Langford had gone home to Australia, which gave Paul O'Connell the chance to make his breakthrough. Gaillimh and Mick O'Driscoll were still around and I was still stuck in the queue. Time was moving on. In March of that season I turned twenty-three. Something needed to happen for me at Munster, one way or another.

For most of that season, nothing happened. I made two appearances off the bench in our six pool matches in the Heineken Cup and was on the field for less than fifteen minutes altogether. For the quarter-final against Stade Français in Paris I wasn't involved. It was doing my head in. The only runs I got were meaningless, after the match had been decided. In those situations you can't make a positive impression. Nobody pays any attention to what you do, unless you cock up. All I wanted was a decent opportunity. The Stade match from the previous campaign was still in my system because I hadn't been given the chance to get it out of my system. In a corner of my mind I believed that the other players didn't rate me. That was probably the worst feeling of all.

Sixteen minutes into the semi-final against Castres I got my chance. Axel went off injured and I was given the nod. I was only on the field a few minutes when Claw was sin-binned so we needed to bring on a prop and I was replaced for those ten minutes. It gave me a chance to think and compose myself.

'This is it now. You've been waiting a year for this opportunity. You've got to walk the walk here.'

There was a yellow-carded Castres player with Claw and they were sitting together in the little holding pen for sin-binned players. I was sitting only a few yards away and the two boys were still roaring and shouting at each other. Claw had a bottle of water and he kept squirting yer man, taunting him and abusing him. I was thinking, 'This is unbelievable, you can't do that.' But he could. Of course he could. It was Claw.

I was looking at this craziness and trying to gather my thoughts. Before I left the field with Claw I had dropped the first ball that came my way. After that I went into survival mode. 'The shit has hit the fan for you here. None of the lads respect you. You know the way they looked at you after the semi-final last year.' Whether that was true or not, it suited me to believe it.

We won, and I put in a massive game. The lads could see that I was pumped up and they gave me every opportunity to carry the ball. Castres kicked it long quite a bit and I got a few chances to run it back. I've spent most of my career doing a lot of things that only your team mates notice. That day I needed to be seen making a contribution, and I grabbed the chance that I was given.

I was glad, too, that I came on in the back row. If I had come on for Gaillimh and played well in the second row everybody would have said, 'Well, that's his position. No big deal.' In people's eyes I had failed at six in the previous year's semi-final. I needed to succeed in that position and put the issue to bed. With Axel off the pitch David Wallace slotted in for a lot of the game at number eight, but we rotated positions. I was probably no more clued in to what I should be doing than I was the year before, but Wally and our scrum-half Peter

Stringer were really good to me. For any of the forwards, playing with Strings has always been a dream because he just marches you around the field. In any case, I wasn't prepared to be used as an excuse for a Munster defeat again. I stood up.

I know it was only one performance and I had come from nowhere, but I believed I had put myself in the picture for the final against Leicester. The key for me was Axel. If he wasn't fit to start I didn't think they'd name an injured player on the bench. Jim Williams had arrived that season and he would be Axel's replacement in the back row, with me slotting into the subs. Whatever the status of Axel's fitness they had a big call to make with Jimmy anyway. He arrived in Munster with a big reputation as a World Cup winner with Australia and he had made a huge impression. He had started every Heineken Cup match that season until injury ruled him out of the semi-final.

On the day the team was named Deccie met some players individually. Jimmy was crying as he left his meeting. More than that – he was bawling. Devastated. As soon as I saw Jimmy's face I knew I was in trouble. If he wasn't starting he was bound to be on the bench. Leaving a player of his stature out of the starting fifteen was a massive decision. Leaving a young fella like me out of the twenty-two was a handy call in comparison.

Deccie broke the bad news and explained his decision. I didn't like what I was hearing but there was logic to it. Paulie was also carrying a knock into the game so he said they wanted cover for the middle of the line-out rather than the front. That meant Micko instead of me. Micko had been ahead of me on the bench all season anyway.

Then Deccie mentioned something that I had written in a questionnaire at the start of the season. We were asked to identify weaknesses in ourselves and I wrote that I didn't think I had the total respect of the other players. It was a hangover from the previous season's semi-final against Stade Français and it was something that was on my mind. I had wanted to be totally honest in the questionnaire and I couldn't see what harm would come of it. Against Castres, though, I had put those doubts to bed. I felt good about myself and my game and I was ready to move on. Deccie hadn't raised the issue with me all season, but now it was being quoted as a reason to leave me out of the twenty-two for the Heineken Cup final. Was it the biggest reason? I don't know. I didn't ask. Paulie's knock was probably the key to their thinking. Why did he need to mention the other stuff? It rattled me. I wasn't expecting it. More than twelve months after the Stade match I was still living with the consequences of that performance. I thought I'd moved on.

For the first time in my life I tried to argue a selection call with him. 'What if Axel has to come off early and Jimmy is straight on? Won't you be short of cover? I can play second row or back row.' I made my argument, but

I didn't push it. He gave me their reasoning and I whimpered back into my corner.

We travelled to Cardiff the following day. Myself and John O'Neill were brought as cover in case of any last-minute injuries. John hadn't played in the Heineken Cup since the Stade match when his try was wrongly disallowed. He hadn't started, he hadn't come on, nothing. Then his world turned upside down. On the day before the match Anthony Horgan broke his hand in a dopey incident with Claw, messing after training. Hoggy was gone and Johno went from being out of the squad to straight into the team. We were room mates on that trip. They would have put us together because we were in the same situation. Now our circumstances couldn't have been more different. Johno had been given the chance of a lifetime and I was still dealing with my shit.

The Munster players who weren't part of the official party travelled on a supporters' plane. They were staying in a different hotel in town and having a ball. John Fogarty rang me, bent out of shape, trying to get me to join them. I had no mind to be with them and I didn't want to be in the team hotel. I probably wanted to be at home, but I wouldn't have been happy there either.

Around the squad, you can't show it. With Munster, sulking has never been tolerated. You might get away with feeling sorry for yourself for a day but that would be the limit. A couple of days before a Heineken Cup final, though, that tolerance wouldn't have existed.

Jimmy spotted that I was hurting and did his best to pick me up. He was probably hurting more than anyone, but he took a minute to look beyond himself. In every way, he brought a lot of class to our dressing room. Everybody else was just looking after themselves. There's no other way to go. Tough calls happen all the time. You can't afford to be distracted or get emotionally involved. I understood that too.

It was a weird experience. Empty. I travelled on the team bus to the stadium wearing my Munster suit and tie rather than a tracksuit. I was in the middle of it and a million miles from it at the same time. I sat with the subs but I wasn't one of them. I went down to the dressing room at half time because that's where everybody was going. I poked my head in and came straight out. I was embarrassed. I didn't want the lads to see me. Irrational stuff. Our media manager Pat Geraghty asked me to do a couple of pitch-side interviews for RTE, and in fairness to Pat that was probably his way of getting me involved. I felt no part of it though. I desperately wanted the lads to win but it killed me to be so close to it and feel like an outsider. It was like being invited to watch other people live out your dream.

Afterwards we stayed on the field to watch Leicester lift the cup. I didn't know what to do with myself. You go around sympathising, like there's been a death in the family. In the dressing room I tried to make myself useful. Asking fellas did they want a cup of tea. Stupid stuff, just to be doing something.

Claw was the first man back in the dressing room. He didn't wait for the presentation. It was his last match for Munster. He took off his jersey, shorts and socks and threw them into the middle of the floor. Then he threw his boots on top of them. I still remember his boots hitting the ground and thinking, 'Fuck. Claw is gone.' I remember my next thought too: 'Horan, you're in. You lucky bastard.' There's a part of this game that's always selfish.

Everyone knew we were going to miss Peter Clohessy around the place. He was old school in lots of ways and he didn't train properly most of the time but he was an incredible player. For a prop he was a serious footballer. He was full of Munster bitterness too. Claw was convinced that nobody rated us and that was his line the whole time. He didn't say much in team meetings but he always gave the impression that he hated whoever we were playing. He'd never say that we should go out and take the head off the other crowd. But he'd go out and give somebody a clip and we'd fall in behind him. Rather than say it, he'd just do it.

Because of who he was he got away with murder. He had a desperate head for names but he didn't give a damn. He often called me Ultan and he often called Mick O'Driscoll Johno because he knew our older brothers before he knew us and he couldn't be bothered remembering our names. On one Ireland tour the lads tried to get Claw to name everyone in the room. I wasn't there but Marcus told me that he didn't know half of them. They were going around the room, one by one, and he'd make a stab at some of the names. They came to Geordan Murphy and Claw said straight out, 'I've no idea who you are.' Anybody else would be mortified, but Claw was shameless.

The problem for me was that Gaillimh wasn't retiring. He stood down as captain after that season but he planned to carry on playing. I was at a crossroads. Gaillimh's career was coming to an end but how much longer was he going to stick it out? Time was moving on for me. Since I made my European debut in October 1998 I had started just one Heineken Cup match in four years. I was twenty-three years old. I had served my time. I needed to make a career for myself. I wanted a future with Munster, but most of all I needed to play. Somewhere.

Just a few weeks after he was sacked by Ireland in November 2001, Warren Gatland had taken over at Wasps. Shortly after that our centre Mike Mullins said that Gatland had been asking about me and that if I ever wanted a move I should give him a shout. I was given his number, and eventually I used it one Sunday. I should have checked the fixtures first because they had a Premiership match that day, but we had a brief chat and we spoke again later. I can't remember exactly what triggered the call but my frustration had been building for ages. At that stage it wouldn't have taken much. After I chatted to him at least I knew I had an option. We didn't speak about money and I didn't clarify if he still saw me as a number six rather than a second row, but he guaranteed me game time and at that point in my career that's what I desperately needed. Gatty said he would come over and meet me if I wanted to take the process to the next stage.

I spoke to my brothers about it. Ultan and Emmett thought I should move, Eddie didn't come down on one side or the other. It was a huge call. I thought if I spent another season rotting on the bench other teams might not want to sign me. After a while you become damaged goods. 'He couldn't make it there. He was trying for years. There must be something lacking.' I was ambitious, but it was important that I was seen to be ambitious too.

The other element in the equation was that Deccie was finishing with Munster to work full-time with Ireland as Eddie O'Sullivan's assistant. If Deccie was staying I believe I would have taken Gatland's offer. For whatever reason, I had failed to convince Deccie of my worth. We never had a conversation about that, but in any case, what could he say? He kept picking Munster teams that didn't include me. We never had a falling out or a cross word but I was getting nowhere, and in my mind he was one of the people standing in my way. I went from spending a season on the bench as the second-row cover to being outside the match-day squad. Whatever he said, I was going backwards.

Before the end of the season Alan Gaffney was

appointed as Deccie's replacement. He came to Cork to meet the squad and was a regular at our matches for the remainder of the year. I asked to see him, and we met in a Cork hotel. I laid my cards on the table: 'I'm only coming to see you because I'm so close to leaving.'

I needed to get a sense of where I stood. I couldn't afford to wait and see how the season would develop. I knew he couldn't guarantee me a place on the team but I needed a serious indication from him that I was in the frame. He gave me that assurance.

'I promise you,' he said, 'no matter who is there, the best second rows will play and everybody will be given a fair chance. You have my word on that.'

That was all I wanted to hear. I suppose if I had really wanted to leave I would have pushed him harder. Maybe that wouldn't have amounted to anything, but the bottom line was that I wanted to be a Munster player. In any negotiations that desire would have weakened my position. Going against the advice of Ultan or Emmett was probably something I'd never done but it showed where my heart was.

For the following season I was given my first proper contract: €30,000 a year. The money was great, but it wasn't about the money for me. I just wanted a chance.

6

Sweet Eighteen

There were two sides to me. I was desperate to improve and get on and for a couple of years all I could see were people in my way. What I struggled to do was get out of my own way. When I look back now, the contradictions are obvious. I wanted to learn and I was constantly looking for stuff that would give me an edge. There was no shortage of people who were prepared to help and I was like a sponge for smart advice and good coaching. But too often it looked like I couldn't learn my lessons. I wanted people to trust me but I was giving them reasons to doubt me instead.

All of my coaches had to deal with this issue. Indiscipline was a big part of it. On the field I wasn't cold enough or cute enough. Things happened, I reacted. Brian Hickey at Con did his best for me but I broke his heart at times. He was part of the Munster set-up for a couple of years and he coached the Con senior team before that. One day, in a key match away to Lansdowne, I cocked up badly. Ken Murphy, our other second row, was yellow-carded after getting involved with one of the Lansdowne guys. I had huge time for Ken and as far as I was concerned he had been hard done by. So, straight from the kick-off, I struck the Lansdowne guy who had hit him. Ken was barely sitting down in the sin-bin seats when I joined him. We were down to thirteen men and we had no second rows on the field.

Brian was freaking. He grabbed me by the arm as I left the field and really laid into me. I pushed his hand away and didn't really listen. At that moment I didn't want to hear it. When I calmed down I knew I was wrong, and later I went over to apologise. He said he was afraid I was going to give him a flake on the side-line. I told him I'd never dream of it. 'You had a mad look in your eye,' he said.

And that was it. On one level, every coach I ever had liked that bit of madness and wanted me to bring it on to the field. But they also wanted me to control it. With Ken off the field that was an opportunity for me to stand up and show a bit of leadership. Instead, I behaved like an idiot. My team mates needed me to dig in and I did something daft.

Brian kept me back for extra training in Con during

the week for punishment, trying to hammer the message home. It wasn't a new message. I knew the message. For me it didn't feel like punishment either. Brian was one of the best coaches I ever worked with. Half an hour of one-on-one attention from him was only going to be of benefit to me.

In different ways, Jimmy Williams tried to help me too. When he joined Munster he settled in Cork and played for Con on those weekends when Munster didn't have a game. He chewed me on the field one day. I had pulled down a line-out and conceded a penalty. It was a stupid penalty to give away, but at the very next line-out I did it again. Jimmy lost it. Ultan was the Con captain and he tried to intervene but Jimmy wasn't having it. He told Ultan to butt out and continued to chew the head off me. He didn't spare me in training either. If I wasn't rolling away from a tackle he'd give me a clip. He could have just pointed out the infringement but he probably figured that a bit of pain was a more powerful lesson.

I accepted all that from Jimmy without a word of argument. I was afraid of my life of him. He was the biggest, scariest man I ever played with or against and when he got angry he seemed to grow even bigger. I was taller than him but in those situations it felt like he was towering over me.

My respect for him, though, was greater than my fear. I respected everything about him: his attitude, his professionalism, his ability. I remember Ultan saying to me, 'You've got to listen to this man, he's setting a whole new standard here.' He was right. I hung on every word Jimmy said. With Munster he brought in practices that are second nature to us now. Apart from Gaillimh he was the oldest guy in the squad but he used to do extra flexibility sessions every week. He used to get a massage twice a week to clear away the lactic acid in his legs. All of us do it now, but back then it wasn't on our minds. I'd say the fitness coaches hated him because he was always questioning stuff. 'Why are we doing this? What's the benefit of it?'

He said something to me one day that totally changed my attitude to training. 'You can't just finish a session here now,' he said, 'and not think about training until this time tomorrow. You have to think about the session before you arrive.'

Apart from that Jimmy transformed our gym work in CIT purely because every one of us was afraid to mess with him. He put down a marker the first day he joined us at the gym. There were a couple of 55kg dumb bells that were used to hold open the doors. Jimmy dusted them down and started lifting them on the bench press. The biggest weight that any of us had ever used was 40kg but within about three months we were all bench-pressing with the 55kg dumb bells. We were a giddy group: myself, Ronan O'Gara, Anthony Horgan, Mick O'Driscoll, Frankie Sheahan, John Fogarty. John Kelly was there too but he was an exception. In the past, we'd get the work done but sessions were slow to start because we were messing and they took longer to finish because we were messing. Jimmy cut that out. We started on time and concentrated while we were doing our work.

That was another contradiction in me. I loved the messing, I was part of it, I enjoyed it, but I had a huge appetite for gym work. Jimmy's work ethic in the gym was everything I aspired to. But if he hadn't cut out the messing, would I have stood up to the lads and told them to cop on? Not a chance. That wasn't me either.

Gaillimh stood down as captain after the 2002 Heineken Cup final and Jimmy was elected in his place. Axel was regarded as the favourite to take over from Gaillimh but in a secret ballot Jimmy was picked by the players in a tight vote. It was a big deal for the Munster captaincy to go to somebody that wasn't from Munster but it showed the impression he'd made on everybody in his first season.

Axel got his chance after Jimmy and went on to be a great captain, but Jimmy was the right man at the time. His approach was different to Gaillimh's and Axel's. He didn't make inspirational speeches; it wasn't blood-and-bandage stuff. He was only interested in the process of rugby. What we were going to do, how we were going to do it. A big thing about Jimmy's team talks was that he always put pressure on himself. 'I'm going to lead the tackle count. I'm going to have the most carries.' He was making a promise to the team that he would lead from the front, and he was true to his word. I really bought into it. I thought it was good to get away from the emotional stuff before matches. There was a limit to where that could take us.

With Jimmy as the new captain and Alan Gaffney as the new coach, the 2002/03 season felt like a fresh start. Me? I continued to get in my own way. In the beginning Alan gave detailed performance reports on every player. We all had to write down three or four key performance goals for every match and then Alan would assess how we'd played along those lines. In one match early that season I gave away five penalties. It came at the end of a week when I had turned up in the wrong gear on Tuesday and been late for training on Thursday. In his report Alan said that indiscipline off the field leads to indiscipline on the field. For the next match I was dropped. There I was, desperate for a chance to play, waiting years for my opportunity, and one of the first things I do is give the new coach a good reason to leave me out. It was crazy.

The other setback I suffered was avoidable too. We played Neath away in the Celtic League and my jaw was broken. It was my fault. I stopped their big number eight Steve Tandy but my technique was terrible and I pulled him down on top of me. He landed, full force, on my face and cracked my jaw. I knew there was something wrong but there were about twenty minutes left and I carried on. In the scrums I could feel my jaw shifting out of place. It was a weird feeling but the pain was bearable and I have a thing in my head about leaving the field with an injury. If there is any way for me to play on, I will.

Later on that evening I knew I was in trouble. I ordered steak at the post-match meal but no matter how small I cut it up I couldn't chew it. I mentioned to Alan that I might have a broken jaw. If I was looking for sympathy, I'd come to the wrong place.

'You deserve to have a broken jaw, mate,' he said. 'That was the worst tackle I ever saw.'

For the December matches in the Heineken Cup I was back in one piece and back in the team. We beat Viadana easily, home and away. Nobody will remember those matches but it was the first time I partnered Paul O'Connell in the second row in the Heineken Cup. We had played together for the Munster U-20s and the Ireland U-21s but his career had taken off after that and mine had stalled. Paulie's breakthrough season with Munster had led to his first caps for Ireland. On both fronts I had ground to make up. He was established in the Munster team now and I was still aspiring to that status. Though he was seven months younger than me he was already the senior partner.

We beat Viadana 64–0 in Thomond Park and scored nine tries in the process. I should have claimed one of them but instead I slipped the ball to Paulie at the back of a maul and he touched it down. He gave me a bollicking for not taking the score myself. That was the start of it.

Gaillimh was still on the scene but he turned thirty-six in the early part of the season and for the first time I felt I was in front in our personal battle. In February 2003 we beat Neath in the final of the Celtic League and we were twenty points up when Gaillimh replaced me with four minutes to go. He was being given the kind of token run that I'd been getting for years. I sprinted off the field just to show them how much I had left in the tank. It was the first competition we won in the professional era and Gaillimh lifted the trophy with Jimmy. Everybody appreciated the gesture on Jimmy's part. Behind it all Gaillimh was still pushing for his place and I was glad of that. I didn't want the jersey handed to me.

In the history of Munster rugby, that season will be remembered for our final Heineken Cup pool match against Gloucester at Thomond Park. We had to score four tries and win by twenty-seven points to qualify and we managed it by the skin of our teeth. None of us could have told you the exact equation before the match. Our only concern was not losing at home. We took some of the things they said and convinced ourselves that they didn't respect us. In those days, that's how we did our business.

For me, though, the biggest game was the quarter-final against Leicester in Welford Road. I wasn't carrying any grievance from the Heineken Cup final the year before because I hadn't been part of that match. The massive challenge for me was playing against Martin Johnson and Ben Kay. Johnson especially.

He was a hero of mine, and I made no secret of it. Irish rugby kids usually don't find their heroes in an English shirt, but my admiration for him went beyond that. He had everything you would want in a second row: he had presence, he was confrontational, he was incredibly hard. In the video of the 1997 Lions tour, *Living with the Lions,* there's a scene where Johnson is cut and he's giving out to the doctor because he's not stitching him fast enough. That image stuck with me.

His status for me never changed. Years later he was coach of an England team that Ireland beat in Croke Park. I was dying to speak to him at the banquet afterwards but when I got to within two feet of his presence I was starstruck. My palms got sweaty and for a second I didn't know what to say. Then he asked me about the knee injury I was carrying. 'I knew you'd play,' he said. 'I knew you'd front up.' I grew about two foot on the spot. As the coach of the other team he was bound to know about our injuries but I still took it as a personal compliment that he knew about mine. A bit of the childish hero-worship was still there.

That day in Welford Road I was desperate to earn his respect. In those days I did a fair amount of talking on the field – shouting and roaring and talking rubbish – but I promised myself that I wouldn't say anything to him. I would have regarded it as disrespectful and I wasn't going to treat him like any other opponent.

The other thing we desperately wanted to do was

mess up their line-out. In the build-up to that game we analysed them to death and Quinny came up with a good suggestion of putting someone into the air at five on their throw. That someone was him, of course. We worked out some of their plays and their triggers and we spoiled or stole eleven balls on their throw.

I was pumped up to the gills. I went for one re-start like a lunatic and basically landed on my head. As the ruck developed I was in a really bad position and anything could have happened. Johnson gave me a nudge to put me in a safer position but I'd say he was looking at me thinking, 'He's off his game.' Our physio came on to give me some treatment and I didn't want to know about it. 'I'm grand, I'm grand, leave me alone.' There was no way I was leaving the field.

The only direct contact I had with Johnson during the match came late in the game. We were in front but they were having a purple patch and they'd just put a great kick into the corner. I flipped off my boot to buy some time and the ref stopped the match. Johnson came over to the ref and told him to play on but he was within his rights to stop the match to get a boot sorted. Johnson would have known I was pulling the piss and the ref probably did as well but there was nothing they could do about it.

Then Johnson stood over me. I didn't realise it was him for a second but all around me the light went out. I was sitting there in the shade. 'Hurry up,' he said. I never tied laces so fast in my life. I didn't give him any back chat either. If any other player in the world had said that he would have got a mouthful from me. He passed one other comment during the match and I let it pass. I had a response on the tip of my tongue and I stopped myself. This was Martin Johnson, the player that I wanted to be. In his career he had done all the things I wanted to do. I was playing against my hero. I wasn't going to spoil that. At the end of the match I wanted him to think that I wasn't a bad player. We shook hands and he said 'Well done'. I never took those two words so personally in my career.

Our dressing room afterwards was one of those places where every joke is funny. For a couple of hours there's a glow of satisfaction and all you want is each other's company. Our showers didn't work and if we'd lost we would have been as sour as pigs, accusing Leicester of sabotage. Instead, we made fun of it. We filled buckets from a tap and threw the water on each other to wash away the suds.

Tom Tierney, one of our former players, was their number nine that day. He came into our dressing room and shook hands with all of us, one by one. There were tears in his eyes and we could all see he was upset. Some of the lads started singing a song that Tom used to sing when he played with us, 'We Are The Greeners'. No visitor to our dressing room ever got a reception like that. It was a special day.

In the semi-final Toulouse beat us by a point in the south of France. For a lot of our players it was the fourth year in a row to lose a Heineken Cup semi-final or final by less than a score. For me, this pain was new. I hadn't played a minute of the finals in 2000 or 2002 and I was desperate to get there.

My worst experiences in a Munster jersey had come in France which, in my mind, gave me something to prove. Fabien Pelous was their captain and main line-out jumper. Two weeks after playing against Johnson, this was another massive challenge. He had lovely hands, great skills, and a hard edge on top of it. Pelous was another guy that I had on a pedestal and coping against him was a big deal for me. I still felt I needed to earn the respect of my team mates and the only place to do it was in the biggest games. I tore into everything, contested every ball, flung myself at the re-starts, made a nuisance of myself at every opportunity, fought it out to the death. I didn't feel out of my depth. I was strong enough for the physical stuff and I could live with the pace of the game. At the end of my first season as a Munster starter I had made a decent contribution in the most important game of our year. In our defeat, it was my only consolation.

With Ireland I had served my time as one of the crash-test dummies in the Glenview Eight. In the autumn of 2002 I was promoted to the role of dirt tracker – not in the team, not even in the match-day squad, but inching ever closer. Because Ireland had performed so badly at the 1999 World Cup we had to come through a qualifying group for the 2003 tournament in Australia. The first game was twelve months before that competition, away to Russia. In Siberia. A mad trip. The food was shocking and the airport was chaotic. We were hanging around in the terminal for ages until somebody realised that the right palm had to be greased to get our flight off the ground.

Marcus Horan and Justin Bishop were two of the other dirt trackers and they pulled me out on the piss the night before the match. The lads were necking vodka and we fell in with a couple of the locals. One of them got thick with me because I didn't join in. 'You're insulting me,' he said. I was trying to explain that I didn't drink but I wasn't getting through to him. I thought it was all going to kick off until Justin picked up the glass and knocked it back. We hailed a taxi to bring us to the hotel and yer man took us through a building site. We obviously didn't know the best way home but this definitely didn't look like it. The thought crossed my mind that we were going to be jumped and robbed. Marcus and Bish were demented from drink which left me on my own against the gang of Russian thugs that were going to pop up any second. None of these irrational fears would probably have occurred to me if I'd just necked the vodka when I was told to.

As dirt trackers we had to wear our IRFU number ones going to the match the following day: blazer and pants, shirt and tie. Marcus, though, hadn't ironed his shirt properly so Keith Wood sent him back to his room and made him do it again. Woody was the captain at the time and as dirt trackers we weren't in a position to argue. Marcus probably looked hung over as well, which didn't help his case. Either way, he was steaming.

In the beginning I kept my mouth shut in the Ireland camp and tried to stay out of trouble. It took a long time for me to get comfortable around Eddie O'Sullivan and I'm not sure I ever did in a social context. I had huge respect for him as a coach and I really believe I learned a lot from him, but I found it hard to be relaxed in his company. When I first joined the squad I was convinced he couldn't see me. It was as if I became invisible when he came near.

It came to a head one day in the team hotel. It was just the two of us in the lift. I walked in and passed some lame remark about the weather. Small talk wasn't Eddie's strong point but even so he didn't respond. The prospect of being alone with Eddie would have made me nervous in any situation, but when he didn't speak I wasn't going to make a second attempt. I know his hearing isn't great but I don't speak that softly and I'm certain he heard me. In any case he could surely see me. There was no good reason why we couldn't have had a harmless conversation, but for the rest of the journey in the lift he didn't open his mouth. No hello, no goodbye, nothing. By that stage I used to slag myself to the lads about Eddie's capacity to ignore me. I went straight from the lift to Marcus and John Hayes. 'Am I here? Can you see me? Do I exist?'

On the training pitch, though, Eddie missed nothing. I got his back up one morning in a contact session and he withered me in front of everyone. Mike Ford was our new defence coach and he was winding me up. 'When are you going to put in a big shot for me, Donners?' I was primed to explode on the next ball-carrier that came round the corner. My innocent victim was David Humphreys. Humph was the weakest ball-carrier we had and the lightest guy in the squad. I melted him. Ronan O'Gara was out injured at the time which obviously made Humph even more precious.

Eddie blew his whistle and stopped the session immediately. He came striding over to me and I half expected a little tribute speech about my tackle along the lines of 'That's the kind of shit we need'. Instead, he embarrassed the life out of me. He was murder for sarcasm, and he let me have it.

'Can you play ten? Can you?'

I didn't know what to say. I was so stunned that it took me a second to rule out the possibility that he was offering me a career change.

'Eh, no, I can't.'

'Then stop running over the only fucker who can!'

Over time I went full circle with Eddie. I realised that it was nothing personal, he had nothing against me, it was just his way. He wasn't one of those coaches that would put his arm around your shoulder at different times or wanted to have something other than a working relationship. He would acknowledge good work in training but as far as he was concerned the biggest compliment he could pay any player was to pick him in the squad or the team. It didn't need any elaboration from him. That was his way of saying, 'You're here because you're good enough. Now, I need you to do this, this and this.' Some of the senior players had a decent relationship with Eddie but I always got the impression that it wouldn't bother him if he didn't speak to a player between the end of one training session and the beginning of the next one.

After a while he realised that I liked the craic and every so often he'd try to join in. Like the old days in school when the teacher cracked a joke I always laughed my head off at Eddie's gags, whether they were funny or not. There were other times, in team meetings, when he was genuinely funny but fellas were afraid to laugh. He'd be going through a match video with his infra-red pencil, stopping the tape and pointing things out. He had a pile of one-liners that he used to reel off. 'You're as useful there as a trap door in a canoe', or 'You're as useful there as a chocolate fireguard.'

I don't know if he was playing for laughs, or what his reaction would have been if people had laughed. He was obviously using these lines to make a serious point, and when the infra-red pencil was pointing at you on the screen it wasn't good news. There were days when I was biting the inside of my cheek to stop myself from laughing but I might have been the only one in the room. I used to take him off behind his back but Guy

Easterby was the only one brave enough to do it to his face. He'd step up to the microphone at the top of the bus and do his routine. Eddie seemed to take it in good heart.

After Russia we went on a ten-match winning run. The buzz around the squad was incredible and it was great to be part of it. What it meant for a fringe player like me, though, was that I was depending on injuries for an opportunity. Malcolm O'Kelly, Paulie, Gary Longwell and Leo Cullen were all ahead of me in the pecking order for the second row. To have any chance of even sitting on the bench I needed two of them to be unavailable.

For the Six Nations match against Wales in Cardiff in March 2003, it happened. Gary and Paulie were out, I was in.

It was a strange and emotional week: the eighteenth anniversary of my father's death and my debut for my country wearing the number eighteen shirt. It was an unbelievable coincidence that meant a lot to Mom. Since I was a kid, that week in the middle of March had only meant one thing in our family. This time we were all able to feel something other than sadness. There was no better way to mark Dad's memory.

It was my first time in the match-day twenty-two and I wasn't sure how to handle it. If I'd been starting I would have been a bag of nerves, but when you're subbing you know there's a chance you won't get on so that takes the edge off it. I was rooming with Rog – Ronan

O'Gara – and every day there were good-luck faxes being pushed under the hotel-room door.

The build-up changed for me, though, at the captain's meeting the night before the game. In all the time I'd spent around the squad in the previous couple of years I'd never been at one of these meetings. Kevin Maggs was playing and his passion for the jersey was respected by everyone. He said his piece and got very emotional. Then he picked me out.

'It's a fucking great day for you tomorrow,' he said. 'I hope you get a result. I know when you're on the pitch you'll give everything.'

Standing for the anthems in the Millennium Stadium blew me away. The Welsh supporters lifted the roof. When we were kids at home watching the internationals we always turned up the volume full blast for the anthems. I stood there thinking, 'I'm living my dream here.' But I wasn't fazed by it. Sitting on the bench, I felt really comfortable. Rog, Frankie Sheahan and John Kelly were all subs too and these were guys I'd won an All-Ireland League with. I didn't feel out of place or in awe of anything.

The match itself was a panic. We were still in front when I came on with about fifteen minutes to go but we were only hanging on. There was a line-out on the far side and I sprinted across the field. You've never seen a sub join play like I did that day. I wasn't going to waste a second. For the remainder of the match I never stopped. If you looked at the footage now I'd probably look like a headless chicken. I was desperate to have one 'moment' in the match. A carry, a big tackle, a catch, something. Fellas said afterwards that I was 'all-action', but I probably achieved nothing. The pace of the game was a complete shock to my system. I had never experienced anything like it. The Heineken Cup didn't come close. By the end my throat was burning.

In the last few minutes Stephen Jones put Wales in front with a drop goal and then Rog responded immediately. He played a perfect re-start, Mal did brilliantly to win it back, and Rog knocked it over from the ten-metre line. We had one more massive scare when Denis Hickie blocked a Jones drop at goal and Justin Bishop probably should have been pinged for offside. Then the final whistle went. Irish players fell to their knees all over the field. I jumped around like a lunatic for what felt like about two minutes. We'd needed a win to set up a Grand Slam match against England at Lansdowne Road the following week so the tension had been crazy.

None of that really concerned me, though. I'd played for Ireland. At that moment, that's all that mattered.

At the post-match banquet debutants are presented with their cap. As I walked up to receive mine the whole place stood up and clapped. I looked around the room and the hair stood up on the back of my neck. Whatever happened next, I had come this far.

7

Stung

I

After my first cap it was seven months to the 2003 World Cup. We were hammered by England in the Grand Slam decider at Lansdowne Road at the end of the Six Nations but that was Ireland's first defeat in eleven Tests. The team was more or less settled. Nobody was screaming for changes.

Making the World Cup squad should have been my goal for the rest of the year but I wasn't thinking in those terms. I didn't line up that target and charge bald-headed for it. Putting it like that probably seems like a lack of ambition, but I don't think that was the problem. Lack of confidence was probably the issue. I had just come through my first full campaign with

Munster and I was still proving things to myself. With Ireland I felt part of the scene without feeling part of their plans. I knew I was learning and I desperately wanted to be there but I probably accepted my place in the rankings. Maybe I accepted my place too easily.

The summer tour was in two parts that year: a Test match against Australia followed by games against Tonga and Samoa. For the Test I sat in the stands but then nine of the first-choice players were sent home and the rest of the squad were given a chance. Gary Longwell and Malcolm O'Kelly were on the plane which left Paulie, Leo Cullen and me for the second row.

Going to Tonga was like being on an old-fashioned tour from the amateur days. The accommodation was rough and the food was dodgy. We were given a lot of this green fish that looked angry on the plate. Nobody ate much. In our rooms at the hotel the air conditioning sounded like the engine of a Suzuki 180. I was rooming with David Wallace and we came up with a plan. We'd suffer the noise for an hour until the room was cool and then turn it off. That was our opportunity to get to sleep until eventually the oppressive heat would wake one of us and we had to rev up the bike again. There was a good spirit, though, on that leg of the tour. We were transported to training on a pick-up truck, all of us standing in the back. No bus, no luxuries.

I played only the last few minutes against Tonga. We

came from eleven points down to win 40–19 in conditions that were incredibly tough with crazy heat and a rock-hard pitch. It was just as bad in Samoa. Maybe worse. For the afternoon kick-off temperatures were in the mid-thirties with blasting heat, like a giant pizza oven. The pitch was covered in weeds but there was no cushion when you hit the deck. My knees and elbows were so badly skinned that they weren't right for two months. During the match nobody could breathe. Even the Samoans were struggling. Our red-haired lads suffered the most. Anthony Horgan made his international debut and had to be replaced because he got sun stroke. He couldn't even attend the ceremony for his first cap that evening. He had a cold towel wrapped around his head, was in an awful state. Jonathan Bell was so dehydrated that he had to be placed on a drip afterwards. The only one of our ginger lads who kept going was Paulie, mostly because he's a lunatic.

Leo started that match too but he dislocated his shoulder after seventeen minutes which gave me my chance. I remember thinking, 'I'm flying fit, our fellas are bollixed already – I'm going to drive on here.' After five minutes I couldn't breathe. My jersey felt like a duffel coat. Getting through that game was a mental challenge as much as a physical one. They weighed us before the game and again afterwards. Some fellas lost 9kg; I lost about six. We beat them handy but it was one of the toughest experiences any of us had had on a rugby field.

The second half of the tour changed my thinking about the World Cup. It gave me hope. I lapped up the training when the squad was cut back. Our sessions were videoed and there were opportunities for one-on-one meetings with our video analyst Mervyn Murphy. The quality of Mervyn's work is so high that sitting down with him is often worth four or five field sessions. It was a chance to do extra homework, and I've always had an appetite for that. Doing more has always given me confidence. Other fellas can get away with doing less. I can't.

If I was going to make the World Cup squad I had to overtake Leo. He was only a year older than me but he had a dozen caps already. We had played together in the back row at the U-21s World Cup in Argentina but he'd broken into first-team rugby much more quickly than I had. Leo had a big reputation from schools rugby too. He'd captained an Irish team that was unbeaten on a tour of Australia and in terms of his career he was always a couple of strides ahead of me.

I remember one day I played against him for Munster U-20s against Leinster U-20s and he levelled me with a great tackle. I took the ball on what we used to call a 'Rambo' run. It was a simple one-out move where the scrum-half gives it to one of the forwards who takes it up. I roared for the ball: 'Rambo, Rambo, Rambo!' And then Leo emptied me. At that moment only one of us felt like Sylvester Stallone.

In September 2003, shortly before the World Cup

squad was named, Munster played Leinster in the Celtic League at Donnybrook. In my mind, this was a final trial. Neither team was at full strength but Leo was playing for them. My brother Eddie had a good chat with me before the game. 'You can't make this into a one-on-one battle. You must play your own game and forget about him.' Still, I couldn't put him out of my head completely.

I don't know how Leo viewed that match or whether he rated me as a serious threat for his place in the squad, but we had a good battle. He tried to wind me up a few times but for once I kept my head. He was perfectly entitled to do it. Everybody tries to play on their opponent's big weakness and I had a reputation for poor discipline. He shoed me in the shins at the back of a ruck and I'd love to have given him a flake. Maybe that's what he wanted too. Nothing personal, just part of the give and take. Anyway, I didn't. Brian O'Brien, the Ireland manager, was at the match and he spotted the incident. 'You did well to keep your head there,' he said to me afterwards. It made the pain worthwhile.

I was at home with Mom when the squad was announced. The players that were left out were supposed to get a call before eleven o'clock. I did my best to disguise my hopes of making it but I had come on in the warm-up games against Wales and Italy and I knew I was in with a real shout. I was wasting my time trying to fool the lads. Quinny rang up pretending to be Brian O'Brien. Normally you'd be wise to a wind-up call like that but I was so nervous that he caught me round as a hoop. I copped on after half a minute but my heart was in my throat by then and Quinny had his laugh at my expense.

Mom and I listened to the squad announcement on the radio in the front room. When my name was called out I took off, roaring and jumping. I ended up in the back garden. I had squeezed in ahead of Leo.

The World Cup was an education. I was a willing learner but I was still leaving myself exposed to hard lessons. On the training field I had another scene with Eddie. He had brought in the policy of 'designated ball-carriers' in the forwards. I had no proof, but I always suspected that Keith Wood was a big influence on that decision. Not only was he the captain but he was the best ball-carrying hooker in world rugby. It made sense that he would have the ball in his hands as much as possible and for the rest of the muppets to get out of his way. Naturally, Paulie was another of the designated ball-carriers.

At training one day a few of the squad players fell in for a turn. For the purpose of the drill Marcus Horan and Victor Costello were the designated ball-carriers, and that status was sacred. Anyway, Horan was pinned down by Kevin Maggs in the tackle and he couldn't step up to make a carry. So I stepped in. I carried the ball as far as I could and made the best of it. I made savage yardage until the sound of Eddie's whistle brought everything to a halt.

'Whoa, whoa, whoa!' he shouted, like a fella trying to slow down a galloping horse. 'Don't fucking move! Nobody fucking move!'

Not for the first time in my short international career I thought this was the moment Eddie was going to recognise my brilliance and bring it to everybody's attention. He walked over to where I had finished up and the second he opened his mouth I knew I was going to be fried again.

'What the fuck were you doing?'

I was still out of breath after my epic break so I took ages to answer: 'Marcus was . . . pinned down . . . so I stepped up . . . to carry it—'

'I don't give a flying fuck if Marcus was in Timbuktu,' said Eddie, 'you're not a designated ball-carrier.'

'But he wouldn't have been—'

'I don't give a fuck!'

The other rocket I got from Eddie at that World Cup, though, was probably more serious. Six o'clock was a regular time for team meetings on that trip and I was nine minutes late for one of them. I had no excuse and I didn't try to make one up. I went for a nap in the afternoon and either I slept through the alarm or I didn't set it properly. When I opened my eyes the bedside clock said 6.01. I was half dressed in my bedroom on the seventh floor when I desperately needed to be in the team room on the second floor a few minutes earlier. I had this terrible feeling of paralysis. I was trying to do everything in a rush but I felt like I was getting nothing done quickly.

After the meeting I went straight up to Eddie to apologise and he let me have it with both barrels. I deserved it. Woody asked me to give him a shout later that evening and we had a really good chat. Being late for a team meeting sent out all the wrong signals, as if I had just come along for the ride. I wasn't in the team and I had no realistic chance of starting, but you can't afford to have that mentality, or to be suspected of it. I couldn't deny, though, that part of me was just happy to be in the squad, and Woody tackled me on that.

'You can't be waiting around hoping it will fall into your lap,' he said. 'You must grab it and make it happen.'

The other annoying thing about being late was that I always took Eddie's meetings very seriously. He went into a lot of detail and after a while I started taking notes. I didn't trust myself to remember everything properly and I wanted to be able to look back over stuff in my own time. As the only player in the room taking notes I knew I'd be slaughtered so I bought a pink Barbie notepad to make fun of myself before the rest of them got a chance. It didn't stop them, but I felt like I was dictating the terms a little bit.

Compared to the World Cup from hell in 2007, this was a dream trip. Our training base was in Terrigal, a beautiful spot on the New South Wales coast, and every day after training we had recovery sessions in the ocean. The locals won't go into the water without wetsuits at that time of the year because it's too cold but it felt like a lovely warm bath to us. We tried surfing, we went on day trips, and apart from the build-up to the Argentina match there was no tension around the place. We had a laugh.

Some of it was at my expense. I was sharing with Simon Easterby who was incredibly neat and organised. In the room he had a place for everything and the stuff he'd need for the following day was laid out the night before. I took my lead from him which meant we probably had the tidiest room in the squad. One day I came back from training, though, and order had turned to chaos. The room was bare. Anything that wasn't nailed to the wall or the floor had been taken. They'd even removed the light bulbs. It was an amazing job. For training the next day we had to pick up spare gear from our bagman Paddy O'Reilly – or Rala as we all knew him.

Immediately I suspected Frankie Sheahan or Simon's brother Guy. It emerged later that Malcolm O'Kelly was the culprit, but by then we had targeted Frankie for our revenge attack. Simon and me turned everything in his room upside down. It took us two and a half hours to get it just right but at this level of guerrilla warfare you must have standards.

We eventually got our stuff back after a tip-off led us to the patio of an unoccupied room.

The standing joke on that trip was Lizzie the Lizard, a dead reptile that we picked up coming home from training one day. She showed up in all sorts of places, usually where she was least expected. Some lads found her in their wash bags. I found her in my pillow case. I knew there was a funny smell in the room but I slept with Lizzie for two nights before I discovered the cause of the stink. That kind of messing always sounds juvenile when you describe it to people living in the outside world but when you're away on a long tour like the World Cup you'd go mad if you didn't have a bit of craic. The World Cup in France four years later was proof of that.

The only downside for me was my role with the laundry. Somebody had to do it, and with only a handful of caps to my name I was an obvious target. Everyone's name was on their stuff but after the gear had been washed it arrived back in a huge bucket. My job was to sift through and put everyone's gear together, right down to matching everyone's socks. It was a nightmare. Rala would sit there while I was doing it but he wouldn't lift a finger to help. If the laundry wasn't done right there'd be murder. I also discovered that a couple of the big shots had a personal arrangement with Rala for their gear to be laundered separately. Rala tried to protect the secret, but after a while it was clear that some players' gear never tumbled out of the bucket. Drico and Woody, definitely. When I started rooming with Rog later on I found out that he had laundry privileges too. They had a special code as well. If they needed something laundered quickly they'd go up to him and say, 'Rala, will you throw that down the Yellow Brick Road.' Later on I was given those privileges too, just to buy my silence.

On the field I probably took one step forward and two steps back. I got a run off the bench against Romania in our pool match and didn't do anything wrong until I refused to swap jerseys after the game. It was my first appearance at the World Cup and my first instinct was to keep the top. I got a bollicking from some of the lads in the dressing room afterwards and Hayes told me to go into their dressing room and swap with yer man. I'm glad I did. It was a novice's mistake.

When I came on against Australia in our final pool match I made the kind of mistakes that were holding back my career. In a tight match I gave away two stupid penalties down at their end of the field. Controllable ones. It released the pressure on them when we were trying to turn the screw. They beat us by a point, which meant a really tough quarter-final against France for us and a quarter-final against Scotland for them. Coming on when a game of that importance was in the melting pot was a vote of confidence. Only four months earlier I'd been the fifth-choice second row with no guarantee of being in the World Cup squad. This was a real chance to make an impact and do what Woody had said: make it happen. Instead, I blew it.

Nobody said anything to me afterwards. That's how bad it was. It was too obvious for words. France murdered us in the quarter-final. The game was over before half time, but Eddie left me on the bench. It was easy to decode the message: he was punishing me for the penalties against Australia.

I couldn't carry on like this.

II

25 April 2004 – Heineken Cup semi-final, Lansdowne Road

We were leading Wasps by ten points when the sky fell in. Nigel Williams, the referee, said I'd killed the ball. Penalty. Lawrence Dallaglio, the Wasps captain, was in his ear straight away. Just as he'd been all day, just like he always was with referees. 'You penalised my player down there and you said the next player was going in the bin.' I was probably gone no matter what Dallaglio said. Williams had already binned two of their players, one of them for the same offence. They'd been as cynical as hell. By the time Williams pinged me the penalty count was 18–5 against them. Didn't matter. I'd put myself in a position where he could do me.

It was a savage hot day and they were coming at us. There were only seventeen minutes left when I was binned and some of our guys were feeling the pace. My stupidity had increased their work load. I sat in the bin, stewing. We were hanging on and holding them out. Then the match exploded in our faces. Just before my ten minutes were up Rob Henderson was binned as well. I was standing on the line, bursting to get back in. We were down to thirteen but the fourth official and the touch judge wouldn't let me on until the ball went dead. Nowadays? I'd probably ignore them and just run on to the field. Back then? I did what I was told.

Rog had been off since the first half with a hamstring injury and Jason Holland was playing out-half in his place. He failed to find touch with a sliced kick, they ran it back, and Tom Voyce scored in the corner. I stood on the touchline watching this, helpless. It was like one of those car crashes on an icy road that seem to happen in slow motion. Both drivers know what's going to happen and neither of them can get out of the way. I felt like one of the drivers. While I was off the field our ten-point lead had been wiped out.

With Hendo in the bin we were going to finish the game with fourteen men, and they had all the momentum. They scored again. Game over. 37–32. Yet again, for the fifth year in a row now, we had lost a final or a semi-final in the Heineken Cup by less than a score.

Sitting in the dressing room, I felt that load on my shoulders. John Hayes was sitting next to me and he looked shattered. My sin-binning had increased the pressure on everyone at a critical time in the match. The pace of the game had been incredible: seven tries on a sunny day. Five for them. The ball never stopped. The last thing my team mates needed was to be running around trying to fill holes that I had left behind.

John Kelly had a few words with me in the dressing

room. Nobody else said anything. Nobody gave out to me either, and that was nearly worse. They were entitled to be angry. In my mind I had cost us the game and I believed that's what they were thinking. I was nearly waiting for one of them to say it just to get it out in the open.

In the post-match interviews Alan Gaffney went out and batted for me. 'It was the harshest sin-binning I've ever seen in my life,' he said. 'We committed one penalty on the ground, they committed eight, and Donncha came in from the side for a marginal penalty. It was only a marginal penalty and he was binned.'

I appreciated his support. He was trying to take some of the heat off me and there were plenty of commentators who thought it was a bad call by the ref. In private, though, I knew that Alan was annoyed. He let things lie for a couple of weeks before we had a meeting. Same old story: my discipline.

It's funny the things that go through your mind. We travelled home on the train and looking out the window there were lines of cars heading south. About forty-five thousand Munster supporters had shown up in Lansdowne Road that day. It was just getting dusky and all you could see for miles were red brake lights, stuck in traffic, crawling home. They were bound to be discussing the match and I imagined what they were saying about me.

In a nightclub in Cork later that night one Munster supporter didn't leave anything to my imagination. I was with a few of the other Munster players but that didn't stop yer man from unloading his frustration on me. Jimmy Williams hunted him away but I went straight home. I had no desire to get involved with a drunk supporter and I had no mind to defend myself either. As far as I was concerned there was no case for my defence. The lads tried to stop me but I went straight out the door. They were going on the piss again the following day but I didn't join them. I didn't go out after a Munster match for two years after that. Until we won the Heineken Cup, basically.

For about two weeks I was in hell. I didn't want to walk down the street, I didn't want to be seen around the place. Even at training I felt ashamed of myself. I didn't talk to any of the others about it. The Munster dressing room is no place for self-pity. Looking back, I probably took everything too much to heart. At the same time, maybe I needed to feel like that if anything was going to change. It was a huge turning point in my career. I couldn't keep on talking about change or getting advice about it or making promises to myself or getting bollickings from other people. I had to do it.

I had three problems that were all related: my discipline wasn't good enough, my relationship with referees wasn't good enough, and because of that I had an image problem. Before a ball was kicked referees expected to penalise me and I gave them too many opportunities. I wasn't taking care of all the little things that make a difference.

My brother Eddie suggested that I sit down with a referee and talk about it. At the time Dave McHugh was the best ref in Ireland with huge international experience. He was working for the IRFU as a regional development officer and he was based in Cork. He agreed to see me, and for the next few months we were in regular contact. He went through everything. We started with the Wasps match and then went back over old videos. He was like an engineer: he examined a side of my game that was structurally unsound and helped me reconstruct it. Neither of us wanted to broadcast what we were doing, even though we often met in public places. I could have used it in interviews to show how concerned I was about my discipline and how hard I was working on correcting the problem but I knew Dave didn't want that attention. The work he was doing with me was so valuable that the last thing I wanted to do was jeopardise it for any short-term gain.

What Dave made me realise most of all was that I wasn't thinking enough about that side of the game. Playing the ref is all about small things. Like, before every match the referee will go into both dressing rooms to say a few words about what he expects from the players. Instead of making an effort to shake his hand, make eye contact and have a couple of words I would just ignore him. I would always keep my head down, and if he saw me I probably looked like I was sucking nettles.

In a lot of cases they already had their mind made up about me. Before one match the French referee Joel

Jutge approached me in the dressing room. 'Today I want you to play, yes, with passion, but no craziness. Play with your heart but no crazy. You listen to me today.' I was completely taken aback. This guy thought I was a nutcase. Paulie jumped in and tried to explain to the ref that there wouldn't be a problem but you're not going to change someone's perception a couple of minutes before kick-off.

Without realising it I was portraying myself in a certain way to them. In that Wasps semi, for example, Joe Worsley was sin-binned early on and as he left the field I gave him a mouthful of abuse or whatever. I didn't think anything of it. But Dave said, you've got to look at that from a referee's point of view. He would have heard it and subconsciously it would have helped form a negative view of me in his mind. When it came to a marginal call, that wasn't going to do me any favours. Dallaglio could easily have been sin-binned in that match but he knew how to play the ref without pushing it too far. I hadn't acquired that skill.

Over the last few years analysing the ref and working out his 'hot' penalties has become a routine part of the build-up to every big match with Ireland and Munster. Back then we didn't go into that kind of detail with Munster. Dave made me do that homework. I went through old videos of our next ref and worked out what things you might get away with and what things you definitely wouldn't. In rugby, gamesmanship, cheating, call it what you will, goes on all the time. If you get caught and give away a needless penalty you're going to be slaughtered in the next video review meeting. If you get away with it everyone applauds it as a bit of 'cuteness'. There are always grey areas where you can take a calculated risk. And if you know the ref you'll have a better idea of the odds.

The key for me was to look at this area of the game in a way that other people did. Eddie O'Sullivan pulled me up one day after a Munster game in the Magners League. The ref was Jonathan Kaplan, who was going to be in charge of Ireland's next Test. I'd given away a good few penalties and Eddie was on my case straight away. From Eddie's viewpoint I had made a bad impression on this referee and he subtly let me know that this could be a factor in team selection. Until I straightened out this problem I was harming myself from every angle.

For the first time in my career I was getting on top of it.

8

Two in a Row

In schools rugby every team has stars that everybody else knows about. In my time St Munchin's had Jerry Flannery and Jeremy Staunton and they were on everybody's radar; Ardscoil Rís had Mossy Lawlor and Paul Neville. I'd never heard of Paul O'Connell. He didn't appear on the list. Anyway, he got better.

He was a year-group below me when we first played together for the Munster U-20s so I was in my second season when he made his breakthrough. We lost to Connacht that season. People probably thought that Munster wouldn't get much from that team. For me, what started there was the most important relationship in my working life and one of the greatest friendships.

We hit it off from the beginning. Over time it became

obvious that we were very different in some ways, but I suppose every friendship starts with common ground. I liked him. He didn't go on with any bullshit. The snobby element in rugby was a million miles from either of us. On the field he was incredibly honest and that appealed to me. I thought at first he was a bit quiet, but the U-20s went on the piss after one of the games and when he got giddy he was a messer. That contradiction has always been there with Paulie. He's the most intense man on the planet, and in that respect he's a lunatic. The fun side of him has never been part of his public image.

We were picked together for the Ireland U-20s and U-21s and the bond we've had as team mates for all of our adult lives started to develop. In one of those seasons we played Wales in Thomond Park and he was unbelievable. The crowd went crazy for him and his performance had an effect on everyone else in a green jersey. People could see very quickly that he was a special player.

For our relationship to work on the field, though, the respect had to be mutual. From an early stage I was at ease about that. There's nothing fake about Paulie. If he didn't rate me he wouldn't have been able to hide it. Before one of the Munster U-20 games I made a speech about what it meant to wear the red jersey and he told me later how much he got out of it. I haven't made many big dressing-room speeches in my career but I remember being pleased that it connected with him. Anyone who has ever shared a dressing room with

Paulie will know the feeling of wanting to impress him.

In the early days of our friendship when we played against each other for Con and Young Munster in the All-Ireland League I never ran my mouth with him. I'm sure the significance of that was lost on Paulie but it was a conscious thing on my part. I didn't make that exception for anybody else. We were opponents on the day but I wasn't going to disrespect our friendship with a few cheap verbals. In fairness, he didn't either.

Competition has been a big part of our relationship, though. As team mates it drives us. I can't remember exactly when it started but I know it didn't take long. I remember an All-Ireland League game when Con beat Young Munster in Temple Hill but he scored a great try at the death when the result was already decided. I was really pissed off that he had a stand-out moment in the match. Leaving the ground, everyone was talking about the up-and-coming second row from Young Munster.

As team mates, post-match statistics became our battlefield. There were some categories, like carries, where he was always going to beat me, but as the stats became more detailed and sophisticated over the years I didn't have to worry about not looking good with the ball in my hands. At the end of every player's stats sheet the positive moments are totalled up, and that's the bottom line. The public watching the match or even your team mates wouldn't spot a fraction of that stuff, but the video misses nothing. That would appeal to

Paulie as well. You might fool some of the pundits but you can't fool the stats.

We also tried to best each other in stuff that wouldn't appear in the stats: getting up off the ground quickly, getting into the defensive line quickly, working hard on the hunt in defence, never walking when we could be running. Tony McGahan, our coach at Munster, picks up on that stuff.

On the field that personal battle spurs us on. If he makes a tackle I want to make the next tackle, except I want to make mine a more dominant tackle than his. And on it goes like that from play to play. I want to have the highest work rate in the pack, if not the team. That's the target I set for myself in every match. Going head-to-head with Paulie is probably the best way to reach that target.

We share a passion for high standards, but he has a different way of expressing it. I call him Keano because he refuses to accept second best. He goes bananas at times if things aren't done right. The difference between me and him is that he's not afraid to confront people about it. He calls me Undercover Keano because I'll tip him off and then he'll do the dirty work. He's always the bad cop. Marcus or someone might come over to me and say, 'Paulie's after chewing the balls off me,' and I'm there, 'Jesus, that's desperate.' I'd give them the sympathy even though I might have been one of the instigators.

Paulie doesn't hold back or spare people's feelings but

the lads will take it from him. They might be sour about it for a while afterwards but nobody would ever question his motives. He doesn't pick and choose his targets either. He'll give out to anybody if he thinks they deserve it, regardless of whether it's a senior player or not.

A couple of times in his career he has been out with long-term injuries, and with Munster especially, one of the places we missed him most was in the video review meetings. He was injured for much of 2010 but he popped in to a video meeting one day and the second he opened his mouth you realised how much of a loss he'd been in that room. Against the Ospreys James Coughlan had given away a penalty under our posts and was sin-binned. Paulie got straight to the point: 'What the fuck did you think you were going to do? Rip the ball and run ninety-five yards up the pitch?' Somebody else could have said that but it wouldn't have had the same impact. Most fellas wouldn't have the balls to say it anyway. When Paulie isn't around in those meetings there are lads who step up to the plate, in fairness, but they can't replace what he brings to the table.

The coaches don't get away with anything either, with Munster or Ireland. If there's a bit of waffle, or if he thinks one of the coaches is going off the point, he jumps in. We might have been shown three great attacking moves by our next opponents and we're all thinking, 'Yeah, they're good at that all right, very dangerous.' Paulie, though, will be thinking beyond that straight away: 'What are we going to do about it?'

On the pitch we have it out. If you heard us during matches you'd never believe we were friends. We argue in training sessions as well but there's never any bad blood. No matter how bad an argument might have been, it never lingers afterwards. Anything he says to me is for the good of the team and I accept that completely. There was a time when we used to get very emotional with each other before matches, nearly beating the heads off each other to get pumped up. Not just in the dressing room but in the way we'd talk about a match in the build-up. After a while, though, we matured and copped on. It wasn't doing us any good and over time we realised that we didn't need it. I know he'll look after his job and I hope as captain he doesn't have to worry about me.

We've never roomed together much – hardly at all – which is probably just as well. I like to have a chat with my room mates whereas Paulie would prefer to be reading than making small talk. He's great craic and he's a social animal but as far as I can see he eats books. I think it comes back to his need to work things out. He wants to be on top of stuff. Like, when the global economy went into recession Paulie wanted to know exactly why it happened. He went out, bought the three best books on the subject, and consumed them. I remember being in his company at dinner one night during an Ireland camp in Dublin when the economist and writer David McWilliams came over with his son, looking for an autograph. Paulie recognised him and began interrogating him about the economy. 'Should

Above left: With Jenny on the bus to our first Six Nations dinner in March 2004.

Above right: Friends and rivals: with Malcolm O'Kelly at a Six Nations dinner.

Below: Taking a ride on the back of a van in Tonga during the 2003 Irish tour with Paddy Wallace, Niall O'Donovan, Keith Wood, Marcus Horan and Arthur Tanner.

Top left: Outjumping Chris Wyatt of the Llanelli Scarlets in the 2005 Celtic League final.

Top right: My relationship with referees is something I have had to work on over the years. Here I am, having a word with Paul Adams during a Celtic League match in 2003.

Centre left: Among some giants of Munster rugby (*left to right*): Christian Cullen, Anthony Foley, Jim Williams and Paul O'Connell (with hair).

Right: In the maul. Determined to shield the ball from Alastair Kellock of Edinburgh Gunners.

Left: Celebrating a crucial try with Marcus Horan in a 2006 Heineken Cup match against the Leicester Tigers.

Below: Diving for a try against Bourgoin in the Heineken Cup, October 2006.

Left: Running in support as Rog breaks through the Leinster defence to score in the Heineken Cup semi-final, 23 April 2006.

Below centre: Celebrating victory over Biarritz in the Heineken Cup final at the Millennium Stadium, Cardiff, 20 May 2006.

Bottom left: Taking a quiet moment to give thanks immediately after the match.

Bottom right: A roaring celebration in the changing room.

Breaking forward for Munster (**above**) against Biarritz in the 2010
Heineken Cup semi-final and (**below**) against London Irish, October 2010.

Top: Alan Quinlan, Pat Geraghty and myself in a happy changing room after the 2008 Heineken Cup final.

Centre: (*Left to right*): Marcus Horan, John Hayes, myself, Paul O'Connell, Rua Tipoki, Jerry Flannery, Denis Leamy and David Wallace celebrating a second Heineken Cup victory for Munster.

Right: Homecoming celebrations in Limerick.

Above: After having been put through our paces by Paul Darbyshire in the Harvard Gym, Boston, 2008. (*Standing left to right*): Alan Quinlan, John Hayes, Rog, Doug Howlett, Jerry Flannery, Paul O'Connell, Phil, Marcus Horan and Peter Stringer. (*Front*): Paul Darbyshire and myself.

Below: At Paul Darbyshire's 40th birthday dinner (*left to right*): Tomás O'Leary, Anthony Horgan, Paul Darbyshire, Denis Leamy, myself, Bryan Carney, Mick O'Driscoll, Denis Fogarty and Frankie Sheahan.

Above left: Closing down on Jonny Wilkinson in the Munster vs Toulon match at Thomond Park in October 2010.

Above right: Dejected on the sideline as defeat to Toulon ends our 2011 Heineken Cup campaign.

Below: A happy squad on a better day. Munster: Magners League Champions 2010/11.

we back out of the euro and go back to the punt?' The poor man was out for a family dinner and Paulie had him under cross-examination.

What it also shows is that he has an open mind. I know that if I find a new dietary supplement that I think is good he'll want to know about it. There are other fellas in the Munster dressing room who would dismiss it without even giving it a chance.

When it comes to rugby I love the fact that Paulie is such a competitive bastard. What I give him hell about is that he has to be so competitive at everything. He was a great swimmer and a talented golfer when he was younger but he chose rugby in the end and applied himself to that. He can't just enjoy golf now, though. He's tearing his hair out if he doesn't shoot a lower score than the last time he played. He'll deny that, but it's true.

Anyway, I'd nearly forgive him when it comes to golf because a lot of fellas seem to get excited about that game. I draw the line when it comes to dopey games in the team room. One night in Ireland camp someone organised a game of Monopoly. There was a sheet on the wall for anybody who wanted to put his name down. Three names went up and then Paulie added his to the list. And that was it. Once fellas saw O'Connell up there they ran a mile from it.

His competitiveness doesn't always impact on other people because his biggest opponent is probably himself. During one Ireland camp he saw a fella doing a one-arm press-up on YouTube. He tried it and failed. That was never going to be the end of it. He went back on the internet looking for techniques, he asked for advice from our three physios and our fitness guy at the time, Mickey McGurn. 'What's the best way?' I walked by the team room one night and there he was, doing it. I burst out laughing. He couldn't just let it go, he had to conquer it.

The best of all was during the 2003 World Cup in Australia. A gang of us went surfing, all of us first-timers, milky-white Paddies down at the beach. The rest of the surfers were togged out in their wetsuits, we were in rugby shorts. The instructor told us, 'Stay in the white water, that's where you'll have most fun.' Who was he talking to? In his mind, Paulie heard a voice from *Point Break*. He followed the experienced surfers, bobbing on his board, waiting around for the perfect wave. When it came, Paulie went for it. All of a sudden the wave crashed and the board came up in two halves. The instructor couldn't believe it. 'I've been surfing for thirty years and I haven't broken a board. He's been surfing for thirty minutes!'

Paulie knows I get a laugh from that side of his personality but he can't help himself. I caught him a beaut in camp one night. We have table-tennis rallies against the wall and we keep track of the record. Stephen Ferris was on a good roll and I spotted Paulie coming in. Fez was miles off the record but I saw an opportunity to wind up Paulie. 'Just play along here, kid,' I whispered to Fez. Then I started counting out loud: 'Sixty-one, sixty-two, sixty-three . . .' The rally broke down but I made sure Paulie knew that a new record had been set. 'Sixty-five is the number to beat now, lads.' Before he left the team room that night Paulie had beaten the fictional record.

Paulie accuses me of being just as bad in a different way. When there are golf outings with Munster I don't go because I have no interest in golf and I wouldn't be any good. Sometimes at training they'll throw out a soccer ball or hurleys, just for a bit of craic. I don't get involved. I know I'm not any good at those games and I suppose I don't want to make a fool of myself – I have other ways of doing that. Paulie holds that against me. 'You're not doing it because you know you're no good,' he says. 'At least I'll keep going until I make myself good at it.'

Behind it all, though, he's a serious messer. When it comes to slagging, nobody gets the better of him. He has an incredibly sharp wit and he'll cut you down in two seconds flat. He'll fight dirty as well. When you have nicknames like Keano and Psycho that leads to a certain image, but he can be as outrageous as any of us.

There was a classic example on the 2005 Lions tour. The coach, Clive Woodward, had appointed Alastair Campbell to handle the media. After his experience with the Labour Party and Tony Blair he probably thought this would be a doddle. A group of rugby players on tour, though, is a different challenge to

Downing Street. One of the juvenile pranks we play is to look out for tracksuit bottoms that haven't been tied properly, pull them down, stick a foot on top of them so that the victim can't pull them back up and, if all goes to plan, push him over. At a big media conference on the Lions tour, in a room full of reporters and television crews, that's what Paulie did to Campbell.

The story that went round, though, was that I had done it. I wasn't even at that media conference. I was nowhere near the room. I was doing interviews a couple of days later and I was asked about my prank with Alastair. It was like people thought, 'It couldn't have been Paulie, it had to be you.'

On the field, nobody mixes us up. Paulie was a leader from the beginning. When we first started playing together for the Munster U-20s I would have felt confident enough to lead the pack because I was in my second season, but after a while I stood back and left him to speak up. He was brilliant at it. He said the right things at the appropriate time.

Over the years that side of his game got even better. He made huge demands on the players around him but he was able to meet those demands in his own perform-ance. That was the key. If he was going to give out to fellas for not being fit enough he had to be the fittest; if he was going to give out to fellas for their work at the breakdown he had to be perfect at it. For his kind of captaincy he needs to be on higher ground, and he is.

As second-row partners I was the one who felt the

need to change. Paulie was the more talented player with the obvious leadership qualities. I fitted in. Nobody told me I should adapt my game, and it's not something I ever discussed with Paulie. For our partnership to work, though, we had to complement each other. There was no point in me trying to do the things that Paulie was better at. If he was going to carry the ball more I thought I could make an impact at rucks and make a contribution with my work rate.

At times my brothers would have urged me to get my hands on the ball more, and part of me would have loved that role. But the shitty work must be done too, and that was my job. It wasn't enjoyable. Most of the time people wouldn't notice what I was doing. The stats would tell a tale when the video analysis was done but the backs on my team probably couldn't tell you whether I'd played well or not. My role involved a certain amount of self-sacrifice, but I was comfortable with that.

In matches, I don't tend to have stand-out moments. There's no glamour in jumping at the front of the line-out. When the throw is called on me it's usually in a defensive situation or when we desperately need to secure the ball. A ball to the front is too slow to launch an attack out wide. Everyone has seen the brilliant photograph of Paulie making a catch in the middle of the line-out against England at Croke Park. It's a wide-angle shot, he's miles up in the air, and it looks spectacular. It's in posters, it's framed on the walls of pubs, it's everywhere. Paulie's career is full of those kinds of photographs. In action shots I don't look like that.

Because we've played so much together for so long – Munster, Ireland, the Lions – our names are always linked. It is clear to everyone, however, that Paulie is the senior partner. At various times over the years I have been in his shadow, even though he has never made me feel like that. I've always believed that he appreciates what I bring to our partnership and that he trusts me. He makes the line-out calls and he has never used that power for his own glorification. On top of everything else he's a selfless player. He calls the ball where he thinks we're going to win it. On the last Lions tour, in 2009, we only played once together and to have any chance of making the Test team I had a lot of ground to make up. He called a lot of ball on me that day. I'm sure that would have changed if I wasn't winning it, but he wanted to give me every chance of making an impression.

On the previous Lions tour, in 2005, we played in two Tests together. For one of the games they got our numbers mixed up. My name appeared on the number five jersey and his on the number four. We swapped shirts so that we would play in our usual numbers but we had a great chat about it before the match and it turned into a very personal thing. The name on my shirt was O'Connell, the name on his was O'Callaghan, and we made a promise to uphold each other's name.

Our experiences on that tour were completely different. Until the last two Tests I spent most of the time with the mid-week team. We were winning matches and having great craic. The Saturday team, though, were having a miserable time. They were struggling on the field, there was no fun in training, there was no fun in the evenings. The way it was structured it was like two different tours. The mid-week team and the Saturday team didn't train together and we had completely different schedules. At one stage I hadn't seen Paulie for about ten days so I called into his hotel room one afternoon. The curtains were pulled and he was sitting in the corner in darkness. I couldn't make him out.

'Are you in here, kid?'

'Come in and close that fucking door.'

He was completely down in the dumps. Even for Paulie, the intensity around the Saturday team was cruel. I didn't realise it until I was called up from the mid-week team. Ian McGeechan and Gareth Jenkins were looking after us and we used to have games of soccer as a warm-up. When I showed up for training with the Test team you couldn't take a breath out of place. I cracked some line during the warm-up and I got a Keano frown from Paulie. Any kind of light relief was out of the question.

The next Lions tour four years later was better for him and worse for me. In terms of results and performances there were difficult periods on that tour and as captain that increased the pressure on Paulie. The English media, especially, seemed to question his position. Paulie rose above all of it. As a leader of that group he commanded the respect of every player. In some ways his whole career had been building up to that moment. If anybody was born to captain the Lions it was him.

Before the last Test he was in bits. A couple of his teeth had been knocked out and whatever repair job had been done he was in terrible pain all that week. His back was at him too and he didn't sleep properly for three nights in the build-up. You could see the suffering in his face. At that stage of the tour there were fellas jumping ship left, right and centre. I couldn't understand that. Fellas were declaring themselves unfit when there was an opportunity to play for the Lions. And there was Paulie, at the opposite end of the scale. He went out on the field in an awful state and played out of his skin. That week, my respect for him went through the roof.

Paulie wasn't always around. During his absences after the 2007 World Cup and the 2010 Six Nations when he spent months recovering from long-term injuries, and at other times over the years, Mick O'Driscoll was my second-row partner, mostly with Munster but with Ireland at times too. I've known Micko even longer than I've known Paulie. We played together with Con and broke into the Munster squad around the same time, in the autumn of 1998. He's a year older than me but he looks about twelve. Benjamin Button is one of his nicknames – the older he gets, the younger he looks.

We spent a long time together on the margins of the Munster team. For a couple of seasons we fought it out to be the second-row cover on the bench. In that race the lead changed hands a few times. It was tough for Micko. He could have made a career at the front of the line-out but jumping at four was probably his natural position and that's where he played, when he played. Shortly after Micko arrived on the scene Munster signed John Langford to play in that position. He was only supposed to come for a year but he stayed for two. By the time he left Paulie was ready to step up. Then Langford came back for another spell.

When Alan Gaffney came in as Munster coach he plumped for me as Paulie's partner, but if Deccie had stayed Micko could easily have got the nod. Around that time one of us was going to have to leave to get our career kick-started. I stayed and Micko went to Perpignan in France for two seasons. It did him good. He came back with a few knocks because they don't spare their players over there, but he definitely came back a better player.

Micko was a serious threat to me when he returned from France but the fact that he'd been away for those couple of years gave me a chance to bed down in the Munster team. I suppose the order didn't change much over the years. If Paulie and I were fit and available, we were picked. I wonder at times if Micko secretly hates us for getting in his way as much as we have. At times it was awkward. There's never any tension between us and we get on fierce well but there were times when Micko was playing really well and was still left out of big games. You feel like sympathising with him but you know that would be two-faced. If he was picked I would be the one on the bench. We're all competitive animals and none of us wants to take a backward step.

After his time at Perpignan he could have gone to any number of big clubs and had a long career as a first-choice player. He decided to stay at Munster and make the best of it. In our set-up he became a huge team player. If he's not in the team he runs the defensive line-outs against us with the same commitment as if he was playing. If anybody is on that side of the line, outside the team, he sets the standard for performance levels in training. Micko was voted the Players' Player of the Year a couple of seasons ago even though, as he said himself, he spent half the season outside the match-day twenty-two. What that reflected was his positive influence around the place.

He has an unbelievable appetite for work. I might arrive at the gym to do an extra session and he'll be in there twenty minutes before me. He wasn't in the Ireland squad during the 2010 Six Nations and because there was a gap in the Magners League schedule all the Munster players were given ten days off. Micko used that time to beast himself in the gym. It was almost like another pre-season. Word of what Micko was doing got around the place and then peer pressure kicked in. Fellas followed Micko into the gym almost because they'd look bad if they didn't.

Over the years he became a leader in the squad. When Paulie was missing and if Rog wasn't around, Micko was often given the captaincy. I've never been given that honour or that opportunity. It might come before I finish but for now it's a hole in my career. It doesn't stop me from speaking up and having my say, and I know the other senior players respect my opinion. What it shows, though, is that Paulie and Micko are perceived differently to me, and I'm probably a bit envious of that. All those years of acting the clown gave me a certain image that has been very hard to shake off.

Even without the captaincy I still regard myself as a leader in the Munster dressing room. I look at the England team that won the World Cup. They had guys like Martin Johnson and Lawrence Dallaglio in their pack – natural captains. But they also had Richard Hill, a guy who didn't say very much but was a huge contributor to their success and produced an incredibly consistent level of performance. I see myself in that mould. Whatever leadership I give to the team I want it to be in my performances. Doing my stuff, week in, week out, with everybody knowing what they can expect from me.

I know I would be nervous about addressing the lads in a group situation. It's a different skill. In Paulie's speeches there are themes that he comes back to, but he works hard to keep it fresh. Micko has a different style, but it works too.

In Paulie's absence we've had good runs of form at different times. It's funny how people react when that happens. We went through a period in the middle of the 2007/08 season when Munster's performances and results were good, the line-out was going well, and people said that we weren't missing Paulie at all. I found that hard to take at the time. I know it would have been meant as a compliment to Micko and myself, but the people who had that opinion obviously had no idea what Paulie brings to our dressing room and the influence he has on the field.

During that period we got a losing bonus point away to Wasps in the first Heineken Cup pool match. It was regarded by most people as a decent result. But we'd been in a winning position halfway through the second half of that game and I couldn't help thinking that if Paulie had been playing we would have closed the deal. He wouldn't have tolerated some of the mistakes that were made and he would have made demands on everyone in a way that I couldn't do or Micko or any of the other lads.

There are other times when people think we can't cope without Paulie, and I hate that too. If anything goes wrong and he's missing, people jump on his absence as the root cause of our problems. Nobody else in our group has that status.

Does he deserve it? Absolutely.

9

Tarzan

Paulie hit me a dig. I probably deserved it. Given that we were team mates and it was only a training session another fella might have just abused me, but Paulie bypassed any dialogue and got straight to the point. Anyway, the rights and wrongs would have to wait until we finished knocking lumps out of each other. I took a swing at him and the swinging continued until we were wrestling on the ground. Simon Easterby and one or two others eventually broke us up but there was a delay while everyone dealt with the initial shock.

My growing frustration was the cause of it. A few days earlier France had beaten Ireland by eighteen points in the opening game of the 2004 Six Nations in Paris. It wasn't nearly as bad as the hiding they'd given us in the World Cup a few months earlier but it wasn't great either. They got a couple of tries in the third quarter to put the game out of reach and I was sent on in place of Malcolm O'Kelly for the last twenty minutes. It was more than a token run. Malcolm didn't have one of his best games and I saw this as an opportunity to step forward. Keith Wood's advice at the World Cup was in the front of my mind: don't wait for it to happen, make it happen.

Early the following week there was an opportunity to do extra defence work with Mike Ford before training started. Extras like that were not compulsory and only myself, Paulie and Simon Easterby showed up. It started off as a technical session, but after a while Mike realised that we were in the mood for some contact. Before it finished we were hopping off each other. By the time the full training session started my dander was up. Wales were coming to Lansdowne Road on the Sunday which meant that the team wasn't being announced until Wednesday, a day later than usual. The extra day's training gave me a chance to make an impression.

In training, though, there are limits. In my anxiety to make an impression I lost sight of that. The old phrase of training like Tarzan and playing like Jane normally refers to fellas who can't produce it at the weekend. I couldn't afford to wait for the weekend. What was I waiting for? Ten minutes at the end? So, in training that day, I was Tarzan. I was on the B team, contesting every ball like it was a full-blooded match and making training harder than it should be for everyone that came into contact with me. After a while Paulie lost his patience. I was off my feet, killing a ball in the ruck, and he flaked me. I was out of order. We both knew it.

Once it was over, though, that was it. There was no bad blood or tension or sulking. He probably knew how important it was for me to train well and look like I really wanted it. It didn't stop him giving me a flake, but we both knew where we stood and we were cool about it.

'You all right, kid?'

'Yeah, no worries.'

We had to kiss and make up on the bus going back to the hotel because those were the rules. A kiss on the lips. From the whole incident, that was the only bad taste.

It wasn't unusual for Paulie and me to knock lumps out of each other at training but we normally did it in our own time. In the week of an international most fellas are looking to avoid heavy contact but we had a different view. Our target was to put each other through six full-on tackles. We'd hang around after training, put on the protective body armour and cut each other in half. Some weeks it would be as late as Thursday, only a couple of days before the game. Looking back it probably wasn't the smartest plan, but the management never stopped us and in our minds we needed it. Going into a Test match, we felt seasoned.

We weren't the only players who did extras. Simon Easterby always joined us, and Rog. It wasn't always tackling either. Some days we did kick-off receptions, other days it was passing or whatever. The idea of doing more was to improve ourselves. In fairness to Rog, he fell in for a lot of the physical stuff too. He liked to take a few body shots before the weekend. Courage was never an issue with him. Rog's problem was that he thought he was trapped in John Hayes' body.

For the Wales match, I was picked. Nobody ever said it to me but I've always believed that the incident with Paulie swung it. They were looking for a reaction from the France match and I probably had the attitude they were looking for that week. I'd say they also wanted to give Malcolm a kick up the backside. So I was in and he was out.

These days the players are told the team the night before it is released to the media so that anybody being dropped has time to deal with the news. Back then it was done on the morning before training. Nobody had tipped me off. The first I knew of my selection was when Eddie O'Sullivan called out my name. I felt like jumping around the place like a lunatic, but I had to act cool. I was too elated to be nervous. That changed when I calmed down.

This would be my first start. My other eight caps had been off the bench, and in terms of the build-up there's no comparison. After training I had to appear at a press conference. I had done one-on-one interviews as a

Munster player but this was a whole new experience. I had never sat at the top table facing a room full of reporters with television cameras in the background and microphones under my nose. When I looked at myself on telly later my face looked red with nerves. At home it was a different week too. People were calling to the house and sending flowers to Mom. Old friends and school mates got in touch to say they were travelling to the game. My brother Eddie took over my ticket allocation so at least I didn't have the hassle of dealing with requests and doling them out.

Malcolm was incredibly good about being dropped. He had about sixty caps at that stage and this was a setback for him. But he was the first to congratulate me and we had dinner together on Thursday night, along with Paulie and Mick O'Driscoll. At least two of my dinner companions had reason to be pissed off with me that week but we never behaved like rivals off the pitch. Mal was a laid-back witty guy who was fun to be around. Every so often he'd turn up late for a team meeting and Eddie would murder him. Once, over in Rome, Eddie ordered him to leave the room when he arrived late. Mal pleaded for leniency but Eddie could be tough in those situations and he didn't yield an inch.

Of all the second rows I've played with he was probably the most naturally skilful and athletic. At times it seemed like he was elastic. He would go up for a ball and then grow another foot or two at the last second. He had the capacity to control a difficult ball with one hand and just do things easily. That's what I was up against. I didn't have his natural talent, but I wanted his green jersey. I had waited patiently for my chance, and now I had it.

Then I lost it. After half an hour against Wales my kneecap went. I was desperate to carry on and I stayed on the field for the next couple of plays but I had no stability in my knee. I could see Stephen Jones, the Wales out-half, eyeing me up for a killing. I was off and Mal was back in. My full debut lasted thirty-six minutes.

I had suffered a patellar sublaxation and a grade two medial ligament tear. I was told that rehab would take six weeks, which would basically rule me out for the rest of the Six Nations. My first instinct was that I could knock weeks off that recovery if I threw myself bald-headed into the rehab. I could have stayed in camp and been treated by the Ireland physios, but you have to wait your turn on the treatment table and they can only give you so much attention when everybody else needs a piece of them too. So I went back to Cork. Ultan's wife, Carol, is a physio and she gave me incredible care. After a couple of days I was doing squats in a knee brace so that there wouldn't be any muscle wastage around the knee. I showed up in the gym at CIT and fellas were looking at me like I'd two heads as if to say, 'You shouldn't be here. You got crocked on Sunday.'

We were playing England at Twickenham two weeks later and it crossed my mind that it wouldn't be the worst game for me to miss. We hadn't won there for years and in our previous two matches against England they'd put forty points on us each time. I watched the game in Mom's house with my brothers. We won by six points and played great. Mal played out of his skin. Near the end he made a try-saving tackle in the corner and all of us in my mother's front room jumped up, roaring. Then the penny dropped and it went very quiet.

My brother Eddie got straight to the point. 'Make yourself comfortable, kid,' he said. 'You could be watching the next few games here.'

I got back to fitness in three weeks and started against Italy in Lansdowne Road because Paulie had picked up a knock. Mal followed up his brilliant performance against England with a try against Italy. For the Triple Crown match against Scotland I was on the bench – back to square one. I came on as a blood sub for Mal in the first half and I charged around like a bull, looking to get my hands on the ball, trying to convince them that they should leave me on the field. It was a ridiculous thought, but you have to cling to something. When Mal was patched up I returned to the bench and didn't get back on.

Ireland hadn't won the Triple Crown for nineteen years and it was a big deal at the time. There was a lap of honour and a lot of excitement around the place, but I didn't feel part of it. One of the papers carried a huge picture of the squad the following day but they didn't have room on the page for everyone. I was standing at the edge and they cut me out of the photograph. That's exactly how I felt: cut out.

I turned twenty-five in the week of that Triple Crown match. I was no longer a greenhorn. It was nearly four years since I'd shown up at the Glenview Hotel for my first squad session as tackle fodder. Time was moving on. The problem, though, was that Mal was going nowhere. For the next two years I couldn't get him out of my way.

Everybody copes differently with being on the bench. I hated it. There were some players in the Ireland squad who gave you the impression they didn't mind. They were in the squad, they were part of the big day, they might get a run and they were happy with that. It used to eat away at me. At times I felt like a supporter with an access-all-areas pass. What was the good in that?

Throughout my career I always resisted it. I never accepted being a sub. As a teenager in Cork Con I put myself on in an All-Ireland League game one day. We were winning by a street, the game was nearly over, I was stripped and ready to go, but it seemed like they had forgotten about me. So I informed the officials that I was coming on for Ken Murphy – eighteen for four. There was an inquiry afterwards about who made that call but I didn't care. I was prepared to take a bollicking for it.

Years later, in 2005, I managed a similar stunt with

Ireland. We were playing Scotland at Murrayfield in the Six Nations. We were miles ahead in the second half and I was doing star jumps on the sideline under the coaches' box trying to get their attention. I was warming up with Gavin Duffy when Mervyn Murphy, our video analyst, asked us if we were going on. Quick as a flash I said we were. I turned to Gavin and told him to start getting stripped. Mervyn must have been miked up to Eddie and the boys in the box and he asked them for confirmation. 'Am I putting on these two lads?' They could have contradicted me but instead they took pity and we were sent on. It's still the only appearance Gavin has made in the Six Nations. Malcolm won his seventieth cap that day, which was a record for an Ireland player at the time. And there I was, trying to scab another appearance off the bench by telling fibs to a member of the management.

With Munster I never managed to pull off a stroke like that, although there were plenty of times when I felt like it. Marcus Horan and myself felt we got a raw deal in Musgrave Park one day in the Heineken Cup. We were both young and bucking to get on the field. It was clear from a long way out that Munster were going to win easily and five minutes after half time Deccie told us to get warmed up. With about ten minutes to go he told us to get stripped and ready, but when the final whistle went we were still standing on the sideline. Munster were under pressure close to the try line towards the end and Deccie had a policy of never making a change when we were defending. We legged it to the dressing room, got showered and were sitting down in our blazers before the rest of them arrived back, covered in muck. We were spotless even before we stepped in the shower. Both of us were mortified.

In the early days with Munster, being a sub really got to me after a while and I did some really stupid stuff to get it out of my system. If I hadn't come on in a match or only played a small part I would go for a long run when we got home. I didn't tell anybody about it. I wasn't doing it for the sake of appearances or to make it look like I was incredibly dedicated. I was probably doing it out of paranoia more than anything else. The others had put in a hard shift on the pitch and I hadn't. I was primed to play and I needed to release that energy.

It didn't matter what time we got home. After one trip to France we weren't back in Cork until after midnight. The others were going for a few drinks, I went for a run. I was still living at home with my mother and I went there to change. It was lunacy when I think about it. I was wearing dark gear without a high-visibility vest and I set off on a route that took me out of the city and on to an unlit country road. I didn't even think about where I was going. It was like Forrest Gump: just run. I had to jump into the ditch at one stage because of an oncoming car. It was such a dark road that the driver had no chance of seeing me. I could have been killed. It was mindless stuff.

Mom was still up when I got home from the run and she could see that it was crazy behaviour. Ultan and Eddie thought it was bonkers as well. At the time, though, there was no talking to me: I was convinced that I had to do it. Whatever frustration or anger I was feeling about being on the bench or not coming on as a sub, this is where I let it out. I wasn't getting into rows with Deccie or any of the other coaches about it, I was taking it out on myself. During the run something would come into my head about the game that day or the fellas that were keeping me out of the team and I'd sprint for two hundred metres, flat out. In the course of a fifty-minute run I might do three or four of those sprints, trying to blow the frustration out of my system.

This went on for about two seasons. Sometimes I'd do the run, get showered and changed and join the other Munster lads in town afterwards. They would be none the wiser and I'd feel a little better about myself.

Then, the next day, I'd do another session on my own. When I was in the IRFU Academy they'd given us a programme that mirrored the exertions of a match. It was devised by Liam Hennessy, who was the IRFU's fitness director at the time, and it involved tons of sprints, two hundred press-ups and loads of ups and downs. It took about seventy minutes to complete and you weren't supposed to do it alone. For me that was the mental challenge: timing myself on a shitty little watch and flogging myself without any encouragement from the coaches or any team mates to share the pain. It was hellish, but at the same time I took comfort in it. I thought of the other lads sitting at home with their feet up the day after the match and I believed I was giving myself an edge.

The reality was, I was doing too much. In my desperation to make a breakthrough I was training like an idiot. On other days during the week I'd do my Munster gym programme in the morning with the rest of the Cork-based lads then do an old Academy gym programme in the afternoon when I should have been resting.

Deccie eventually found out and he confronted me one day in CIT. He didn't spare me. He said I was letting down my team mates, which was the last thing on my mind. But he was right. Because of the way I was carrying on I was compromising my physical condition and my capacity to perform in a match if I was needed.

I believed I was turning myself into the fittest player in the squad, but the stats told a different story because I wasn't training smart. I was putting myself through extra sessions when I was tired and doing more harm than good. It got to a stage where I almost had an addiction to training. I loved the buzz it gave me, I loved the way it made me feel. It was a release for my frustration and I couldn't get enough of it.

Deccie put an end to the madness. I was banned from doing extra sessions in the gym on pain of a fine. The figure he mentioned was €1,000, and at the time I was probably only earning about seven grand. I don't know if he would have followed through on the figure but in any case I got the message.

I've never lost the desire to do extra work but over time I learned how to manage it. I learned where to stop. The urge to take out my frustrations in the gym from time to time didn't leave me either but I did it in a more controlled environment. In Ireland camp Mickey McGurn, our fitness guy, knew my frustrations and helped me to unload them. In a Munster context I would ring Aidan O'Connell, who was our strength and conditioning trainer and brilliant at his job. If I needed to do a hard gym session on a Sunday he would come in and supervise it for me.

With Ireland the post-match fitness session for the subs is always a good blow-out, but I sometimes needed more than that. If I hadn't started the match I got into a routine of going to the gym the following morning and Mickey would join me there. He had an incredible ability to push you to your maximum output. He knew I wanted to smash myself and he stood over me while I did it. But he would have devised the session and he was supervising it so we both knew I was operating within acceptable limits.

This went on until the 2006 Six Nations. By then my head was wrecked from being a sub. In the two years since my first start for Ireland until the end of the 2006 Six Nations, Ireland played twenty-three Tests. I had been available for twenty of them and started only four. On five occasions I didn't even come off the bench.

Niall O'Donovan was the forwards coach under Eddie O'Sullivan and I knew Niall from his time with Munster. I expressed my frustration to him at one stage and he laid it on the line for me. If I wanted to get into the team ahead of Paulie or Mal then I needed to do more when I got my chance. That sounds a pretty obvious thing to say, but everyone's performance was so carefully monitored and analysed that they could quantify every player's impact. Supporters or reporters came away from a match with an impression of who played well, but the Ireland management were getting a print-out from Mervyn Murphy that went way beyond who looked good in the television highlights.

Niall wanted all the forwards to have fifty 'moments' in a game. A 'moment' would be a carry or a tackle or winning line-out ball, but it would also be a positive contribution at a ruck or a maul. To reach fifty 'moments' required a really big performance, but if Paulie and Mal were hitting that target it wasn't enough for me just to match them; when I got my chance I had to get to the next level. That was the point Niall made to me, and that was the size of the challenge I faced.

The issue came to a head during that 2006 Six Nations campaign. Paulie was injured for the autumn internationals at the end of 2005 and I'd started all three games against New Zealand, Australia and Romania. As a team we didn't play well: Australia beat us, New Zealand slaughtered us. But I had played two

Tests for the Lions that summer. In my mind I had served my apprenticeship.

When the Six Nations came round, though, I was back as a sub, as if the Lions tour and autumn internationals had never happened. Paulie was fit, Mal was preferred, and I was on the bench. I made an appearance in every game during that tournament but the only one I started was against Wales when Paulie was injured. We won, Paulie came back, I was left out.

I was sick of it. It wasn't my style to confront the coach. It still isn't. I don't have that confidence in myself. But for the first time in my Ireland career I looked for an explanation. Why was I left out? What did I have to do to change their minds? I felt like a soft touch. It was like they knew they could leave me out and I wouldn't kick up a fuss. Around the camp I had a reputation as a fun-loving fella, a bit of a messer, a bit of craic. In a close call that image probably didn't help me. I should have been going bananas and throwing the toys out of the pram. It had been going on too long. I had proved myself with Munster, I had played two Tests for the Lions. What more did I need to do?

In fairness to Eddie O'Sullivan he didn't try to give me a bullshit explanation. He didn't pick out a couple of areas of my game and tell me to go off and work on them. He wasn't hiding behind my faults. He said it was a fifty-fifty call but he was staying loyal to Mal as one of the senior players and somebody who had played well for Ireland for a long time. In years to come, he said, I would probably get the benefit of that loyalty when younger players were coming through. I'll never forget the bottom line: 'It's a bollix for you,' he said, 'but you just have to suck it up and get on with it.'

What else could I do?

10
Pride

As a kid I watched *Living with the Lions* until the videotape was worn out. I could recite passages from the dressing-room speeches word for word. I never tired of it. On that 1997 tour the Lions won a Test series in South Africa for the first time since the early seventies. To me, those players were giants. Did I dream of following in their footsteps? I wasn't the only boy with that dream.

Making the 2005 Lions didn't enter my mind at the beginning of that season. I signed a new contract with the IRFU without any bonus clause for making a Lions Test appearance. For all the established internationals that was a standard part of their deal, but nobody suggested it to me and I never thought of raising it.

What chance did I have of playing for the Lions? In 2004 I started only three Tests for Ireland, including the filler fixture against the USA in the autumn.

At Christmas I received a card from Clive Woodward, the Lions coach. It was specially designed with the Lions logo for that tour: The Power of 4. God knows how many were sent but I was surprised to get one. I didn't boast about it or make a joke about it either. I barely mentioned it to the other lads in Munster. It crossed my mind that every international with two arms and two legs probably got one of those cards but I wanted to hold on to the thought that it might mean something.

The 2005 Six Nations was a wash-out for me with just three appearances off the bench, but Clive showed up at a few of our training sessions. I always wanted to look good in Ireland training sessions because I was trying to impress Eddie and Niall, but when Clive was there I felt nervous about looking good. I might have said to people that I had no chance of being picked but, deep down, that's not the way I felt. Somebody was going to get slagged for training like Tarzan in Clive's presence and I was prepared to take that chance.

In early March I was picked to play for the Northern Hemisphere against the Southern Hemisphere in an aid match for victims of the Boxing Day tsunami disaster. Clive was in charge of the team and Eddie said that they were seriously looking at me for the tour. He gave me a brilliant piece of advice: 'Don't try to reinvent the wheel. They're interested in you because of the way you normally play. Don't think you have to change to impress them.' If he hadn't said that I probably would have run around like a blue-arsed fly, looking to make carries. Instead, I made sure I was at every ruck and maul. Jimmy Williams, by now one of our coaches in Munster, slagged the hell out of me for not touching the ball, but being a hero with the ball in hand wasn't my normal game.

I was at home with Mom when the Lions squad was announced. Just the two of us. We didn't have Sky Sports News so we were glued to the radio in the front room. When I heard my name I went bananas. Mom was bawling. It takes a lot to make Mom cry.

After Munster lost to Biarritz in the quarter-final of the Heineken Cup I trained my arse off for the tour. The Lions training camp was in the Vale of Glamorgan Hotel, near Cardiff. When I checked in I enquired about my room mate. 'A Mr Hill,' I was told.

Richard Hill.

It might be hard for people to understand that a professional sportsman can be in awe of somebody else in his profession but my admiration for Richard was child-like. It was hero-worship. I rang my brother Eddie immediately. I was like one of those kids that appeared on the television programme *Jim'll Fix It* years ago. It seemed like Jimmy Savile had arranged for me to spend some time with a hero of mine.

Richard wasn't one of the big stars on the England

team that won the World Cup in 2003 because he didn't have a glamorous job. Other forwards on that England team had a higher profile, on and off the pitch, but you could see how much his team mates appreciated him. His tackle count and his work rate were incredible. They couldn't have been such an effective pack without his contribution. Most of all he was selfless, and that appealed to me. That's the way I saw myself. In an ideal world I would have wanted all my team mates to think of me in the way that Richard's team mates thought of him.

They say you should never meet your heroes, that it's bound to be a disappointment. It hadn't been the case with Martin Johnson, and it wasn't the case now. Richard was good company, and as one of the senior players in the squad he put me at ease. When he was going for a coffee he'd invite me along, and two minutes later I'd be sitting down with Lawrence Dallaglio or Matt Dawson. The key to a Lions tour is getting along with people that you're knocking lumps out of in the normal course of events. From watching Dawson and playing against him, for example, I had a firm opinion of what he was like; when I met him, I discovered that I had been completely wrong. He was one of the soundest guys you could meet. A Lions tour is full of surprises like that.

Team bonding was a big focus of our time in camp. I'm all in favour of the concept but I didn't buy the techniques that were used. They broke us into groups and got us to do a giant painting. It was basically colour by numbers but the colours had to be co-ordinated so it forced you to interact with other people. It did nothing for me. I had to draw a rhino in my corner of the canvas and I stuck a cigarette in his mouth.

The other thing we were asked to do was pair off with another player and share our life stories. Effectively, you were interviewing your partner and he was interviewing you. I was paired with Stephen Jones, and neither of us took it seriously. The outcome of the interview was put into a red book that everyone was given so you could turn to a page containing the life story in brief of any player in the squad. It was handy for breaking the ice with players that you knew nothing about – although they wouldn't have discovered much about me from reading my page.

That contrived team-building stuff has never worked for me. For a pack to come together there are a few ways of doing it, in my opinion. Let them kick the shit out of each other on the training field, put them through savage scrummaging sessions or let them go out on the piss for a night. You can call me old-fashioned but I believe those are the best ways. When you're in a Test match and the chips are down there's nothing to be gained from how well you dovetailed with somebody on a giant painting.

Other stuff, though, blew me away that week. People often talk about attention to detail, but this was off the scale. With the gear allocation they wanted to make sure that everything fitted absolutely perfectly. If your tracksuit wasn't sitting on top of your runner they wanted to adjust it. 'Sir, can we let it down another inch for you?' Everyone was given a memory stick for their laptop that contained incredible detail about our itinerary on tour – where we would be visiting and what we would be doing almost hour by hour.

Former players were invited to speak to us about the Lions, and they produced video packages of old matches that would bring a lump to your throat. That's what they were designed to do. Everything about that camp hammered home the message that you were privileged to be a Lion but that you also had a responsibility to the jersey.

When it came to goal-setting, nothing was off limits. We were broken into small groups and Danny Grewcock, the English second row, was one of the players in my circle. I couldn't believe how blunt he was: 'I don't want to go to New Zealand and be told that the line-outs are up to us to work out. I want them to be sorted out now, before we leave.' I was thinking, 'You can't say that.' But he could. He was a senior player and he was prepared to challenge the management rather than assume that everything would be all right.

My goal was to make the Test team. I didn't broadcast that ambition. Five second rows had been named in the squad and in everyone's estimation I was number five on the list. None of the other second rows – Paulie, Mal, Grewcock and fellow Englishman Ben Kay – were worried about me. I liked the idea of starting from that position.

The regime of touring suited me too. I liked the intensity of it and the opportunity to get into a routine and the chance to do more. In Lions company, though, I wasn't alone in that thinking. On one of the first days in camp I decided to go to the gym for a sneaky extra weights session. When I opened the door the place was jointed, packed with English players. The other impressive thing about them was that they were confident in their own fitness programmes. They weren't distracted by the Lions fitness trainers or any other outside interference. At the time I was very open to outside influence and I was prepared to try anything. They had the confidence to believe in their own routine.

Even before I arrived in camp I knew the standards I would have to reach in terms of physical conditioning. A few weeks in advance they sent us a sheet with fitness targets, depending on your position. For the forwards there was a big emphasis on what we could lift in the gym. The numbers were broken down and given different labels: Lion, Lion Cub and Pussy Cat. I looked at the sheet and was shocked by how much of a Pussy Cat I was. I showed it to the fitness lads in Munster, Aidan O'Connell and Damien Mendes, and they gave me great programmes to raise my levels in a short space of time. Aidan put my mind at ease as well: 'Do you have to get to that level to know you're playing good rugby?' Clearly, the answer was no.

When I got into camp I didn't know exactly where I stood. The first time I saw Danny Grewcock in the gym I couldn't believe what he was lifting. He could do whatever he wanted with the weights. I remember seeing Dallaglio for the first time in the gym and thinking that I'd never seen a fitter, stronger man in my life. He was chiselled. The 2001 Lions tour had made a huge impression on Ronan O'Gara and he'd come home with a different attitude to being a professional. Before I went on tour I thought I was a good professional, but the experience opened my eyes too. I could feel myself having the same experience that Rog had had.

They tested us from the beginning. Very early on they put us through a savage strength-endurance session involving wrestling, tug-of-war, lifting weights, then sprints. I was paired with Ben Kay. There was a head-to-head element to the session that I liked. It wasn't supposed to be competitive, but it was in my mind. I wanted to let Kay know that I would be on his tail for the next six weeks.

They had picked three Irish second rows: Mal, Paulie and myself. Mal had had a bad experience on the previous tour and I know he was desperate to make up for it but he never even got on the plane. An injury in camp ended his tour before we left Wales. I always liked Mal and on a personal level I felt sorry for him. Being selfish, though, I really wanted him to be on the tour so that we could take our personal argument into a different arena. I had failed to take the green jersey off him but I really believed I could push ahead of him on the Lions tour. In my wildest dreams I wanted to end the argument in New Zealand and come home as the obvious partner for Paulie in the Ireland second row. When Mal got injured I lost that opportunity. Whatever I achieved on the tour, part of me thought that people would point to Mal's absence and that would keep the argument alive.

A couple of days before we left for New Zealand we had a warm-up match against Argentina in the Millennium Stadium. I was picked to start. It wasn't anybody's idea of the Test team but I was just glad to be up and running on the tour. In the team meeting before we left the hotel Ian McGeechan presented me with my jersey. He was in charge of the mid-week team on this tour but he'd been everything to the Lions in his long career as a player and coach. On the 1997 tour to South Africa he had been the head coach. He had no idea how many times I'd watched his speeches on the video.

He handed me the jersey and shook my hand. 'You're growing,' he said. Two such simple words had never given me such a lift.

There were a few things that defined that tour above everything else: the spear tackle on Brian O'Driscoll in the first minute of the first Test, losing the series 3–0, and the internal division between the Test team and the mid-week team. Like the weather, you couldn't get away from any of those things. And none of them were good.

For the first half of the tour I was with the dirt trackers, or the Mid-week Massive as we called ourselves. For those few weeks we led a separate existence from the Saturday team. Obviously there were fellas on the Mid-week Massive who were gutted not to be in the Saturday team, but most fellas made the best of it and we had good craic. The warm-up before training might be a game of soccer, the lads were allowed to have a couple of beers after the games, and we had sing-songs on the bus.

We took the piss out of ourselves too. Rob Henderson's version of the Travis song 'Driftwood' was still alive from the previous tour ('We're driftwood, touring with the Lions, we only play on Tuesdays, Tuesdays'), and we changed the chorus of another song too: 'If we crash would anyone care, do they know we're even here?' For example, in the build-up to the first Test members of the mid-week team were refused entry to the video analysis room because we weren't in the match-day twenty-two. What did they think we were going to do? Sell our secrets to the All Blacks? There was an element of paranoia around the place that was uncomfortable, and that incident caused some bitterness among the mid-week players.

We probably felt like second-class citizens at times, even though they didn't treat us like that. The same level of military organisation applied to us. Auckland was our base, but when we were travelling for matches we put a sticker on our bags in the team hotel and we wouldn't see the bags again until we walked into the hotel room at our destination. After a while, though, you start taking things like that for granted. It was no consolation to be treated like royalty when what you really wanted was a place in the Test team.

As I mentioned earlier, Clive hired Alastair Campbell as the media manager for the tour. With his background in British politics not all of the English players were happy with his inclusion. I enjoyed him. I didn't know much about his working life so I just took him as I found him. Alastair's first initiative was to put up a 'War Wall' in the team room. The idea was to find negative comments or articles in the New Zealand press and pin them up. I suppose the idea was to get our blood boiling and maybe develop a siege mentality. But after three days there was no space left on the War Wall for any more cuttings and the Wall was retired.

When you're on the mid-week team you cling to the hope of being promoted, and for a tour to be happy as many players as possible need to have that hope for as long as possible. On the 2005 tour, the hope died quickly for a lot of players. The Saturday team lost to the New Zealand Maori in the third game and suddenly a bit of panic set in. For the Wednesday game against Wellington they picked the guts of a Saturday team again, and after that it was obvious to a lot of fellas that the fifteen for the first Test was already picked, probably before we'd even left home.

A lot of things changed after that first Test, though.

New Zealand walked all over us, and Brian O'Driscoll, our captain, was out of the tour after a desperate tackle wrecked his shoulder. The controversy about Brian raged in the media for days and soured the atmosphere around the tour. In the meantime the Mid-week Massive carried on to Palmerston North for a match against Manawatu that we won by over a hundred points. I was replaced at half time. Clive told me I was coming off rather than Ian McGeechan. Four days before the second Test that was a good sign.

I didn't do anything extraordinary to get picked. I trained consistently well and I suppose I played consistently well. My performances were full of all the usual things, the things they had liked about me in the first place. Nothing special. After losing the first Test by eighteen points there were bound to be changes, and maybe they liked the idea of having a second-row partnership that had played a lot together. I didn't ask for an explanation and I wasn't given one.

The next few days were mad. At the press briefing I was bounced from one interview to the next. The number of reporters on that tour was unbelievable. I was drained by the end of it because you couldn't just relax and be yourself. I had to watch everything I said in case I said the wrong thing.

Hector Ó hEochagáin, an Irish broadcaster with a madcap style, was following the tour in a camper van to make a light-hearted documentary. I was doing a line of television interviews and I could see he was in the queue to speak to me. Normally I'd have no problem having the craic, and I'm sure he knew that I had a reputation as a messer, but at that moment he was the last person I wanted to speak to. I made a promise to myself going on that tour that I wasn't going to act the ghoul. My brother Eddie had put it well: 'Think about Lawrence Dallaglio, Richard Hill, Jonny Wilkinson and all these guys. Are they looking for somebody that will stand up in a Test match or somebody doing the fool?' Hector would have wanted me to do the fool for a couple of minutes and I didn't need that temptation. I didn't want to make light of something that was massive in my life. I was living my dream and, at that moment at least, it wasn't a laughing matter. Hector started asking me about Paulie, hoping to get a bit of slagging going, but I just played it dead straight. I've no doubt he was disappointed but I felt I couldn't let my guard down for a second.

I had never been so nervous before a match. It didn't help that we were rooming on our own. When your head is wrecked coming up to a big game you need to be sharing a room with somebody who's suffering in the same way. Rog and John Hayes were very good for calling and taking me for cups of tea but I was still tormented.

I managed to lose the SIM card for my Irish mobile phone which meant I didn't pick up the millions of goodwill texts until I got home and replaced it. That was no harm. Dominic Crotty faxed a beautiful letter to the team hotel. We played together with Munster for a few years and then he moved to the States when his career finished. Dominic was always a diamond and it was an incredibly thoughtful thing to do. I don't think I ever thanked him, but I appreciated every word he wrote.

In the build-up to the match they gave us a dietary supplement called Focus. For consumption you added a bit of water. It had the texture of paste and it tasted horrible but I never got such a buzz from anything in my life. There were no labels on the pot and they wouldn't tell us what was in it. I've no doubt it was full of caffeine and taurine, a key ingredient in Red Bull. I don't know what else it contained, but the effect was to enhance whatever emotion you were feeling. After one of the matches Shane Horgan couldn't stop crying. He was a bit down about not getting a run off the bench and disappointed about losing the match, but to look at him you'd swear there had been a death in the family. He wanted to stop crying but he couldn't. In the first Test Paulie pole-vaulted over one ruck early in the match in a crazy manoeuvre and I've no doubt he was acting under the influence of Focus.

It didn't matter what they gave us, though, New Zealand were just too good. Martin Corry came on for me near the end but I wasn't disappointed with my performance. I did all right.

Now trailing 2–0 we couldn't rescue the series and the tour was coming to a bad end. Some fellas would have swum home at that stage. Even in the dressing room after the second Test some fellas looked to me like they were separating themselves from the group. It didn't feel like a collective loss, the way it should.

Andy Robinson, the forwards coach, approached Paulie in the dressing room and asked him about some line-out that had gone wrong. It wasn't the time or the place. We had just lost a Test series with the Lions in New Zealand and he wanted an explanation on the spot about a specific line-out malfunction. The line-outs were Robinson's responsibility, they hadn't gone well in the Tests, and he was feeling the heat. Bringing it up at that moment, though, was the wrong thing to do. To an extent, it reflected the atmosphere in the dressing room. A lot of individuals were only concerned about themselves. Nobody was thinking about the giant painting back at the Vale of Glamorgan and the unity it was supposed to bring.

Under pressure from the players the line-out calls were changed for the final Test. Shane Byrne, our hooker with Ireland, led the charge. He called round to my room and asked me to speak up in the argument as well, but I couldn't get involved. I was hardly in the Test squad a wet week. I didn't feel that I had the authority or the confidence. Anyway, the argument was won without my contribution.

What was it that Danny Grewcock said? He wanted the line-outs sorted before we left Wales. We were still trying to work them out nearly seven weeks later.

Other coaches were feeling the pressure too. Phil Larder had been the defence coach when England won the World Cup and their defence was brilliant in that tournament. The Lions tour had done nothing for his reputation, though, and in training on the week of the final Test I thought he was washing his hands of us. He gave us the impression that we had disgraced him. I couldn't understand that attitude. Coaches give out all the time and apportion blame but, in my eyes, he was distancing himself from the players. I couldn't accept that.

By then I was different from everybody else on the tour: I was the only one who didn't want it to end. If they'd told me we were carrying on for another six months I would have said, 'Brilliant!' Playing for the Lions had been a lifelong dream. I was prepared to put up with anything.

Gareth Thomas took over as captain for the final Test. The Welsh lads really respected him but I found nothing inspirational in what he had to say. His speech before the match was poor. It struck the wrong tone. New Zealand had crushed us in two Tests and we should have been bursting ourselves to burst them. Instead he went on about 'doing our best'.

Then he said something that really stuck in my throat: 'I know we all want to get out of here . . .' We were preparing for a Test match. That thought shouldn't have been entertained for a second. Anybody who had that thought should have kept it to themselves. Thomas was captain of a Lions team against the All Blacks. It should have been one of the greatest days of his career. The only thing on our minds should have been winning and salvaging some pride for the jersey. Instead some fellas were feeling sorry for themselves and only thinking of the plane home.

We lost. Did we prepare like we were going to win?

The end was an anti-climax. Losing a Test series 3–0 hadn't been part of the dream. For me, though, it had been a positive experience. I had gained from it. I'd learned. I'd got better. I'd soaked up everything about it. I'd loved it.

I went home to resume my battle with Mal.

11
Glory Be

21 January 2006, Thomond Park –
Munster 31 Sale 9

Big Heineken Cup games against English teams in Thomond Park were part of our story. More often than not it was in the final pool match with our qualification for the quarter-finals in the balance. That wouldn't have been how we planned it, but most years we had cocked up somewhere along the line, always on the road. In the 2005/06 season Sale had beaten us handy in the opening round of games and we were chasing our tail after that. To give ourselves any chance of getting out of the group we had to beat Castres away in our second last game, and we did.

Everything clicked that night and we murdered them.

But that still left Sale in Thomond Park. To qualify, we had to win. To have any chance of a home quarter-final, we needed four tries for a bonus point. Sale were top of the English Premiership at the time with a team full of internationals. Until then we had never lost a Heineken Cup match in Thomond Park, but that didn't kill the fear of losing. That fear was built into our psyche. We knew it was there but we didn't let it become a negative thing. We drew on it.

We have a routine for those big Saturday games at home. The Cork-based players stay in the team hotel on Friday night and the Limerick lads join us on the morning of the game for the various walk-throughs: line-outs for the forwards and whatever the backs do. The Clarion Hotel is right in the middle of town, on the riverside, so there isn't any pitch or big park nearby. We go to the scrap yard next door. It's not private but we're not concerned about that. People watch from the gate and from bedroom windows in the hotel; some of them take photographs but they don't bother us. The surface in the scrap yard is slippery sometimes and when it is we go to a small patio area behind the hotel. If the hooker overthrows to the tail the ball is in the Shannon. That focuses his mind.

Because of television those games have often been at tea-time under floodlights. For atmosphere, that has always been the best time. The crowd arrives long before kick-off, and some of them would have been in the pubs since early that afternoon. For the Sale match they sang during the warm-up. You notice it, you feel it. You're a professional rugby player preparing for the pivotal game of the season but it's impossible not to be affected by something like that. The atmosphere that night was probably the best we ever played in.

There were days when we had to remind ourselves that the crowd and the Thomond Park atmosphere weren't going to get us over the line, but there was never a time when we didn't appreciate it. There was never a thought in our minds of shutting out the crowd and just playing the match. We want them in there with us. It doesn't matter how many times I've experienced that atmosphere it always makes me nervous, and you can't fake that feeling.

For us, the build-up is never left to match day. It starts at the beginning of the week and gradually winds up. We're always looking for loose comments in the media that we can seize upon. That week one of the Sale players said that they were 'looking forward' to coming to Thomond Park. We twisted that into an insult. Thomond Park had a reputation as one of the most intimidating venues in European rugby. I'm sure the Sale player didn't mean to be disrespectful but that's how we chose to interpret it. Paulie picked it up and ran with it.

'They think they know us. They think they know what it will be like to play us in front of our own people. They don't know what's coming.'

Paulie spoke brilliantly that week. He has an incredible

gift for saying the right thing and catching the mood. I never get tired of listening to him. He's direct and he can be emotional and some days there are tears in his eyes, and every time it gets to me. By the time he's finished I'm prepared to walk barefoot on broken glass. In the huddle that day he spoke about family and friends. Other players could talk about the same things and it wouldn't have the same impact. He has a way of putting it across. It's part of his charisma. It's not easy to impress the players in our dressing room but he does it.

'They should see what it means to you,' he said. 'The people that know you best should see that you're different today.'

That close to kick-off it's about feelings more than words. When the whistle blows it's about actions. Sébastien Chabal, the giant French forward with the long hair, was Sale's talisman. He fielded the kick-off and Paulie nailed him the second the ball arrived. I joined in with Denis Leamy and Anthony Foley and we drove him back about twenty metres. He's such a proud bastard and such a strong man that he didn't go to ground and he managed to get the ball back on their side, but the tackle had set the tone for our performance. Every team has what Mervyn Murphy calls 'momentum builders' and he was that player for them. The crowd went ballistic, and we tore into them.

By half time we had three tries on the board. The fourth try and the bonus point didn't come until the first minute of stoppage time, but it wasn't unusual for us to leave it late.

On those nights after big games in Thomond we all end up back in the Clarion. There's a room upstairs just for players and their guests. Mostly it's family but you'll always put in a word for one of your buddies at the door. You'd warn them not to annoy anybody and then you'd see one of them telling Rog what he should have done. It happens to all of us. Sometimes one of the guests will drive you bananas but you know he belongs to somebody else in the room so you put up with it. After a big win you'd put up with anything.

After a while a video of the match is played in the corner and all the players gravitate towards it. The wives and girlfriends freak out. It's meant to be a social occasion and there we are, glued to the television. It's like a teenage disco with girls and boys at opposite sides of the room. On those nights when you win, everything is funny. Somebody falls over or gets a shoeing or misses a tackle and every comment gets a laugh. In all the time we spend together training and travelling and playing that feeling only exists in that room for those couple of hours. It's a special thing.

23 April 2006, Lansdowne Road – Munster 30 Leinster 6

I made CDs for the car. I couldn't listen to the radio. They never stopped talking about the match. Every hour: news, previews, interviews, ticket competitions. I put a bit of thought into the CDs. I didn't just want them to be noise in the car or a distraction from the match. I wanted them to be part of my build-up. I picked songs that I knew would cue certain thoughts and moods. I downloaded music from *Gladiator* and speeches from *Any Given Sunday* and stuff from Muhammad Ali ('I'll show you how great I am . . .').

I had met the McNulty brothers, Enda and Justin, through a mutual friend, Mick Kearney, and I looked to them for advice. They were still playing Gaelic football for Armagh at the time but motivational speaking and sports psychology was their business and still is. They gave me some CDs and some ideas and I worked them in. Apart from that, I was sceptical about sports psychology at the time. I've changed my mind completely on that subject, but back then it didn't do anything for me, or I didn't open my mind to it. Either way, I wasn't a believer, which was no place to start.

When he came back as Munster coach that season, Deccie made a sports psychologist available to us. Some of our lads swore by him, but his methods didn't work for me. One of his techniques was 'bin-day'. He would prompt us with a text and we'd have to unload all our negative thoughts in a text back to him. He wanted to hear the doubts we had about ourselves and then he would replace them with positive thoughts. I tried it at first but after a while I stopped replying to the texts. It was no reflection on him.

For that week, though, I could have done with something to help me get through the build-up. It was nothing like 'butterflies in your tummy'; it was a horrible, sickening feeling in your gut. I had a constant feeling of nausea. It was torturous. I knew what it was like to suffer before big games but it wouldn't usually kick in until travelling day. This followed me around all week. I couldn't shake it off.

After training on the Wednesday I cooked some fish and after I took one bite I suddenly got paranoid that it might make me sick. I put it in the bin and stuck on some chicken and pasta instead, just to be safe. I think a lot about my diet and I'm always mindful of what I eat but I had never done something like that before.

I knew some of the other lads would be suffering. I asked Paulie how he was feeling, dying to hear that he was tormented with nerves too. It somehow makes it more bearable if you know somebody else is in the same boat. Wrong man. He probably could have gone fishing that Wednesday and forgotten about the match. He wasn't entertaining my anxieties. 'It's a big game, you've just got to get ready for big games. We've played them before.' But this wasn't like any other big match we'd ever played before. In the history of Irish rugby there had never been hype like this.

On the day of the game we had our usual team meeting in the hotel before we got on the bus. Fellas can seem loose and relaxed all day until that meeting. At that point everyone's demeanour changes. Walking into the room I caught Axel's eye, and then John Kelly's. They were both pale as a sheet. So was Wally. So was I. Strings was fizzing around the place. Everybody deals differently with nerves: some people go quiet, some people need to talk and be heard, for their own benefit rather than anybody else's. We'd been through so much as a group that we knew what to expect from each other in this situation. You don't want anybody to start behaving differently.

There was a good feeling in that room. Everything I saw and heard gave me confidence. I absolutely believed we were going to win. You've heard that a million times from winning teams after the final whistle. Every Leinster player probably had the same feeling that morning. In that team meeting, though, I had a good feeling about us. At that moment, that was all that mattered.

Leinster were favourites after their quarter-final win against Toulouse in the south of France. We had struggled to beat Perpignan in Lansdowne Road on the same day. Leinster had really turned us over in the RDS on New Year's Day too and a lot of us had bad memories of that experience. People thought their back line would tear us apart again. It was set up perfectly for us: underdogs with chips on our shoulders. Nicely bitter.

Lansdowne Road ought to have been a home venue

for them, but Munster fans outnumbered Leinster fans by about three to one. The stadium was covered in red. None of that would matter, though, if we couldn't rise to the occasion. We did. We started like a train and finished like a train. Leinster had a good spell in the middle but they didn't really lay a hand on us.

Playing a big match against so many players that you knew was strange. It raised the stakes and made all of us more desperate to win. At the same time, I didn't want to behave in a way that was disrespectful to people I shared an Ireland dressing room with. For one thing, I kept my mouth shut on the pitch.

Except for Felipe Contepomi. Something about him always loosened my tongue. We had a history of run-ins going back years and it came to blows one night in Lansdowne Road. We actually apologised to each other after that match. You couldn't say we buried the hatchet but most of the hostile exchanges after that were verbal. Off the field, I didn't know him at all. He was probably the kind of fella that you'd love if he was your team mate, and I know he was very good to Timmy Ryan years later when they were both at Toulon. On the field, though, I didn't like him.

He was in brilliant form that season. On New Year's Day he scored two tries against us and he was cock of the walk. Running out after one of his tries he flaked me on the shoulder, and after the other one he cupped his ear to the Munster fans. We couldn't allow him to have that kind of influence again. We got after him from the start and he cracked very quickly. His kicking went to pot and he got into a fight with Leamy. I don't know how the row started but it suited us more than it suited them.

Being on the back foot and playing badly didn't shut him up though. Paulie had one of his monster games that day and Contepomi wondered out loud if I was being paid from Paulie's wages. Like I was his shoe-shine boy. It was a good put-down and Leamy knocked a laugh out of it. On another day or at another time in my career something like that would have wound me up. I would have chased him until I nailed him; I would have been fishing him out of rucks. That day, I let it pass. I had too much work on my plate to worry about him. When he missed his kicks I was one of the fellas reminding him about it, but apart from that I left him alone.

That evening the overwhelming feeling was relief. You can't enjoy anything about a game like that except the result. We had lost so many semi-finals and finals that losing another one didn't bear thinking about. It was grand to wake up on Monday morning without having to avoid people in the street or avoid the papers, and for a short while you have this feeling of invincibility.

That doesn't last long. In the final our reputation was on the line again. If we lost another one people were going to think of us as chokers. Some people already did.

20 May 2006, Cardiff – Munster 23 Biarritz 19

You can't prepare for everything. Outside my room at the Vale of Glamorgan Hotel was a table-tennis table. It wasn't a special feature of the hotel. Somebody had organised this table to help fellas relax on the night before the final. The only part of the corridor wide enough to accommodate it was outside my room. With Munster, Marcus Horan was my room mate. He checked in first. He knew I'd freak. He was already in the room when he heard my reaction from the corridor.

'Ah, for fuck's sake!'

I like to go to bed early. I can stay awake talking for the next two hours but I like to be under the sheets. Then the ping-pong started. I took a deep breath and decided not to get worked up. I buried my head under the pillow. Then the crowds started arriving and the noise got louder. Shouting, roaring. I went out and tried to reason with them. Kept my cool.

'Lads, keep it down, will ye? We're trying to get some sleep here.'

No joy. I stuck my head under the pillow again but I couldn't sleep. So I sent Marcus out to stop the racket. He didn't come back. The noise got worse, and when I couldn't stick it any more I went out myself. There was Horan, holding a bat. Talk about sending a boy to do a man's job. At that stage I confiscated the ball. I didn't care what they called me or what damage it did to my reputation as a fun-lover.

By then, we'd had our team meeting. It went as well as we could hope. In these meetings the mistakes of the past dictated how things were handled. Not everybody was expected to speak, like they were before the 2000 final. Emotions were kept in check. Among the players the only speakers were the voices we always respected: Axel, Paulie and Rags – John Kelly. Rags spoke with a lot of passion and emotion and with a direct message: we can't just hope it happens for us, we must make it happen, we must grab it.

Deccie played a famous speech from the *Coach Carter* movie: 'Our deepest fear is not that we are in-adequate. Our deepest fear is that we are powerful beyond measure. It is our light, not our darkness that most frightens us . . .'

Over the years Deccie always tried different motivational techniques. There was a clip from *The Lion King* that he was fond of too and we saw that a few times. With that kind of stuff you're not going to connect with everybody. It didn't do anything for me but I wasn't suffering that week like I did before the Leinster game. I hadn't played a minute of the other two finals that Munster had lost. I felt like I was carrying the bitterness without the baggage.

On Saturday morning we went through the line-outs and if someone had said the game was starting in two minutes I was ready. I had this feeling of destiny about the whole thing. You can't rationalise it but that's how I felt. They had really good second rows and a very strong defensive line-out but we had analysed them to death and made some alterations to our set-up that they wouldn't be expecting. Paulie was carrying an ankle injury into the game and we didn't expect him to last eighty minutes but he was more than ready to start. Even if his ankle was bent the other way he was still going to play.

For a match like that there is comfort in routine. My routine doesn't change from one game to the next, big or small. The lads accuse me of being superstitious, and maybe they have a point. I think they're waiting for the day when part of my routine falls down and my head explodes. It'll never happen. The routine is part of my preparation and I pay attention to it, just like my video analysis or my diet.

I have the same training kit and I wear the same pair of jocks for every match. Washed, before you ask. For every game I get a new pair of short white socks that I wear under my rugby socks. I've done that since my school days. I also have a holy cross on a chain that I found on a rugby pitch one day while I was playing for Christians. I keep it in a make-up jar that my sister Emer gave to me along with a few other religious bits and pieces. I get slagged about the jar but I've never tried to hide it. I'm not a religious fanatic but I do have faith.

I often take the cross out of the jar and say a prayer. Usually I give thanks: for my family, for my team mates, for the life I've been given. I feel privileged, and I thank

God for that. I never pray to ask for anything, but before the Biarritz match I couldn't stop myself. I didn't kneel down with that intention, it just barged into my prayers.

'Please, God, just let us win this game.'

They scored first. Try. Poor tackle by John Kelly. We gathered behind the posts. No panic. John put his hand up. A mistake. Forget it. Drive on. Nothing was going to rattle us.

Our plan was to take the game to them in every way. Be confrontational. Go for the jugular. We had penalty chances in the first half-hour but declined to kick for the posts. Rog looked at Axel and they didn't even need to speak: kick it to the corner. Let's go for them. Mentally, we wanted to break them.

Our first try came as a result of that attitude. We played phase after phase, down the field. Fellas wanted the ball. Trevor Halstead demanded it. He ran over two fellas to score, a horse of a man. Shortly after he arrived I asked him to spot me on the bench press one day. I was lifting what I thought was a decent weight, 130kg. He was appalled. 'For such a big man,' he said, 'you lift terrible. For your size you should be lifting 170. Don't ever ask me to spot you again.' He was completely serious. Trevor could have lifted any weight he wanted. From close range, at full speed, those Biarritz defenders stood no chance.

Paulie called a lot of ball on me at the front. He's very

good at weighing up the opposition line-out on the hoof. He can work out at a glance where they're weak. He was heavily marked that day and he called the ball where the risk was smallest. Even though most of it was only bread-and-butter ball it got me into the game quickly. Later in the game I had to take a pressure ball inside our 22. Even though it was the final of the Heineken Cup there was no special formula: I had to chew the top off it, like Ken Murphy had shown me in Con years before.

In every respect our set pieces were good. Against French teams you can't start thinking about winning unless you nail the scrum. For the Strings try on the short side our scrum was like a rock. If they had moved us an inch in any direction Strings wouldn't have been able to score like that. Hayes was the key to it. They couldn't shift him. I still had my head down in the scrum when Strings scampered over the line. That's how quick it was. The lift it gave us was massive. To score off first phase feels like a freebie. None of this grinding through the phases like we did for Halstead's try. Just a clean score: scrum, short-side break, touch down.

The pace of the game was savage. There was no bedding-in period. It started at a hundred miles an hour and never stopped. When the roof is closed in the Millennium Stadium and the stands are full it can feel very stuffy down on the field. At half time I was so drenched from sweat that I had to change everything from shirt to socks.

Just after the break Rog put us ten points ahead. They hadn't threatened another try since scoring in the first couple of minutes and part of me thought they hadn't a hope of scoring another. We were hunting them down like a pack of dogs. Then they had their spell in the match. We couldn't get field position and they started to turn the screw. Dimitri Yachvili landed three penalties, we didn't score for half an hour, and suddenly it was a one-point game.

The penalty that Rog faced with eleven minutes to go was pressure. Everybody in the stadium knew the importance of a four-point lead with the clock winding down. Apart from Yachvili they had other guys who could land a drop goal given half a chance. I wouldn't have wanted anybody else in the world to take that kick for us. Rog had been through everything with this team. I knew he'd have the balls to nail it.

They threw everything at us but we finished the game on our terms. When they desperately needed the ball in the last minute, we had it. Strings put the ball into the scrum near halfway and we left it there until the stadium clock turned red. Leamy had the ball at his feet, dreaming about the moment he was going to kick it into the stand. With Strings around he didn't stand a chance.

The final whistle was the most beautiful sound. Other lads spoke about relief. For me it was joy. Pure joy. I collapsed to the ground. My knee was sore and I was empty with exhaustion. I left everything out on the field. That's the promise we'd made to each other.

I could see a few of the lads bouncing around in a circle. At that moment I'm not sure I would have been able for that. Wally was the closest player to me and we embraced.

After a couple of minutes I got another lease of life. Lads who weren't in the match-day twenty-two managed to get on to the field, begging and stealing to get past the security men. Seeing them was the best bit of the celebrations. Some of them had been drinking all day and they were steaming. They added a different dimension to the madness on the field. It must have killed a few of them not to be involved but they didn't show it. They were part of us, and they would have known that.

After the slow lap of honour and the presentation of the trophy I ran towards the tunnel before any of the others. I wanted to be on my own for a couple of minutes in the dressing room. I felt that my prayer had been answered and I had this nagging guilt that I should never have asked in the first place.

I knelt down in the corner and said another prayer, of thanks.

12

Messer? Me?!?

In December 2006 Munster played Cardiff Blues in the Heineken Cup. If anybody remembers that match it will be for the moment late in the game when my shorts ripped and I needed a replacement pair. In a situation like that there is no privacy. I was wearing red jocks. Tight fit. Flaming red. Getting a new pair of shorts shouldn't have been a problem except that the game was nearly over and our kit-man, Jack Kiely, was already loading the van, hoping to make the next ferry. There was a delay while they rooted around for something and in the end they handed me a pair that wouldn't have fitted Strings.

All of this probably took a minute or two but it felt like an eternity. The referee was Christophe Berdos and

I could tell that he was anxious to re-start the game. 'You are not in the correct uniform,' he said to me. Talk about stating the obvious. We had a line-out close to their 22, there were four minutes left and we were seven points in front. So I threw away the shorts and ran over to take my place in the line-out.

There was a bit of crowd reaction, and anybody who knew me back home would have been thinking, 'Typical Donncha, acting the ghoul. He'd do anything to get a laugh.' It was a classic case of my reputation as a messer leading everybody to only one conclusion.

In this case, it was the wrong conclusion. I wasn't doing it for a laugh. Playing rugby is the most serious thing I do. My only thought was that I needed to be at the line-out. I wasn't thinking about the embarrassment of not having a pair of shorts on. Earlier in that season Paulie had his tooth knocked out in a collision. He handed it to one of the medics, got up off the floor and carried on. One day against Clermont, Rog's ear was hanging off; they stitched him up and he carried on. I wasn't missing any body parts, all I was missing were my shorts. I accept that it didn't look good, but I was prepared to contest the line-out in my underpants if the only alternative was not contesting the line-out at all.

Planning without me, Paulie had already shortened the line-out and put David Wallace in my position at the front. It meant that when I took my place Wally was automatically in a lifter's position. He said to me and Paulie afterwards that he thought it was an elaborate wind-up at his expense – to make him lift me in my jocks. This is what one of my oldest team mates thought I was capable of in the middle of a Heineken Cup match. What chance did I have of convincing the rest of the world?

The contrast with Darragh Hurley was funny. He had just come off the bench for his first appearance in the Heineken Cup and, as a prop, it would have been his job to lift me. He was so wound up, he said, that he didn't give a damn. 'If you had been wearing a tutu,' he said, 'I wouldn't have noticed.'

The reaction over the next few days was crazy. Pat Geraghty, Munster's media manager, was snowed under with requests to interview me. For three days I turned my phone off. I'm well able to laugh at myself but I didn't think this was funny. I was totally mortified and I wasn't prepared to laugh along.

There were two games with Cardiff, back to back, so they came to Thomond Park the following weekend. Unbelievably, my shorts ripped again. This time none of the lads thought for a second that this might be a joke. Leamy could see the look of absolute horror on my face and he gathered a couple of the lads round in a circle while I was changing. That's what should have happened a week earlier. The problem for me was that they probably thought I wouldn't mind making a fool of myself in public.

That impression would have come from me.

* * *

I am a messer, but I've changed. I used to be a serious messer. Pulling pranks or being part of pranks has been part of me as long as I can remember. When I was a kid, Emmett used to call me Trickster. In those days it was small-time gags like putting tea bags in his shoes or interfering with his aftershave. In school, if there was messing going on I was close to the middle of it. In Christians we used to capture pigeons and release them into the rafters to torment the caretaker. It was childish stuff that seems stupid now but it gave us a laugh at the time. That's the way it is with pranks: you have to be there.

As I moved into adulthood some of that childishness stayed with me. If I'd been forced to get a proper job in the real world I might have had to grow up more quickly, but the world of professional rugby wasn't that kind of environment. The Munster dressing room that I walked into was full of messers. A lot of it involved finding somebody's weakness and poking fun at it, without mercy. You needed a thick skin to survive and you needed to be quick with a sharp line if you were going to win those battles. There's a motto in our dressing room that all new players are made aware of immediately: 'Welcome to Munster. Leave your feelings at the door.'

Paulie has always been good in exchanges. Axel too, in his day. I remember a match against the Border Reivers in Scotland when their hooker called Axel a 'fat bastard'. Rather than take offence, Axel cut him dead: 'Are there no mirrors in your house?' The hooker was a big man and everybody who heard the line broke out laughing, including his team mates. The sound of that laughter would have been more devastating than any dig Axel could have given him.

I don't back off in the slagging matches but I don't have that kind of quick wit. Practical jokes have always been my thing. The story of the duck shit has been trotted out a million times, but there might be one person who hasn't heard it.

It was a Munster training camp in Breaffy House Hotel. We had some time off in the afternoon and we were bored. That was a lethal combination.

It started off innocently. There was a pond in the grounds of the hotel and we took cornflakes from the team room to feed the ducks. The ducks were delighted, and we soon realised that they would follow the cornflakes if we set a trail. We had them halfway up the path when the punch line came to us in a moment of inspiration. The management team were having a meeting and it dawned on us that we could entice the ducks up to the door of the meeting room and hunt them inside. In the end they needed a bit of encouragement from the boot of our Aussie second row Dave Pusey, but the plan worked.

As ever in these situations you don't think about the consequences. Once they were inside the room the ducks got a bit of a fright and, loaded up with cornflakes, they started to leave deposits all over the place. Jerry Holland was the Munster manager at the time and he caught me red-handed. Hayes and the rest of them had left the scene by then. Holl murdered me, and I spent the next couple of hours cleaning up duck droppings.

Because I was a messer, that also made me a target for pranks. Paulie knew my weaknesses better than anybody and he wasn't slow to exploit them. He was in Ireland camp once with time on his hands and I was at home, recovering from an injury. Knowing my appetite for training aids, he called to say that he had found a brilliant new device on the internet, an isometric core enhancer. It was a completely fictional story but I took the bait, hook, line and sinker. I gave Paulie my card details to buy one for me. Before I knew it, Paulie and a couple of others were sending flowers to people at my expense.

Shortly after I started training with the Ireland squad Keith Wood nearly caught me too. He was a brilliant table-tennis player and I was useless. If you gave me a tennis racket I wouldn't have been able to get the ball over the net, let alone do it with a little bat. There was a rule that if you lost 11–0 the penalty was to do a naked run. That involved stripping on the team bus on the way back from training, getting out at the bottom of the hill leading up to the Glenview Hotel and running to your room. I knew nothing about this, but everybody else did. When the score reached 7–0 word spread like wildfire and fellas crowded around our match in the team room. I was defenceless, and only a double-fault on Woody's serve saved my dignity.

Making a fool of yourself is one thing; feeling like a fool is a different thing. I've done that too. When Christian Cullen arrived in the middle of the 2003/04 season the excitement surrounding his signing was massive. Here was a superstar of world rugby coming to Munster. He came just in time to join our Christmas night out in Kilkenny, which would have been an eye-opener for him.

People say it's important to make a good first impression with a handshake, so for my special welcome I got a hand buzzer from the joke shop. It was a poor gag. Christian didn't know what to make of it, or me. Everyone could see I was embarrassed by his lack of reaction and the lads laughed at my expense rather than his. It turned out that Christian was good fun and had a dry sense of humour, but I had made an eejit of myself yet again.

By then John Fogarty had left Munster. He was my partner in a lot of the messing that went on. We got our first Munster contracts around the same time and we shared the same sense of humour. When Rog had the head beaten off him by Duncan McRae on the 2001 Lions tour, myself and Fogs turned it into a routine where we re-enacted the incident in full detail, complete with Rog's deadly wagging finger. We put on this act in all sorts of venues, including airport departure lounges. The lads enjoyed it. Even Rog saw the funny side.

We turned up to a fancy dress party once as a pantomime horse, partly because we were both broke and it was cheaper to split the price of one costume than hire two. I was the head and neck and he was the backside. Before we handed it back we decided to give it an outing at Munster training. We arrived early and just stood in the middle of Thomond Park.

A prank like that doesn't interfere with anybody else. Fellas either appreciate it or they don't. One bout of stupid messing, though, cost Fogs his place on the bench for the 2002 Heineken Cup final. We played Ulster in Ravenhill a couple of weeks earlier and we were basically wrestling in the hotel room on the night before the game. Unlike WWF, though, this was a situation where somebody could get hurt. I fell off the bed, Fogs landed on the point of his shoulder, and he didn't recover in time for the final. There was no sense to that.

For the following season Munster let him go, and he joined Connacht. I started a 'Bring Back Fogs' campaign which was harmless enough until a pre-season team meeting to elect the next Munster captain. Gaillimh was stepping down and picking his successor was a serious business. We were asked for nominations and, from the back of the room, I proposed Fogs. It wasn't witty and it was the wrong time to say something foolish. Alan Gaffney had just taken over as Munster coach and he came back at me like a flash: 'If you don't shut your mouth you'll be joining him.'

Jerry Holland was still the manager, and he spoke to me about it afterwards. He wasn't happy and he gave me the clear impression that I could have been shipped out just as easily as Fogs. When we were together we had the capacity to behave like nutters and they seemed to think we were better off apart. Separating us wasn't the only reason that Fogs went to Connacht, far from it, but it probably suited them to give me a jolt.

I was slow to change. In my own mind I was always able to separate acting the jackass from preparing seriously for professional rugby. Halfway through the 2005 Lions tour Gareth Thomas asked me what the story was. 'Everybody is asking me what gags you've been playing and I said, "I haven't seen any."' If you only met me for the first time on that tour you probably would have said I was dull.

My image, though, was one-dimensional. I was the clown, and I kept reinforcing that image in public. When Munster won the Heineken Cup in 2006 we were named Team of the Year at the RTE Sports Awards. I was one of the players sent along to accept the trophy and Brian O'Driscoll was going to make the presentation, live on television. I tried to do a deal with Drico. I offered to stumble up the steps on to the stage like a drunk if he agreed to drop the trophy as he was handing it over to Paulie. I couldn't get a straight answer. 'I'll see,' he said, 'I'll see.' That didn't stop me from going ahead with my part of the plan. I fell up the steps without actually hitting the floor. Gay Byrne, who was hosting the show, must have thought I was pissed. He didn't ask me any questions but I caught him trying to sniff my breath. Drico nearly cracked up but he held his composure long enough to hand over the trophy.

As the years went on I got tired of the image. For one thing, I knew it was selling me short. I had reached a certain level in my career and achieved certain goals by working incredibly hard and constantly looking to improve myself. That side of me was being overlooked. In the years when I was struggling to make a breakthrough with Munster and Ireland I felt at times that my image as a messer was harming my chances, but I couldn't shake it off. My behaviour kept it alive.

I alone was responsible for it. I played up to it. In later years, if I was asked to speak at a corporate function, I would tell them about the gags and the pranks, partly because I believed that's what they expected to hear but also because it was easy. I knew how to play that part.

Paulie appeared on *The Late Late Show* with Ryan Tubridy one night towards the end of 2010. No matter how many interviews you've done, those situations are never comfortable. So Paulie started slagging me about fake tan, the studio audience got a laugh out of it, Ryan Tubridy seemed to enjoy it, and Paulie carried on with a couple of other gags about me. Straight after the show he sent me a text. The last thing he'd wanted to do was sit there on national television and answer questions about himself; jokes about me were his escape route. 'I could sit there and have ten minutes of hell,' he said, 'or I could slag the shit out of you.' He wasn't apologising, he was just explaining. No problem.

Around the same time Alastair Campbell was a guest on the show. We'd got on well during the 2005 Lions tour and we still exchange texts every so often. When I heard he was going on I sent him a quick one-liner, and he brought it up during the interview, along with another story or two about the Lions tour. Between Alastair and Paulie my reputation as a messer had been cemented on the biggest chat show on Irish television.

A couple of months later it was my turn to be a guest. My work with UNICEF was the reason I was invited on to the programme and this was an opportunity to show the public other sides of my personality. Instead, I stumbled up the steps to my seat and immediately started playing up to my image. I took the easy option. To get through the interview I gave people what they expected to see.

By then I was a thirty-one-year-old husband and father with a long career in professional rugby behind me and huge ambitions for the years ahead. The audience would have got a small flavour of that, but not much. That was my fault.

Years after the incident with the ripped shorts, one of Ultan's boys, Ted, saw it for the first time. His teacher was explaining to the class about computers and the internet, and knowing that my nephew was one of her pupils she put 'Donncha O'Callaghan' into a Google search. The video footage was there, on YouTube. When she clicked on the website I don't think she had any idea what she was going to find. I'm sure she didn't. It wasn't something that you would choose to show to a class of five-year-olds.

Anyway, my nephew got a little bit upset. The other boys in the class were probably laughing and my nephew was confused. Why was I playing rugby in my underpants?

I had to meet him and explain: it wasn't a joke.

13

Winter in Croke Park, Summer in Spala

Before the match against England at Croke Park in February 2007 I got a phone call from my nan, Joan Roche. Nan lived in Mahon, a suburb of Cork city, and she was a fierce GAA supporter. I've played in Heineken Cup finals with Munster and been involved in Triple Crowns and a Grand Slam with Ireland, but the only time I ever saw bunting outside Nan's house was when Cork were in the All-Ireland final.

Nan was into her eighties at the time but a fantastic character and a big player on the bingo circuit, mostly in the GAA clubs around town. They all seemed to know her as my grandmother, and when Munster or Ireland were going well she played it up. One of the bingo announcers entered into the spirit of it, poking a bit of fun at me: 'With a tan, number four.'

I rang Nan more often than I called down to see her. During the season we spend so much time in camp or travelling that we're not at home as much as we would like. When I rang she'd give out that I hadn't called down.

'But Nan, we're playing Wales tomorrow.'

'In what?'

'The Six Nations.'

Anyway, she rang me before the England game.

'I haven't got a clue about rugby,' she said, 'but I'm telling you now, you can't lose to that shower in Croke Park.'

'I know, Nan.'

'If ye do, I'll never be able to go to the bingo again.'

We didn't need to be told. The first rugby game in Croke Park was against France, and we cocked up. There was so much talk about the venue and managing the occasion that we might not have talked enough about our opponents. They came at us like a train and for the first twenty minutes dominated us up front. When that happens you wonder if your head is in the right place. If we're honest with ourselves, I think we were a bit in awe of the whole thing.

The atmosphere was different to what we expected. Not as good. A bit weird. It wasn't like Thomond Park or the best days in the old Lansdowne Road where the crowd were part of the match and you took energy from their involvement. For one thing, the crowd seemed far away. Normally when you win a line-out you can hear an instant crowd reaction, but it was like those satellite delays you see on television. The cheer didn't reach your ears until you hit the ground with the ball. In spite of all that we should have won. They caught us with a last-minute try when we failed to deal properly with a re-start. Criminal.

The build-up to the England game was even more intense, but we handled it better. There was talk of bomb threats, and during the captain's run on Friday we could see them sweeping the stand for any suspicious devices. There was a greater security presence than we had ever seen. This was the game that everybody had been talking about once the Gaelic Athletic Association made the decision to open up Croke Park for rugby and soccer. We understood that it was more than a rugby game. People have different views about what it did mean or what it should mean or if too much was made of it. You can argue about all that. What we knew was that losing wasn't an option.

You often hear players saying that you have to separate the match from the occasion. Most of the time that's the best way to approach big games. This time, we couldn't look at it in that way. We had to stand up to the occasion and all the things it meant to people. Drico put it best in the team meeting on the day of the game. 'If you think this is just another international match,' he

said, 'you're one hundred per cent wrong.' Our balls
were on the line.

Before the match we lined up along the red carpet to
shake hands with President Mary McAleese, as usual.
She always says something appropriate but not serious.
This was the exception. 'Today is the day,' she said to
me. 'We need a big one.' At that moment I felt like I was
going to war. It was like getting your orders from the
commander-in-chief.

I noticed that her hand was sticky. I'd shaken her
hand enough times to know that hers wasn't a sweaty
palm. Rugby players use a substance called handball
wax. It's an adhesive that you spray on your hands and
arms to reduce the risk of dropping the ball. It came
into rugby through Olympic handball and it's very hard
to get off. Using soap and hot water isn't enough. Unless
you scrub it with a special oil it'll come back as sticky as
ever five minutes later. I put it on for the warm-up,
clean it off before I meet the President, then apply it
again before the game starts. To my mind that's basic
good manners. Somebody, though, hadn't done that.

It immediately struck me that it must have been one
of the English lads. Of course she shook hands with
other Irish lads along the red carpet before she got to
me but I ruled all of them out as suspects without
giving it a second thought. It was only a small thing but
I thought it was disrespectful. On another day, it
mightn't have struck me at all.

I wasn't emotional during our anthem but I really

wanted to belt it out. Normally you can hear yourself singing because not all of the crowd would be putting their hearts into it, but that day I couldn't hear myself. In the build-up nobody was sure what would happen during 'God Save the Queen'. You could feel the tension in the crowd before the band started up. It would only have taken a couple of ghouls to start shouting or booing and ruin it for everybody. Everybody who experienced the silence will never forget it. It really got to me.

And then we drew a line under it. My feeling was that the English players should be treated with total respect until the first whistle blew and then we should flake the life out of them. Conor O'Shea, the former Ireland international, had been asked to talk to the English players about the history of Croke Park and its significance in Irish life. Whatever they learned that week couldn't make them understand. As far as I was concerned they would never know what it meant to us.

Drico said that, in our careers, this game would be judged on its own, and he was right. It didn't matter which English team turned up that day, they didn't stand a chance against us.

By the time we got to Rome on the final day of the Six Nations we still had an outside chance of winning the championship on points difference. At half time, though, we were only eight points up and Niall O'Donovan gave the forwards an unmerciful bollicking. That was the thing about Eddie O'Sullivan and all the coaches he had working with him, they were incredibly direct and honest. There would have been no thought in their minds that they should come into the dressing room, stroke our egos and emphasise the positives. After two minutes in that dressing room it was the last place in the world you wanted to be.

Against Italy it's all about physicality in the pack, and Niallo basically said we hadn't been man enough. Straight out. The video might have told a different story later on, but at that moment he made us feel like we were betraying ourselves and the jersey on our backs.

In the third quarter we put on nineteen unanswered points and blew Italy away. By the end we had racked up eight tries and fifty-one points, but in the last minute Italy hit us for a score on the counter-attack after a bad turnover inside their half. When the final sums were done later that evening every point was crucial.

It all came down to France's match against Scotland in Paris. They kicked off later than us and when we got back to the team hotel the match was being shown on a small television in the lobby. The game was nearly over, Scotland were losing, but they weren't dead yet. Against the run of play they scored with a couple of minutes left and if they didn't concede again we would be crowned champions. It was too good to be true.

France launched one last attack and in stoppage time they got the try they needed. To prolong our agony the decision was referred to the television match official. The score was awarded.

We had a recovery session scheduled for the swimming pool in the hotel. Because of the France match it was delayed, but John Hayes just carried on regardless. He had no interest in watching the other game, standing around the hotel lobby with supporters and a television camera waiting for our reaction. He'd run a mile from that.

I was next into the pool after Hayes and I tried to tell him about the game in Paris.

'Hayes, France won.'

No response.

'Fuck it, we were close enough.'

Nothing.

The whole idea of Scotland doing us a favour in Paris probably didn't appeal to him. If we weren't able to close the deal ourselves on the field I'd say he wouldn't have cared much about it. I'm not sure he was wild about the thought of winning a championship anyway. It was probably a Grand Slam or nothing for him at that stage. But you couldn't be sure with Hayes. He didn't see any need to share his feelings or his inner thoughts with the rest of us. He doesn't care what anyone thinks of him. Nobody had any problem accepting him the way he was.

When we did finally win the Grand Slam Hayes didn't even hang around for the celebrations. We were herded on to a stage outside the Mansion House in the centre of Dublin and made a show of ourselves. When I noticed he was missing I sent him a text: 'Where are you?'

'I'm at home, watching ye fools on the telly.'

Secretly he enjoyed the messing too, but mostly as a spectator. We're all going to miss him when he's gone. There was massive respect and affection for him in the Munster and Ireland dressing rooms. He was the kind of player that only his team mates could fully appreciate. The pundits who were critical of Hayes would never buy a line like that, but you can't fool the people you play with.

After we're all finished playing you wonder how many of us will remain friends. A lot of us have spent the best part of ten or twelve years working together, sharing the same dreams, ambitions, disappointments, triumphs. Being in the trenches from week to week creates a lot of closeness, but how much of that will last when we go our separate ways?

I keep telling Hayes that we're going to be friends. He seems to have a problem with that.

'O'Callaghan, if you come near me, I'll shoot you.'

'I'm going to call down to you on the farm in Cappamore and say hello.'

'O'Callaghan, I'll only see you down the barrel of a gun. I swear, I'll fucking do you, O'Callaghan.'

I don't think he means it. He's a softie at heart.

I can't remember when I felt I had won my battle with Malcolm O'Kelly for the Ireland jersey. Even now, with seventy-odd caps, I never feel relaxed about my place. I used to get good-luck texts from family and friends on the night before a team announcement, but when I became established on the team those messages stopped. I couldn't understand that because my anxiety hadn't gone away.

Mal had been injured for the summer tour in 2006, and that was my big chance. We started with two Tests against New Zealand and finished against Australia. It could have been a brilliant tour but it ended in exhaustion and failure. In the opening Test we blew a great chance to beat the All Blacks for the first time in our history. A week later we rattled them again without looking like winning. By the time we got to Australia we had nothing left in the tank.

Me? I was buzzing. Tours have always suited me. I like the way our days are structured. Busy. Laid out. The week starts with a game and finishes with a game. The preparation is intense and focused. I loved that tour. In the first match I made twenty-one tackles, more than any other player on the pitch. Depending on the opposition, a score in the mid-teens would usually lead the tackle count, and it would generally be one of the back rows. That day, though, Niall O'Donovan's words were ringing in my ears: 'You need to do more.'

Work rate was my thing. My athleticism was good, I did my job in the line-out, but most of all I worked hard. That's what I brought to the party. Against the All Blacks, if your tackle count wasn't up you weren't doing your job properly, but I had never achieved a figure like that before. That was my big statement. Mal had talents that I could only dream about, but he couldn't match me for work rate. To overtake him, that's where I needed to take the battle.

From the beginning of that tour to the end of the 2007 Six Nations Ireland played eleven Tests and I started ten of them. More than that, I played eighty minutes in every match that I started. Mal had replaced Paulie against Australia at Lansdowne Road in the autumn of 2006 and he'd started against the Pacific Islands a week later. But he fell out of favour for the 2007 Six Nations and Mick O'Driscoll forced his way into the match-day twenty-two. Either way, I had won Eddie's confidence. When Ireland went on a short tour to Argentina in the summer of 2007 the players that were seen as the first fifteen for the World Cup were left at home, and I was in that group.

The World Cup started in September. My build-up began as soon as Munster lost to Llanelli in the quarter-final of the Heineken Cup, at the end of March. Looking back, it was crazy. I structured my whole life around the World Cup. I didn't go out for meals with friends in case I ended up eating the wrong foods, or in case I got to bed late. In the normal course of my life I watch everything I eat but some days you'd relax and allow yourself a treat. For me, that would probably be a hot chocolate. I wasn't even doing that.

As soon as Munster were out I was thinking about peaking again for September. I spoke to Aidan O'Connell, our fitness guy with Munster, and Mickey

McGurn, the fitness guy with Ireland, and asked them for programmes that would keep me going until the end of the season and into the summer. Come the World Cup I wanted to be in the best shape of my life. Gary O'Driscoll, the Ireland doctor, got wind of what I was doing and I know he was worried about it. He thought I'd be burned out. That was the only reasonable way to look at it. I had entered a tunnel, though, that was leading all the way to France.

The players who weren't on the summer tour to Argentina or who weren't at the Churchill Cup in America went to Spala in Poland for a pre-season training camp. We'd been going there for years. It was our private place of torture. I went there first at the beginning of Eddie O'Sullivan's reign, before I was a regular member of the squad. Mick Galwey pulled out at short notice and I was called up. Gaillimh had been around long enough to know what he was missing in Spala.

The camp was situated on the edge of a forest, miles from nowhere. There were no luxuries or comforts, everything was basic. The beds were just foam mattresses that were much too small for me if I stretched out. It didn't matter. At the end of a day's training in Spala you'd have slept on a window ledge.

The food was terrible too. They would put strawberries in your soup and yoghurt in your pasta. They fed us fish that was chewy and tough. Every dish was supposed to be incredibly healthy, and I've no doubt they were. The pre-World Cup camp was only a week, but going back the years we had much longer stays, up to three weeks, and on those trips fellas needed a break from the food.

Our bagman Rala – Paddy O'Reilly – always has a stash of sweets and chocolates. During Ireland camp Rala's room is usually busy with lads calling in for a piece of kit or just for a chat; in Spala they were looking for treats more than anything. Rala called them 'lu-lus'. He had everything you could wish for. It was like Willy Wonka's Chocolate Factory in there. Curly-Wurlys were a big favourite, but the range of stuff was massive. The nutritionist frowned on this carry-on and Rala's room was raided every so often. Being a fence for illegal sweets isn't for the faint-hearted, but Rala knew that he was performing a service for our morale. Whenever he was raided he changed the location of his stash and re-loaded.

I've prided myself on never taking a sweet from Rala, but in Spala the temptation nearly broke me. I asked him once where the stash was and he thought I was cracking. I held tough. That's what Spala was about, though: pushing us to the point of breakdown.

The day began at seven when the medical staff monitored your physical condition before breakfast. Training started soon afterwards and, with a few breaks, it continued until seven in the evening.

There were two weights sessions, a fitness session, a skills session, two cardio sessions and two sessions of cryotherapy in the ice chamber. The cryotherapy was supposed to speed up your body's recovery. None of us were sure if it worked, and from what I understand scientists are divided about its value. I believed in it, one hundred per cent. I don't think we could have got through the volumes of work, day after day, without the ice chambers. Anyway, we trooped in there, six at a time, stripped down to gloves and boxer shorts, braving temperatures that you wouldn't get in the Arctic.

When fellas cracked, the tension turned into fights on the training field. You could see it in fellas' faces. Everyone looked strained, nobody was happy. In the early years, especially, the training schedule was crazy. It was Sylvester Stallone in *Rocky III*, except that this was for real. They assured us that three weeks of pre-season in Spala was the equivalent of two months' training at home. One year we did fitness tests with Munster about a month later and the lads who hadn't been in Spala posted the same scores as the rest of us. Maybe the benefits were more long term.

During our long stints at Spala they used to take us away for weekends. Two stick in my mind. One was a night in Krakow, an absolutely beautiful city. We ate steak and slept in hotel beds with duvets – all the things we take for granted that suddenly felt like the greatest luxuries in the world.

The other trip was a visit to Auschwitz, the Nazi concentration camp. It is an incredible place, but it was the wrong time for us to see it. We were all worn down from camp and starting to miss home. Even if you visited Auschwitz in a good frame of mind it would be impossible not to be affected. A lot of our guys were in tears and a couple of guys got physically sick. There's always craic on our bus trips but nobody opened their mouths on the way back to camp. In my rugby life I've suffered a lot of shattering defeats but I've never experienced a low like we all felt that day. Nobody complained in Spala for the next week. Nobody gave out about the beds or the food or their blisters or the savage training.

The training camp before the World Cup was much different. It was only a week, for a start, there were just thirteen or fourteen of us, and we ripped into it. Fellas were producing personal bests in all kinds of exercises. Some of us were doing extra work in the gym on top of the schedule that was laid out for us. It was probably sheer madness but that was the mood in the camp. Everyone was there to burst a gut. For team bonding, it was brilliant. When the group is that small you don't fall into the usual cliques. Everybody is suffering and helping each other to get through it. Having said that, there were exceptions to that mentality. Among rugby players, compassion has its limits.

The only exercise I couldn't handle was in the pool. Water is my kryptonite. I swim like a stone. The drill was to swim a length, get out, do a load of press-ups, run down to the other end of the pool and start again. Mickey McGurn knew it wouldn't suit me and told me to give it a skip. The thought of not doing it would have killed me. Instead, I nearly killed myself in the pool. I was taking on more water than the *Titanic*. At the end of every length I was barfing on the poolside to get the chlorine out of my stomach. All the other lads were finished long before me and, in typical fashion, they thought my suffering was hilarious. They know how much pride I take in my fitness and being able to handle the work load. If they ever think I'm getting above my station now they throw the pool session in Spala back in my face. I got through it, though. That's what Spala was all about.

On the last day in camp we had a tough field session. All of us were pumped up, keen to finish the week on a high. Tackling was the last drill, and Paulie lined up Hayes for one of the biggest hits of the season. Hayes could see what was coming and he had no intention of being a helpless victim. Just like he did to me years earlier, Hayes swung his hip and his arse at the last second and laid Paulie out. He was lying on the grass, flattened, like all the air had been left out of him. Everyone's first reaction was panic. Paulie was groaning, and I knew exactly how he felt. When I got a stinger off Hayes I thought the world was going to end, and I wouldn't have minded if it meant being released from the pain.

On the same day Rog twisted his knee in a seven-on-seven match. It was the same knee that he had damaged a couple of years earlier, and leaving the training camp that weekend nobody was sure if he was going to be all right or not.

Paulie eventually came round and Rog's knee injury wasn't as bad as everyone had feared, but, looking back, it was probably a key day in our build-up to the World Cup. Everyone got a fright, including the management. Turning up in France without Paulie or Rog, or both, was unthinkable.

People said that the management were wrapping us in cotton wool by not sending us on tour to Argentina. At the time the commentators didn't have a problem with that and neither did the players. When we assembled in Limerick for the next training camp a few weeks later, though, there seemed to be another layer of cotton wool. The contact sessions weren't as fierce as they had been in Spala. We weren't instructed to ease off, and if the management noticed the reduced intensity they didn't make an issue of it. The reality was that getting to the World Cup in one piece was on everyone's mind.

When the tournament came round we were under-cooked, and that attitude was part of the reason. But that was only one aspect. There is no simple explanation for what happened in France in the autumn of 2007.

14

Nutella

For the World Cup we stayed in a hotel on the outskirts of Bordeaux, in a place called Bordeaux-Lac. Bordeaux is a beautiful city with lovely streets and buildings. From our hotel we didn't have those views. We were close to an industrial estate, a hypermarket and a greasy spoon café. The 'Lac' referred to a man-made lake about a five-minute walk from the hotel. It was a featureless place that didn't even have wildlife, but when things turned sour during that tournament it was a quiet place to go and throw some skimmers on to the water. You wouldn't choose it as an oasis of tranquillity, but everything is relative.

The hotel was fine. Not great, but fine. It played no part in our failure. During that World Cup we would have been miserable in the most beautiful hotel in France. If we had played well we probably could have lived with the food too. In the circumstances it contributed to our despair. Small things, big things – all of it snowballed.

Why does it matter? Because when you're in camp, dinner is a social occasion. It passes the evening. It puts you in good form. In the Killiney Castle, our team hotel in Dublin, there's a brilliant chef, Sean Dempsey, who prepares the most fantastic meals for us. You look forward to going for dinner at seven in the evening and it could be nearly nine o'clock before you leave the dining room. You're stuck in the hotel anyway so you may as well be happy about it.

In Bordeaux, the food in the hotel was terrible. The irony is that I'd spent months watching every morsel that went into my mouth and only eating the best food I could lay my hands on. When we got to the tournament we could barely finish what was on the plate. Some nights we didn't. We went off and tried to find restaurants but there was nowhere decent close to our hotel. Other nights we used to walk round to the hypermarket and pick up something handy to fill the gaps. I made a lot of Nutella sandwiches. I can't look at it now. The flavour of Nutella is the bad taste of the 2007 World Cup. Ruth Wood-Martin, our nutritionist, was tearing her hair out. She was doing her best to work with the chef in the hotel and we lived in hope that the next evening's meal would be better. Generally, it wasn't.

So, dinner was no longer a social occasion. Fellas trooped back to their rooms, moaning and hungry. When morale is low everything feels worse. In a way the food summed up our tournament. We thought we had every angle covered coming into the World Cup and in the end we couldn't even get the basics right.

We didn't arrive with bad morale, far from it. During the build-up we had spoken openly about our ambition to win the World Cup. When we were handed an itinerary that didn't account for our movements after the quarter-final Shane Horgan raised it immediately in a squad meeting. We had no interest in the 'give it a lash' mentality that other Ireland teams entertained in the past. We went there to be successful. We believed we would be successful. We thought we could win it.

Our build-up wasn't ideal in the end, but I don't remember being worried. We got away with murder against Italy in Belfast, didn't play well in Scotland and had a ridiculous match against Bayonne in the south of France. That was the filthiest match I ever played in. There was gouging and biting and cheap shots. At the first line-out one of their guys grabbed my balls; later on, one of them head-butted me while I was lying on the ground. Paulie and Drico tried talking to Wayne Barnes, the referee, but he would have needed a hundred pairs of eyes to see everything that was going on. They had no interest in playing ball.

The odd thing is that it wasn't even a physically intense match, which is what we desperately needed.

They were miles off Test level. It wasn't even at Magners League intensity. We'd have been better off with a training session, except that we weren't really getting stuck into each other at training. It was a catch-22 situation: we all wanted to get to the World Cup in one piece, the management didn't want to put the first fifteen at risk, but we needed to get battle-hardened before the battle started. The idea of the Bayonne match was to get a tough game under our belts, but that match was just dangerous. Long before the end all I was thinking about was getting off the field without being injured or sent off. Drico wasn't so lucky. He suffered a facial injury, just above his eye, and for a while it looked like he'd miss the first couple of games in the tournament. Shane Horgan had already been injured against Scotland. We didn't need any more injuries, but we needed more contact work.

We got the balance wrong. During the build-up we were probably making excuses without even realising it. The Italy match was our first run out so we were bound to be rusty; we heard after the Scotland match that they'd been kicking lumps out of each other for the previous month so they were closer to match fitness; the Bayonne game was a write-off, forget about it. All of those thoughts amounted to excuses. We weren't reading the signs.

I think we were all convinced it was going to click into place. It's easy to be critical in hindsight and see the mistakes that were made, but I had complete faith in our preparation and the plan that had been put in place. Right up until the end I was certain that everything would somehow come right for us.

Eddie O'Sullivan reckoned that the games against Namibia and Georgia would put us spot on for the big games in the pool against France and Argentina. Instead, those games exposed us. We were expected to beat Namibia by fifty or sixty points and we ended up winning by fifteen. After a good opening twenty minutes it turned into a poor performance. That was the start of the criticism back home. One way or another we were going to be in the spotlight. When things are going badly the spotlight becomes part of the problem.

We went to the beach the day after the Namibia game, and photographs were published in the papers the following day. 'Beach Boys' was the headline in one newspaper. Underneath it read: 'Irish lads sun themselves after narrow victory over minnows Namibia'. At the 2003 World Cup in Australia we stayed on the coast and went to the beach every day after training. Nobody said a word about it. Now, it felt like we were accused of committing an offence.

As things got worse, small things played on your mind. A trip to a vineyard was organised for one of our free days. I don't drink, I have no interest in wine, but I thought it would do me good to get out of the hotel and get away for a few hours. When I stepped on the bus, though, I saw that some reporters and a couple of photographers had been invited too. I turned back straight away. Our World Cup was going down the toilet; I didn't want a picture of me at a vineyard to appear in the papers the following day. It was probably ridiculously paranoid, but this wasn't a normal situation.

There was no panic after the Namibia match but that performance had a knock-on effect. Instead of making a couple of changes for the Georgia game, which might have been the original plan, Eddie fielded the same fifteen. It was obvious that we were short of match practice and that was the priority now. For a certain number of players in the squad, playing against Georgia was their best chance of making an appearance at that World Cup. Now that chance had been taken away less than a week after the tournament had started. Everybody's troubles were their own.

I remember looking at the Georgian players as they walked out and thinking they were all the same shape. You couldn't tell the second rows from the scrum-half. They all seemed to be about 6ft 3in, eighteen or so stone and square. It was the most physical game I'd ever played in. They were like the world's hardest junior team. Every time they got the ball they wanted to run over the top of us. After every hit you were rocked. It didn't matter a damn what scores we had posted in our fitness tests in Spala. This was old-fashioned rugby, dog eat dog.

We couldn't get away from them, and the longer they stayed in the game the more hope they had. When they scored their intercept try in the second half all of them seemed to grow an inch. Were we starting to panic? Yeah. Were we barking at each other and losing the rag? There was a bit of that. Panic, though, isn't just about arguments. It's much more serious when fellas go quiet. That's the worst thing that can happen. A quiet pitch is hell because it makes it feel bigger. When the communication drops, everybody is more isolated. That's what we were dealing with – not enough possession and too much silence.

Georgia were camped on our line, looking for the try that would destroy us and our World Cup. They were picking and jamming, picking and jamming, and we were hanging on for dear life. When they finally got over the line the referee went to the television match official. The replays seemed to show that Denis Leamy got his hand under the ball before it was grounded and the try wasn't given. From what I could see Denis got his hand under the ball after it had been grounded. The TMO didn't have that camera angle. We got away with murder.

We won by four points, but it felt like the worst defeat of all time. Our dressing room resembled an Accident and Emergency ward. Sore bodies and ice packs all over the place. It was quiet too. Everyone was looking for a bit of direction. Clarity. We needed to be told, 'Do this, do that, and everything will be all right.' But nobody had the instant answers we were looking for. We didn't know what was wrong.

Our response was to train even harder. Georgia had bullied us so we belted lumps out of each other in training on Monday and Tuesday. Every coach wanted more time to work on his area so the sessions became crazy long on the week of the France game. Over the years with Eddie, training was strictly managed. Every one of the specialist coaches knew how much time he had for his segment of the session, and when Eddie sounded the hooter they had to finish. After Georgia, Eddie swallowed the hooter. We'd been preparing for the World Cup for months and all of a sudden we were cramming for the biggest exam: France in Paris.

That game was on a Friday night. On the Tuesday I felt exhausted. We were doing too much. I was in the best shape of my life. I shouldn't have felt tired three days before the biggest game of our World Cup. Wednesday was our day off and I spent most of it in bed trying to recover some freshness. I went for a rub in the morning and spent twenty minutes at the lake, just so I could say to myself that I got out of the hotel. The rest of the day was spent in and out of bed.

Against France we were terrible. Flat. Dead. They had lost their first match to Argentina and they were under pressure too. We thought we could exploit that, keep it tight, make them worry. But we never got into their heads. We defended badly for a couple of tries and it was over long before the end. There's nothing worse than knowing that you have no way back with twenty minutes left. Chris White was the referee and we thought he blew us off the pitch. In the end he wouldn't even talk to Paulie. We were on his back so much he wasn't prepared to listen to another word. We were nearly pleading with him for decisions. It was another sign of our growing desperation. We bitched about him afterwards, but he wasn't the reason for our performance.

To qualify from the pool we needed to beat Argentina and score four tries for a bonus point. To everybody on the outside it looked impossible. I believed we could do it. I was convinced that we were being put through this terrible punishment but it would be worth it in the end. Even before the France game we were still talking about topping the pool. When I look back, I think we were in a state of denial. We couldn't work out what had gone wrong, we couldn't work out ways to fix it. All we had left was irrational belief.

We heard all the stories about disharmony in the camp. We kept hearing them for months after the tournament. Every one of them was ridiculous. Some of the lads used to go searching for them on internet chat rooms, or people at home used to send them on by email. On the bus going to training Frankie Sheahan or Brian Carney used to read out the 'Rumour of the Day'. It was a bit of light relief for us. I can't remember most of them now. I know it was rumoured that Geordan Murphy had walked out of the squad, and there he was, sitting on the bus listening to this rumour. People also said that Drico and Strings had had a row, and you'd walk into the team room and there they were playing table tennis. After a while Frankie and Carns were adding arms and legs to the rumours just for the craic.

There weren't any fights or flare-ups. We were just miserable. Somebody seemed to be on the verge of cracking every day. There was no point hopping the ball with lads or trying to create a bit of fun because it would have been false. Nobody would have bought it. The social committee didn't come up with great out-ings or activities for our days off, but nobody was giving out about it either. In ways, we probably needed to get away from each other on our free day.

The other thing that strikes me is that maybe we should have gone on the lash after the Georgia match. I've come full circle on this issue. Compared to when I started with Munster and Ireland there is very little drinking now during the season, but I'd always found it hard to accept that professional athletes should drink at all. Now, I think it can be useful in certain situations. Maybe after that Georgia match we just needed to let off some steam. Going on the lash would have been alien to us after all the work we'd put in, but maybe that was part of the problem – we were too uptight, too intense.

We threw everything at Argentina. Our physicality in the first twenty minutes was through the roof. To use Eddie's phrase, we went out on the field like 'mad dogs in a meat house'. But they played it smart. All they had to do was stop us from scoring four tries, and spoiling other teams has always been their greatest strength.

Then they scored first. A simple 8–9–14 move down the short side from the base of a five-metre scrum. We'd spent twenty minutes in training during the week thrashing out how to defend in that situation and then they scored from it at the first opportunity. When you shoot yourself in the foot like that, what chance do you have?

After the try, Felipe Contepomi was running his mouth on the way back. 'You go home tomorrow.' He was right.

We scored two tries but we never looked like scoring four. Up front we were beaten again. For the third game out of four at that World Cup we lost more collisions than we won. As a pack, we couldn't get away from that damning reality. I was replaced by Mal in the second half, just like I was against France. I live and die by my stats, and at that World Cup I didn't reach the standards I demand of myself. I couldn't explain it, and it wrecked my head for months afterwards. I couldn't have done any more in the build-up. I couldn't have been more careful or committed. I couldn't have wanted to succeed any more than I did. And I failed. We failed.

That night I drank Coke and ate chocolate ice cream for the first time in months. That was my blow-out.

It affected everyone differently. During the tournament you could see it was getting on top of Eddie. Conviction was his greatest strength. He told us how it was going to be done, we listened and obeyed. Not everyone agreed with him all of the time but we trusted him. At the World Cup, though, he started asking us for feedback. Some coaches operate in that way, but in Eddie's case it was a significant change of approach that we didn't expect. I always had huge time for Eddie because I liked being told exactly what was required of me. Whether he was right or wrong, he knew exactly what he wanted and that kind of certainty suited me. By the end of the World Cup he didn't seem so sure of himself. One way or another, all of us were rattled.

When we flew into Dublin we were shepherded into a private area at the airport, away from the public. If we had won the World Cup we would have been shepherded into the same area, but in these circumstances it felt like we were being hidden away. Like we were coming home in shame. I felt ashamed, but I wanted to front up. I didn't have a problem meeting people and letting them say whatever they wanted to get off their chests. At one stage I made a move to pick up my bag and one of the lads called me back. 'Not that way, there's a quieter exit over here.' I got the feeling that they'd have liked us to arrive into Cobh by boat under cover of darkness.

I went away to Spain with Jenny for a couple of weeks. I brought the World Cup with me. For a long time I couldn't shake it off. A couple of days after I returned to training with Munster Deccie called me into his office. He produced a photograph from the Argentina match. Their number eight, Gonzalo Longo

Elia, had me pinned to the ground and I had my arms outstretched so that the match officials could see that I was the victim in this incident. I was so conscious of keeping my discipline that my first thought was to make sure I didn't get a yellow card; in the past my first instinct would have been to throw a dig. Deccie said he never wanted to see me in that situation again. In a way it clarified the problem I've always had: coaches want me to be a little bit mad but they don't want me in the sin-bin. Striking that balance has been the constant challenge of my career.

The photograph did look terrible. It summed up my World Cup. Trying desperately to do the right thing but unable to do anything. Helpless.

15

Hearts and Minds

As far as I could see, everything was fine. Munster were back in the final of the Heineken Cup, the World Cup was out of my system, my form was good. Or, I thought it was good.

After we beat Saracens in the semi-final most of the first team was rested for a mid-week match against Ulster in the Magners League a few days later, but I was back in the team against Llanelli. We didn't play well. They led by fifteen points at the break and we beat them with a penalty in the tenth minute of stoppage time. Got away with murder. Micko came on for me with twenty minutes left but that wasn't unusual and I wasn't concerned.

Then Deccie rang on Monday evening. It was strange

to see his name flash up on my mobile phone because outside training or matches we didn't have much contact. The moment I answered I knew something was up. Before the Heineken Cup final we had one match left, against Glasgow in the Magners League. After that there was a two-week break to the final, so it was an ideal game to put the first fifteen on the pitch. That's why he was ringing.

'I don't have a place for you on Saturday,' he said.

I was waiting for him to say that I needed a rest or that he was minding a few players before the final but he didn't elaborate. He left it hanging.

I can't remember what I said to him exactly. My mind was racing so fast that I didn't work out all the implications straight away. My instinct was that my place on the team for the final wasn't really under threat and my first thought was that I needed to play against Glasgow to get ready for Toulouse.

I blurted out something about this not being ideal preparation. And then Deccie completed the message.

'Like everybody else in the squad, you're in my thoughts for the final.'

That was it. My place was under threat. Or, I believed it was. Or, that's what he wanted me to believe.

It was a short conversation, and when I came off the phone I considered ringing him straight back. But I probably knew it wouldn't get me anywhere, and anyway, I was too rattled.

I'd known Deccie a long time but that didn't mean I

could always work him out. Was I really under pressure or not? Years earlier at the U-19s World Cup he'd pulled a stunt with team selection for the opening match that made half of the first fifteen think that they were under pressure, including me. I couldn't believe that I found myself in that situation again. Not now.

I went upstairs and broke down. Jenny and I had moved in together by then. She was in the front room watching telly but I didn't want her to see me in this state. About twenty minutes later she followed me upstairs. It was the first time she'd seen me cry. She was worried that something seriously bad had happened. While I was sobbing I tried to explain about the phone call from Deccie, and at that moment she probably thought that she'd moved in with a head case.

At the same time, she knew how much it meant to me. And so did Deccie. That's what was killing me. My life revolved around being ready for rugby. I did everything by the book. Part of me was worrying to death about being left out of the final and part of me was angry. In my mind I didn't deserve this. My performances on the pitch and at training didn't deserve it.

I didn't ring any of the other Munster lads but I called Eddie, my brother. He just said I needed to calm down. I couldn't. I was so rocked that I couldn't sleep that night. Every time I turned it over in my head I thought I knew what Deccie was doing, but that didn't convince me that everything was going to be all right.

We trained the following day in Garryowen and I

heard that Marcus and Leamy had received the same phone call from Deccie. 'No place for you on Saturday, in my thoughts for the final.' So I called them and we arranged to meet round the back of the clubhouse ten minutes before training. We agreed that we weren't going to show any sign of weakness. We were going to train full on and not wave the white flag.

A couple of minutes after training started myself and Leamy had a scrap. I jumped on him and gave him a slap and he gave me a kick in the balls as I was being pulled away. The rest of the session had an edge after that. Is that what Deccie wanted all along? It occurred to me afterwards that the three of us should have waltzed around training with a hangdog expression rather than play into Deccie's hands. But he would have taken that into account when he picked us for his plan. He would have known that myself, Leamy and Marcus were incapable of reacting in that way.

The other lads could sense that something wasn't right. After training Rog and Paulie asked me what was up and I was honest with them. I told them what had happened and how I felt about it. I know Paulie raised it with Deccie. I don't know the ins and outs of that conversation but before training on Thursday there was a meeting at Charleville Golf Club. Myself, Leamy and Marcus were asked to stay back afterwards along with Paulie and Quinny.

Deccie's tone was much different to that of our conversation on Monday. He took a softer line. He told us that he had full faith in our ability and then he started into a speech about discipline. The team's discipline hadn't been good against Llanelli and he was harping on about it. Were the three of us carrying the can for that? He didn't make that clear. The bottom line seemed to be that our places weren't under threat for the final.

Over the years we've always had a good relationship. Deccie has a heart as big as himself and he cares about people. Not every coach has that quality, and in that role it's not strictly necessary. Eddie O'Sullivan, for example, didn't pretend to be interested in your life outside rugby. At a post-match dinner he wouldn't automatically know the names of all the wives or girl-friends at the table. If he knew one name we'd be impressed. He was good in other ways, though, and I took a lot from our player–coach relationship.

Deccie is different. Man-management is one of his great strengths. When Jenny gave birth to Sophie, he sent flowers. It was a genuine gesture from a genuine person and we both appreciated it. He looks after the small things that make a difference. When he bumps into one of my brothers he greets them by name and has a word. They appreciate that he remembers their names and they'll always mention it to me. He's concerned about your well-being as a person and he makes time to ask. I don't need a life coach and Deccie doesn't intrude in that way, but when he occasionally asks about my life outside rugby I know that he's not doing it for the sake of appearances.

Early in my career with Munster I probably frustrated him at times. Deccie was a school teacher before rugby went professional and I'm sure I reminded him of the messers at the back of the class. I was immature, and it showed. He believed that I needed a kick in the backside every so often, but by 2008 I was well beyond that stage. I was a seasoned international with a Lions tour, a Heineken Cup and two World Cups under my belt. In my rugby life, being professional about everything was all I cared about.

Getting ready for Toulouse was going to consume me in the days and weeks leading up to the final. I didn't need to be put through the wringer about team selection. The anxiety drained me. If you look at photographs after the final there is a massive cold sore on my face. That came from the stress of all this.

Deccie is the most successful coach in the history of Irish rugby because he gets most things right most of the time. Did he get this right with me? Probably. Did it hurt? Absolutely. Had I the balls to tell him straight out? No. I should have. I didn't. We carried on as before.

We had work to do after the Saracens semi-final. We'd played ourselves into a hole in the second half that day and were nearly buried in it. Alan Gaffney was in charge of them and he knew a lot of us from his time with Munster. I suspect he remembered what I used to be like too. Straight from the kick-off Kris Chesney clattered me off the ball, full in the face with his arm and shoulder.

They expected me to react and that's what they wanted. Chesney was a beast of a man, about 6ft 6in, and a scary-looking bastard. He'd been around a long time as well and he knew all the tricks. Every chance he got during the match he twisted my tail. Back in Alan's time with Munster I would have given him a thump in the first minute but I'd changed. It clicked with me immediately, and I didn't fall into their trap.

There was a penalty decision on our 22 right at the death that went our way but could easily have gone theirs. It should never have come down to a one-score game but when you survive those situations there's a lot to gain. Straight away it put us on the back foot. Leading into a big game we've always been better off in that position. Tony McGahan was our defence coach that season and he ripped into us at the end of a video session the following week. The next day at training he had good drills to consolidate everything he had said in the video meeting, and our build-up for Toulouse started there.

On the Tuesday before the match they took a risk. Normally the sessions would be light that week but at the end of the Tuesday session our fitness guy Paul Darbyshire took us away and murdered us. By the time he was finished all of us were blowing hard. Then he called us in.

'Just know,' he said, 'that Toulouse haven't gone through that today.'

It wasn't for our bodies, it was for our heads. We might not be fitter than them but we all believed we'd something extra in the tank for the last twenty minutes in the Millennium Stadium when everyone would be blowing hard. It was probably madness to do a session like that so close to the match, and who knows if it made any real difference, but when you're looking for the tiny fractions that will get you over the line everything is on the table.

Over the years with Munster Marcus was usually my room mate, but he had a cold that week so he was in quarantine. Marcus has the immune system of a wet paper bag. If anybody in the squad has a cold he picks it up in a matter of seconds. We call him Stevie, after the character in *Malcolm in the Middle*. They put me with Tomás O'Leary instead, a young fella playing in his first Heineken Cup final. I had half a notion that I'd put him under my wing. A senior pro looking after the rookie. After ten minutes I realised that he was in charge. Tomás is the coolest guy you'll ever meet. He was made for that stage.

For me, it was much different to the 2006 final. I had no doubts. I knew the level of performance that was required and I was satisfied that I could reach it. Toulouse were the Manchester United of European rugby and they were favourites. That suited us fine. Deccie could play the role of underdog in his sleep. He said all the right things in public and pressed all the right buttons with us.

Fabien Pelous was my direct opponent. For years he'd been a hero of mine. Pelous had everything you could ask for in a second row; he had silky skills but he wasn't afraid to get stuck in, and he was a leader. During the week I watched as much footage as I could get my hands on. Rugby, though, is not like hurling or football or even soccer where you can mark your direct opponent from first whistle to last. I studied him in the line-out and at kick-off receptions and worked out how I could be a nuisance in those areas.

Pelous was their captain, and he lined up alongside Paulie in the tunnel. While we were waiting to be beckoned on to the field I stared across at him. At one stage he looked round and caught my eye. I must have looked to him like a dog with rabies. That's what I wanted him to think. I wanted him to believe that my only purpose was to make this match a nightmare for him. He might not have given me a second thought.

Anthony Foley was left out of the twenty-two for that match. He had been our captain in 2006 and a leader in our group for many years. This was his final season as a player and it must have ripped his heart out not to be involved. He didn't show it though. He didn't distance himself from the team in the days leading up to the match. He made a contribution where it was appropriate and was a positive presence around the place.

The way he conducted himself as a professional rugby player was an example to everyone. At Munster training sessions nobody was more focused. He never

2011 RBS Six Nations: (**Above**) Winning line-out possession against France, and (**below**) breaking through a tackle against England.

Top left: (*Left to right*): Emily, Paulie, myself and Jenny in the garden of Nelson Mandela's house in Soweto during a break from the 2009 Lions tour in South Africa.

Top right: On top of Table Mountain in Cape Town with Paul O'Connell, John Hayes and Alan Quinlan during Ireland's Rugby tour to South Africa in 2004.

Centre: Out for dinner with team mates and good friends Peter Stringer, Jerry Flannery and Marcus Horan.

Left: With Mom during the Lions tour of New Zealand in 2005.

Top left: Messing with 'Rala'.

Top right: On Safari – Lions tour to South Africa, 2009.

Centre left: Rooming with BO'D.

Centre right: 'Keano' and 'Undercover Keano' on the 2009 Lions tour to South Africa.

Below right: A proud and memorable day. Leading the British and Irish Lions out as captain against the Southern Kings XV, Nelson Mandela Bay Stadium, Port Elizabeth, South Africa, on 16 June 2009.

Below left: Enjoying a joke with John Hayes.

Above: Taking an ice bath after the Six Nations Championship game in Rome, 15 February 2009. My shoulders were red raw after that game.

Below: Post-match dinner in Italy, February 2009. A great night in our Grand Slam year.

Above: Ireland: 2009 RBS Six Nations Grand Slam winners!

Below left: Presenting the RBS Six Nations trophy and Triple Crown plate to my nan.

Bottom left: Meeting President Mary McAleese with her husband, Martin.

Below right: Meeting the Queen.

Bottom right: With the trophies after the game in Cardiff, 21 March 2009: Paddy Wallace, myself, Declan Kidney and Brian O'Driscoll.

Top: Jenny and myself on our wedding day, 23 December 2009, outside St Columba's Church in Douglas.

Above left: With Jenny and Sophie (one day old) at the Neo-natal Ward in Cork University Hospital on 25 July 2010.

Right: A family holiday in Spain, summer 2011.

Top: On a UNICEF visit to a boys' school for Zimbabwean refugees in South Africa, 2009.

Centre: Visiting a displaced family after the earthquake in Haiti, 2010.

Right: This young Haitian boy (*on the left in centre photo above*) was determined to make his home presentable despite the terrible conditions.

From the high of defeating Australia (**above and right**) to the despair of losing in the quarter-final to Wales (**below**), the 2011 Rugby World Cup in New Zealand had some very memorable moments, not least the tremendous support we received at each match from the thousands of Irish fans who made the trip.

wasted a session. Every time he togged out he brought intensity to his work. In the gym the Limerick lads used to slag him that he was the only man who could do a thirty-minute bike exercise in twenty-five minutes. There was a serious point in that, though. That was the example he set.

On the field, other leaders had emerged. We had a couple of new guys, but overall we were an experienced team going into that final. The benefit of that is composure. It comes out in small things. In the very first minute Denis Hurley conceded a five-metre scrum. Like Tomás, this was Denis's breakthrough season and his first European final. He made a poor decision, but there was no panic. It was a bad start and it put us on the back foot straight away but nobody said a word to him. It was just inexperience on his part. It was fine. I remember walking back to the scrum thinking, 'This is what we have to do now.' Next ball, let's go.

That attitude defined our performance. For Denis Leamy's try in the first half we hammered him over from a couple of metres short. A try like that always looks like brute force when in fact it's all about team-work, co-ordination and composure. To get over the line he needed a shove from me and he needed Quinny to clear away the tackler on the outside. The three of us needed to be ready to go at the same moment.

Denis was just about to pick and go when I told him to wait. When you're that close to the line and you sense a chance the hardest thing to do is delay, but he listened to me, he took a couple of seconds, I got myself organised, and we went for it. I roared at him to keep his feet while Quinny was his 'outside clean' – basically taking away the tackler's legs. Strictly speaking that's illegal, but Quinny made a career from getting away with infringements. When it comes off people call it cuteness. If he hadn't done it perfectly the try would have been disallowed. If he hadn't done it at all Leamy wouldn't have scored.

A few minutes earlier we'd had a possible try sent upstairs to the television match official. Paulie stood next to the referee while the rest of the forwards walked back to our half assuming that the score would be given. When it wasn't we had to march back down for a scrum. Paulie said it was an amazing sight, the seven of us running back towards the Toulouse line looking like lunatics: tight and together and prepared to scrum our heads off. He couldn't imagine what the Toulouse players were thinking. That vision, he said, was nearly worth more than a try.

Paulie called a lot of line-out ball on me that day. It's never ideal to attack off ball thrown to the front but he was very closely marked, and so was Quinny at the tail. Paulie never thinks about himself in these situations. Wherever he believes we will win possession that's where he will call it. Toulouse were willing to leave us to win the ball at the front because they believed they could defend that all day. Paulie's attitude was, 'Fine, we'll take it.'

Afterwards a lot of people said that we played no rugby. Part of me didn't care what people said and part of me was annoyed. Dougie Howlett scored an incredible try just after half time that was whistled back for a forward pass. The ball went through half a dozen pairs of hands and if Toulouse had scored it everyone would have described it as typically brilliant.

At the same time, whenever one of their backs got the ball I was terrified. You didn't want to be caught in a one-on-one. Even if we were thirty points up against them you wouldn't have been able to relax. We were never that far ahead and they drew level early in the second half after a brilliant try from Yves Donguy. That's when we needed composure and experience.

The amazing thing was that Pelous was the first man to crack. Quinny wound him up until he could take no more. Pelous probably couldn't understand a word that he was saying but eventually he gave Quinny a kick in the backside and he went down like he'd been shot, tearing the arse out of it. We didn't score while Pelous was in the sin-bin but it happened shortly after their try, and it checked their momentum.

A few minutes after Pelous returned to the field Rog put us in front with a cool penalty – 16–13. We were in a winning position, and this was a test of our experience. When we had the ball we had to control it. If we gave them an inch they could have murdered us.

There were a good few minutes on the clock when we started picking and jamming in their half. Nobody was hiding, everybody volunteered for carries. Rog was roaring at Tomás for the ball but Tomás couldn't get it off us. If you weren't supporting Munster you would have said it was ugly. So what? Our only concern was winning. For the Toulouse players it was physically draining. Every tackle took something out of them and every pick and jam took something out of the clock. One fumble or knock-on and the game would have been in the melting pot again, but we had the control and the accuracy to keep it going.

The final whistle was different this time. The emotions in 2006 were relief and elation. It felt like we were doing it for everybody who had shared our heartbreak for years and it felt like we had thrown off a great burden. This time it was more for ourselves. To prove that we were a really good team we needed to come back and win it again. Against one of the giants of European rugby, we had met the challenge.

When the whistle went I tried to jump but my legs cramped up. Every ounce of energy in my body had been thrown into the battle. The intensity had been incredible. I was sore and spent. About an hour after the match I was asked to do interviews. To get to the press conference I had to walk down about twenty steps. I couldn't do it without holding the hand rail and taking each step slowly. I was crippled by tiredness.

The emotions of the build-up had worn me out too. Once I knew I was playing I'd parked all the other stuff that went before, but it hadn't left my mind and it hadn't left my system. Deccie went around to every player in the dressing room and we had a moment together like everybody else. It was his last game as Munster coach and he had gotten us over the line again. So much of what Munster had become over the previous ten years was down to him.

We never discussed our phone conversation and the days that followed. I never told him how much I was hurt by it and he wouldn't have guessed. Later that evening myself and Leamy were chatting about how hellish that week had been. Darragh Hurley was listening.

'But didn't it work?' he said. 'Ye both trained well in the build-up and ye both played well in the match.'

Maybe he was right. Maybe it did work. I guess when you win it makes everything right.

16

Slam

In professional sport, goodbyes are strange. Somebody that you saw every day, somebody that you promised to die for a few times a year when the occasion demanded that kind of promise, is suddenly gone. You think that you'll stay in touch but so many of the things that you had in common existed in the dressing room and inside the four white lines of the playing field. Beyond that world, the relationship can't be the same.

At Christmas 2007 Munster lost John Kelly. His contract was coming to an end and the next offer on the table wasn't very attractive. You could say they forced his hand, but most of us would probably have accepted whatever offer they made and hid away from the real world for another while. John wasn't like that. He had a career as an accountant waiting for him and he decided that now was the time to jump and go for it.

He was an established player when I arrived on the scene and over the years he commanded a huge presence in our dressing room. In training he set standards and made sure that others reached them. On match days he helped to set the tone. If our dressing room was quiet before an ordinary Magners match, he'd come up with something to get us going. It's rare that you come across a fella with his qualities.

After his last game in Musgrave Park he made a brilliant speech in the dressing room. I remember looking at him thinking, what a heartless game it is. This is how it ends, on a miserable December night in the middle of the season. I went over to him and said all I wanted to say. The lads were going for a few drinks in Douglas but I couldn't face it. I didn't want to go out and pretend it was a great laugh and act the maggot because it upset me to see him go. He had been a great player for Munster, but somebody decided that his time was up and he was gone.

It's different with coaches. No matter how good they've been for your career or how much success you've shared there is always a distance between you and them. That was the case with Eddie O'Sullivan especially; he didn't seek our affection and he didn't need it. When it all went wrong I still felt sorry for him, though. Whatever we lost as a group at the 2007 World Cup, we couldn't recover it during the 2008 Six Nations.

To a certain extent Eddie changed in front of our eyes. The absolute conviction that he brought to team meetings and the training ground slipped a little. With twenty minutes to go in the Wales game at Croke Park the system was basically thrown out the window by the players and we started playing a different game to the one Eddie had laid out for us. If that had happened at any other time in his reign as coach there would have been blood on the walls at the next video session, but he seemed to accept it. Losing to Wales with Warren Gatland as their coach would have been a bitter pill for Eddie with their personal history. Around that time nothing was easy for Eddie.

We finished the campaign away to England at Twickenham with only pride at stake. The rumours flying around were that it was going to be Eddie's last game whether we won or lost. Eddie wasn't himself that week. Maybe he knew that his time was up. If he did, we weren't told. Not everybody would have been sorry to see him go. Worse than that, I felt some players were hiding behind him, blaming Eddie for our performances instead of looking at themselves. I stayed away from whatever bitching was going on. He'd been a good coach for us, and I was loyal to him. He could have been leading us into the fires of hell but I was willing to follow him.

The performance against England was a shambles. We started well and they murdered us after that. We were beaten after an hour's play. You could see them trying things with the ball and enjoying themselves. That's more humiliating than any scoreline.

We caved in that day. It was the first time I had experienced that in a green jersey. There had been other bad beatings, but this was different. The World Cup had been a disaster but every time we took the field at that tournament we believed in what we were doing and we believed we were going to win. At Twickenham we didn't believe in anything.

In his dressing-room speech afterwards Eddie didn't say that he was finished but there was a downbeat tone to his words. At one stage he said, 'Whatever will be, will be.' I'd never heard him say something like that before. He seemed to be saying that it was out of his control now. In a sense, we were out of his control now too.

Eddie went to the press conference and when he came back only myself and Andrew Trimble were in the dressing room. There was a drinks reception for the players upstairs but I had no mind for it. There was some booze in the dressing room too, and Eddie started talking to us about a lovely beer that he'd tasted in America. Andrew and myself were probably the only teetotallers in the squad and it would have been funny if the situation wasn't so serious. This wasn't the time to stop Eddie in his tracks. He was rambling, and we let him off. He probably couldn't face the drinks reception upstairs either.

We all got a text from Eddie a few days later to say that he was stepping down. Instead of texting back I wrote him a letter. I must have ripped it up ten times before I put it in the post. I wanted him to know that I thought he was a good coach, that I appreciated the things he had done for me, that he had made me a better player. I don't know if the letter reached him. I've met him a few times since and he's never mentioned it. It wouldn't be his style to bring it up anyway. I'm glad I did it though. It was important to say goodbye properly.

So, we started again. Michael Bradley was in charge for the summer tour of Australia and New Zealand but Deccie had already been appointed as the new head coach and he took over in the autumn of 2008. Around him was a new team: Paul McNaughton (manager), Les Kiss (defence coach), Alan Gaffney (backs coach) and Gert Smal (forwards coach). It was typical of Deccie. Just like with Munster he surrounded himself with excellent people and got them working together. He didn't have a problem with delegation or sharing the stage, and that made him different from other head coaches. That attitude is the key to his success.

Gert came with a big reputation. He was South Africa's forwards coach when they won the 2007 World Cup and had been involved with Super 15 teams before that. We met him first in Cork for a pre-season fitness camp. He's a big man with a quiet manner, polite and likeable, but there's real presence about him. On YouTube there's footage of him throwing a haymaker in a Currie Cup final years before. It's a side of him that we've never seen, but it makes you think. If he says it's Christmas, I'm singing Christmas carols.

I was a little on edge because in my mind I was starting from scratch again. He was coming in with a blank sheet and I didn't know whether he rated me or not. Gert could have watched us on video a million times but I chose to be a little paranoid. I've been down that route many times looking for motivation: 'We're all on square one here. How am I going to show this guy that I'm different to the rest?'

When you're starting a new relationship it's funny how little things have an impact. At breakfast, Gert was inclined to shake hands with everyone as he said good morning. The most you could expect from a lot of our fellas at that hour of the morning was a grunt. I think he was taken aback by that. Among the South Africans and New Zealanders that played with Munster I noticed the same expectations: all of them were liable to greet you in the morning with high fives and good humour and expected a similar greeting in return. It probably exposes our reticence as a people. We're not good at warm greetings or goodbyes. Finbar Quaid, a friend of mine who spent some time living in Argentina, says that the locals over there call it 'The Irish Goodbye'. At the end of the night, when we've had enough, we're liable just to slip away without a word.

Another local habit irritated Gert. As a Cork person I often refer to people as 'boy' or 'kid'. It's a common way of speaking around here. They can be terms of affection when talking to people that you've known for years but they can just as easily be used in conversation with strangers. Without giving it a second thought I used those terms with Gert and he found them disrespectful. He pulled me aside and raised it with me quietly. 'I'm your coach' was his basic point; 'boy' and 'kid' weren't appropriate ways of addressing somebody in authority. I accepted his point straight away, without argument. He understood that it was a Cork way of speaking and that I didn't mean to be disrespectful in any way but it was grating on him. I'm glad he didn't allow it to fester. If he'd said nothing I would have kept at it and it would have wrecked his head. I didn't need to have that status in his life.

It was only a tiny thing and it didn't affect our relationship in the slightest. I liked him from the start. His determination to get things right and his attention to detail were incredible. He knew what he wanted from us and that's exactly what he demanded. There was no grey area; it was black and white, and I need that from my coaches. He's very straight and very harsh but he can be generous too. A compliment from Gert makes you feel six inches taller.

There were days on the training pitch when he said, 'This is the best line-out I've ever worked with', or 'I've never seen that drill done as well as that'. And there were days when he ate us. One of the exercises we go through on the week of a match is working out how to defend against the opposition's line-out. The starting pack lines up against subs and squad members who play out the opposition's calls, but if they're not concentrating or putting their hearts into it then the exercise is useless. Before one of the autumn internationals in 2009 the shadow pack weren't having a good day and Gert didn't spare them.

A couple of weeks later many of the first fifteen were being rested for a Test match against Fiji at the RDS and it was our turn to be the shadow pack. Before we could even think about taking our eye off the ball Gert made our responsibilities clear: 'These guys have been selfless on your behalf in recent weeks. Now it's your turn.'

Gert made a lot of changes. The code for our line-out calls, for example, had no pattern, which made it harder for new guys to pick them up. We had one called Greystones. Why? Because that's where we trained the week we devised it, years earlier. Another was called Easter Bunny. Why? That was Simon Easterby's nickname. Simon wasn't even in the squad any more; he'd retired after Eddie's last game. New guys that joined the squad were given this sheet of line-out calls with bizarre names and you could see their faces drop. When Gert came in he binned those calls and put a system in place that made it clearer for us without making it any easier for the opposition.

For the autumn internationals in 2008 we were trying to deal with a lot of change all at once. Les Kiss had different defence systems which we needed to absorb very quickly, and all together it was too much. We were trying to recover from twelve months of playing poorly, embrace a change in direction from our new coaches and win Test matches. It doesn't happen just like that. New Zealand beat us out the gate in Croke Park and we had our usual dogfight with Argentina. It was ugly, but for our seeding in the 2011 World Cup draw it was a match we needed to win, and we managed it.

In that match we had a much better grasp of what the coaches wanted us to do, even though it mightn't have looked like it. Did we think we'd turned the corner? No.

People seem to believe that we won the 2009 Grand Slam in a December 2008 training camp at Enfield. None of us had that impression at the time. Looking back, I don't believe it now either. Months later details of what went on at Enfield leaked out in various interviews, and to my mind it was given a significance that it didn't deserve.

The big revelation in the media was Rob Kearney's contribution to a brain-storming session. We were broken up into small groups to discuss issues, problems, where we were going, where we wanted to go, how we were going to get there. It was a blank sheet and no subject was off limits. In those situations, though, there are no guarantees that every subject is going to come up.

Rob had the courage to raise a difficult issue that must have been on the minds of other players too. He said that when he watched Munster play he saw a special spirit and he wondered if we could match that spirit with the Ireland jersey. He chose his words carefully and it wasn't intended to be a dig, but the implication was clear: did the Munster players in the Ireland squad give more to the red jersey than the green jersey?

Rog was the facilitator in Kearney's group and he brought that issue to the meeting without saying who had raised it. He stressed that it wasn't said in a hostile way but it was obvious that this subject was going to generate a response. As the debate got going, Rob put his hand up, identified himself as the source and explained his thinking. Fronting up like that gave his words even more weight.

Nobody took his head off. None of the Munster players accepted that they gave any less for Ireland than they did for Munster, but at the same time it made us examine our consciences. Were we different in Ireland camp? Did it mean less? The answer was no. Emphatically. Was Rob right to bring it up? Yes, absolutely. If that issue was lurking in the background it needed to be brought out into the open and confronted.

At training later that day myself and Marcus Horan made a point of speaking to him. Rob was still a young guy with only a couple of international seasons under his belt. It took a lot of guts to raise this issue and we wanted him to know that we respected him for doing it.

There were no hard feelings. The issue had been dealt with and we were moving on.

On the week of the France game a couple of months later, though, it was on my mind again, and I know it was on the mind of other Munster players. 'Our commitment to this jersey was questioned,' we all thought. 'We need to deliver a performance that blows the question out of the water.'

After the Grand Slam, nobody talked in public about the night we went on the piss in Rome. To my mind, that was more important than Enfield for bonding us as a group. Like all the best nights, it wasn't planned. After the post-match dinner the Italian players drifted away and we were left to our own devices. One table started getting bigger and bigger until eventually every Irish player had pulled up a chair. Because there was no match the following weekend the lads were allowed a few beers and after a while a sing-song started. The craic was good and everyone was comfortable in each other's company.

We went from there to a nightclub in town and stayed out until all hours. By about four in the morning Rob was only fit for his bed. We hailed a taxi and bundled him into it. He wasn't feeling great so we had to roll down the window and he stuck his head out for a bit of air. He only rejoined us when he had something important to say.

'Lads,' he said, 'we're fucking going places.'

After a night out like that the slagging is always

brilliant. Without slagging you can't have team spirit. On the journey home nobody was safe. Rob's line, though, was the quote of the day. The story went around the place at breakfast and it was thrown at Rob the second he got on the bus. He got it in the neck all the way home. Drunk or sober, Rob was setting the agenda.

France came to Croke Park for that opening game of the 2009 Six Nations. They had spoiled our first appearance there two years earlier, they had turned us over at the World Cup, we hadn't beaten them for years. I had never played on a winning team against them. At some stage you have to stand up and say, 'Enough is enough.' For us, that was the day.

It was an incredible match. The ball was flying and France would always expect to win a game like that. During the week they made no secret of the way they were going to play and we interpreted that as laying down a challenge. At Enfield we did a lot of talking about how we wanted to play. This is how Deccie operates. Unlike Eddie, he was never going to impose a pattern on us. He had his thoughts but he wanted to hear everyone's feelings and then come up with a consensus that he believed would work. For the France match everyone was on the same page, coaches and players. Once we agreed on a way forward, everyone bought into it.

Even though they scored a couple of tries, our

defence was really good. They battered our line late in the game when they needed two scores to rescue the match. We refused to give them one. Our new defensive system had taken a bit of learning but Les Kiss had presented it in a way that was totally convincing. He was almost spiritual on the subject. To him, defence was the soul of every team. It was what you were prepared to do for the man next to you. In defensive situations, if you put yourself first the system breaks down. Les wasn't dogmatic about his system either. If you did something that was outside the plan he would want to tease it out rather than come down on you like a ton of bricks. He would never say that what you did was absolutely wrong, but by the end of the discussion you would realise that the system worked to everyone's benefit.

Italy were next. Playing them in Rome is different to all the other games in the Six Nations. Up front, it's a war. If you show any sign of weakness they'll jump down your throat. They're not interested in the space on either side of you, they want to go straight over the top.

Italy always target the scrum, and a couple of days before the match one of their former props identified Marcus as a potential point of weakness. Marcus didn't see the interview but it was brought to his attention and we all heard about it. I knew he was angry, and he carried that bitterness into the match. So did I. We've been team mates for a long time but we're friends too.

When the first scrum collapsed, Martin Castrogiovanni

fixed Marcus with a stare and gave him a mouthful. 'It's going to be a long day for you' was the gist of it. I heard it and roared back at him. I roared a couple of times in case he didn't get the message. I was right behind Marcus in the scrum and I put absolutely everything I had into every shove. There's a picture of me in the ice bath afterwards and my shoulder is red raw. In the second scrum we murdered them, and that set the tone for us. Castrogiovanni went off after about half an hour. I don't know what was wrong with him but he came back mid-way through the second half. We hardly missed him. By the time he returned we had the game under control.

In a normal Six Nations, Italy is the most physical match of the championship. That year it was England in Croke Park. The first twenty minutes were off the scale. They were incredibly direct and every contest for the ball was savage. I pride myself on my fitness but I spent half the time trying to get my breath back. Instead of a Test match it felt like the most hectic club game of all time – two teams trying to knock the life out of each other. We had plenty of the ball but we couldn't break them down. Anyway, the ball didn't seem to matter very much. It was all about giving punishment and taking it.

They really targeted Drico and roughed him up. Some of it was legitimate, some of it wasn't. At one stage it looked like he might have to leave the field but he dusted himself down and kept going. His try was typical: a fearless lunge for the only inch of ground that

England had left exposed on their try line. In a match like that, one try was massive.

Everything about it was much different to the England game two years earlier. There was no hype about national anthems or possible protests. We weren't burdened by the thought that it was more than a match.

There was only a point in it at the finish. In the dressing room everyone was shattered. We were too tired to celebrate. Looking around the place all you could see were damaged bodies and exhausted faces. It was still a good feeling. That hour after a match in a winning dressing room is the best feeling in rugby.

The following night we went to see Snow Patrol in concert. We should have had a private gig in the team hotel on the Thursday night before the game but Jamie Heaslip declined the offer. I've been a member of the Entertainments Committee over the years and I always hated it. You get no thanks and whatever you do somebody is going to give out. This was a monumental cock-up though. As it turned out Jamie knocking back Snow Patrol was probably the greatest source of entertainment in the Ireland camp for a long time.

Jamie claimed that he hadn't realised they wanted to come in and play for us, he thought they wanted to come in and say hello. As far as Jamie was concerned there'd be enough hellos after the gig on Sunday night when we'd be introduced to them backstage. It was a feeble defence that was blown out of the water. We tormented him about it. Every time he walked into the room that week we booed him, and for his penance we forced him to write a letter of apology to the band. From then on he wasn't allowed to make a decision without running it past two other members of the committee.

The craic was good that week. It was a happy camp. You might think that slagging and banter and taking the piss out of people are not important but you can't do it unless you're comfortable in their company. Jamie had been around for a couple of seasons but he was still one of the new generation that had made a break-through after the 2007 World Cup. We all got along fine from the beginning, but there's a difference between being nice to somebody – your standard 'nice' – and having a relationship where slagging is permitted. If that permission doesn't exist slagging can lead to bad feeling, which defeats the purpose of taking the piss in the first place.

We had a mini-camp in Cork during the Six Nations and the Entertainments Committee had a few bob to spend. The committee's only source of income is fines imposed for all kinds of concocted offences. It means that the kitty is never empty. So, we decided to go bowling in costume. Rog, for example, was made to look like the Fine Gael leader Enda Kenny. The best outfit, though, was for Paulie and Gert. They had struck up a close relationship very quickly and the enormous mutual respect between them was obvious to everyone. So we got them a giant pair of boxer shorts that they could wear together while they were bowling. It was a *Dumb and Dumber* kind of gag that worked out beautifully.

In Ireland camp, Rala is vital to the overall mood. We always say that a happy Rala is a happy camp. To be honest, that probably isn't a great rule of thumb because he tends to be in good form most of the time, even if we aren't. During that Six Nations he was under more stress than usual. One of his jobs is to compile the daily itinerary and distribute it to the players every evening. The information for that needs to come from the management, and the management meetings in that first season under Deccie seemed to be taking longer and longer. So Rala had to wait, and there were nights when the itinerary didn't arrive until eleven in the evening. None of us minded, but it was a golden opportunity to torment Rala.

During that Six Nations, Rala decided to spice up the itinerary with his Thought for the Day. It was a big hit until Rala ran out of thoughts on the week of the England game and he started asking around for suggestions. All kinds of stuff started to appear on the itinerary. My contribution was 'Measure twice, cut once'. It was a throwback to working on the sites as a young fella. One of my jobs was to cut the plasterboards for my brother. He'd give me perfect measurements, but as the day wore on I'd get sloppier and sloppier and I might be out by an inch or two. That was a waste of plasterboard, and Emmett would be fit to put the trowel down my throat.

I don't know how many times Deccie measured his team selection before the Scotland game but he cut four players from the fifteen that beat England. Jerry Flannery, Jamie Heaslip, Tomás O'Leary and Paddy Wallace were replaced by Rory Best, Denis Leamy, Peter Stringer and Gordon D'Arcy. He told the lads that they weren't dropped, they weren't being rotated, they just weren't starting. He didn't want them to think they'd been playing badly and he didn't want them to think they'd be coming straight back into the team for the final game against Wales. It was the old Deccie strategy, designed to put the wind up everyone in the squad. It worked, as usual.

As a coach, there's nothing you can say to make a player feel better in that situation. When Tony McGahan took over from Deccie as Munster coach he asked the players how we wanted him to handle those situations. Did we want a phone call, did we want an explanation on the spot or the following day? Denis Fogarty gave the best answer. 'Dumper,' he said, 'when you tell me I'm dropped I'm going to put down the phone and say to myself that you're nothing but a bollix no matter what you say to me.'

It's true. When you've been dropped there's nothing a coach can say to make you feel better about it. I also think there's no point in giving an explanation straight away because you're not really going to take it in.

Deccie spent a lot of time that week talking up Scotland – beware of this, beware of that. I take notes at all the team meetings during the week so that I can reflect on the key points the day before the game. I remember thinking that I had more notes that week than I did before the New Zealand match. We had almost talked ourselves into a state of paranoia. In hindsight, maybe that's the best way to be against them. A year later they came to Croke Park, we weren't really worried about them, we decided to play like the Harlem Globetrotters, and we lost. Anyway, going to Murrayfield there was no fear of that happening. It was difficult, like we'd convinced ourselves it would be.

Jamie was released from the bench when Denis Leamy took a knock in the first half, and his try turned the game. It was a great break by Strings. I trailed him through and for a second I thought I might get the scoring pass. Then Jamie blew past me. Over ten or twenty metres I had no chance against him. When it comes to running, I'm more of a Kenyan in my make-up. Had it been 800 metres to the line I'd have fancied myself.

It was an odd atmosphere in the dressing room afterwards. Nobody was going bananas. It almost felt like a loss. Rala put on some Christy Moore music and Deccie turned it off. The dressing rooms in Murrayfield are small and the management wanted to have a chat, I think. He wasn't being a spoilsport for any reason. There wasn't much craic to begin with.

We were seven days away from a game that would define our careers.

* * *

On Sunday we watched England play France on television. At the end of the BBC coverage Jeremy Guscott was asked who he thought would win between Ireland and Wales the following week. He half laughed and said, 'Wales – Ireland will choke.' I didn't watch any more of it. I thought, 'To hell with him.' But I thought about it again later on, and he had a point. There had been too many crunch games over the years where we had come up short. Sometimes we had been miles short.

We didn't think of ourselves as chokers or bottlers. It wasn't something that we ever discussed. But that was the other side of not winning this match. That's how people would see us, once and for all. Some defeats have the capacity to scar your career, and this would have been one of them.

On a week like that the days drag the closer you get to kick-off. Early in the week was fine. We were busy. Training, meetings, rubs, our routine. For a bit of fun myself and Geordan Murphy organised a sprint race for the management team on Thursday. There was some resistance but we refused to tolerate any non-runners. We came up with a handicap system according to age, with the oldest getting the greatest head starts. This brought out the competitive streak in a few of them and we had to deal with various objections. Rala had the race in the bag until five metres from the line when he went down as if he'd been taken out by a sniper. He was later diagnosed with two pulled hamstrings.

Friday was completely different. After the captain's run in the morning the rest of the day and most of Saturday were hellish. It was a late afternoon kick-off which made it worse. It felt like time was going backwards. After all these years I still don't have ways of taking my mind off big games. Other lads watch movies or read or play computer games. On the journey to Cardiff about eight of them were playing a Mario Go-Kart game on their DSs. I was sitting next to Hayes and we were shaking our heads like two old-timers. It was like being on a bus trip to Fota Wildlife Park with a gang of twelve-year-olds.

I need to sleep well early in the week because I know my sleep will be broken closer to the game. After breakfast on Saturday I put my head under the duvet and tried to get some more rest but I was only fooling myself. Paulie called in for a chat. He wasn't suffering nearly as badly as I was. That didn't make me feel any better.

I needed to get into my pre-match routine, but that didn't start until after our line-out session. When we finished, Gert spoke really well. For a game like this we needed somebody with his mentality. He was a World Cup winner from a rugby culture that didn't accept being second best. This was a day for us to be greedy. That was his message: reach out and take it. He spoke passionately about his confidence in us. I believed every word he said. I knew that his faith in us was completely sincere. After his speech I was buzzing.

As soon as the match started I was stuck in the middle of it. Ryan Jones came through late on Rog and an alarm went off in my head. I knew Ryan from the Lions tour and he's a real nice guy – no badness in him. So if he's having a pop at Rog, imagine what the rest of them have in mind. They were going to target him and try to get him off the field, just like Wasps tried to do in the 2004 Heineken Cup semi-final when Warren Gatland was their coach. My instinct was to lay down a marker here. I grabbed Ryan and gave him a piece of my mind. I probably shouldn't have got involved but we couldn't let them think that they could hit Rog with cheap shots and get away with it. Playing with Rog is like playing with your sister – you have to mind him.

Wayne Barnes was the referee and he told myself and Ryan to calm down. I ignored his advice. I gave Mike Phillips a bit of a slap later on and Barnes reversed a free kick to us and awarded a penalty to them. Paulie tried to argue the call with Barnes but I knew I'd been stupid. Phillips used to be easy to wind up but he's changed in the last couple of seasons.

Barnes is a good ref, and as an away team you never feel like he's going to be intimidated by the crowd. But I think we got under his skin. Our penalty count was massive. Managing relations with the ref is part of the game and we didn't manage it well that day.

He wasn't the reason why we trailed 6–0 at the break, though. We had most of the territory and it felt like we were playing most of the rugby but we couldn't turn it into points. At half time there was frustration but no panic. We knew we were playing well enough, we just had to make it count.

Our two tries came quickly after half time. The first ten minutes of the second half had been a strong period for us in all our games that season. Those scores put us in control and we should have put the game to bed but our indiscipline allowed Wales back into it. Stephen Jones kicked two penalties. Then a drop goal. They were in front with less than five minutes left.

This was it. Shit or bust.

We gathered behind the posts. Rog was certain we were going to get one more chance. I don't know what the others were thinking but everyone seemed calm. I said to Rog, 'Just make sure the re-start's contestable.' Normally he's brilliant at that, but his kick went too far. After that Wales cocked up. Phillips passed the ball to Jones standing inside the 22 and he kicked it straight into touch. Line-out to us, deep in their territory. That mistake was huge.

We won clean line-out ball and started going through the phases. By then Strings was on the field in place of Tomás and he thrives on these situations. There's nothing he does better than bossing a pack. You can nearly switch off and go on to auto-pilot. He'll call every carry and every play. I could hear Rog outside screaming for the ball but he wasn't going to get it until Strings decided the moment was right. When the pass came it was perfect and, like so many times over the years,

Rog did exactly what we needed him to do when the pressure was on.

I flicked off my boot immediately to stop the play. One of the Wales players had gone down straight after their drop goal, just to make us stew on the scoreline for a minute. Stephen Jones abused me. 'Get out of the way!' Barnes was there and he knew that I was entitled to get attention in that situation. There was nothing wrong with me and everyone knew what was going on, but sometimes you can make the laws of the game work in your favour.

That wasn't the case a minute later. I don't blame Paddy Wallace for what happened. He was trying to poach the ball at the breakdown, and to my eyes he was entitled to go for it. The breakdown laws were a mess at the time and it was a real high-wire act. To give yourself the best possible chance you had to play on the edge of the law, but when you put yourself in that position the call can go against you.

The penalty was just inside the halfway line. Straight away Paulie gave me the job of making sure they didn't steal an inch. I was standing there, pointing, telling the ref, 'I know where the mark is.'

I looked at the clock and thought, 'This is all over, there's nothing we can do here.' I said a silent prayer as Jones lined it up: 'God grant me the serenity to accept the things I cannot change . . .'

I didn't follow the flight of the ball, I just looked at Jones. When I turned round the ball was in Geordan

Murphy's arms. Geordie is the most skilful player in our squad – he could do anything. I was just saying, 'Please, Geordie, don't muck around, don't take any risks, just kill it.' The clock in the stadium had turned red and Paulie was running around like a lunatic. We'd won.

It was an odd sensation. How many times in your life does a dream come true? I should have felt ecstatic, but that's not how I felt. Not at first. I hated the way the game had finished. For a game as big as that I hated the fact that we had been depending on Stephen Jones to miss a kick. To win meant the world to me but I'd have preferred it if we'd been camped on our line defending like dogs for ten minutes rather than celebrating Stephen's missed kick. That feeling passed though.

I think I was the first person to speak to Paddy Wallace after the final whistle. I knew all about giving away crucial penalties in big matches. I knew he would have been disgusted with himself, even though it didn't cost us the match. I tried to make a joke of it with him.

'Jesus, Paddy, thank God you gave away that penalty – otherwise I would have got the blame.'

After the presentation ceremony I found my mother in the crowd and gave her my medal. It's something I've done with every medal I've won since I was with Cork Con. In a way my whole rugby life had been poured into this one. Marie treated them all the same.

17

A Wounded Lion

It was the morning after we had beaten Western Province, six days before the first Test on the 2009 Lions tour to South Africa. Ian McGeechan, the head coach, asked for a quiet word before breakfast. He got straight to the point.

'I want you to lead the side on Tuesday.'

My instant response was delight. Captaining the Lions was the greatest individual honour of my career. I told Ian how proud and grateful I was for the opportunity.

There shouldn't have been any downside to this news, but my next thought was the first Test. Test players are never risked in the last mid-week game. Being captain didn't change that. If I'd thought about it

303

a bit longer I would have left it at that. Instead, I wanted some hope for making the Test team, and I basically asked him for it.

'If you don't mind me asking,' I said, 'what's the story with Saturday?'

'The Test team will be picked on Wednesday.'

He was probably a little taken aback. He had just paid me one of the biggest compliments of my life. I had never been offered the captaincy of any rugby team, by anybody, ever. This recognition had come from the most successful Lions coach in history. I should have been floating on air, but I couldn't get the Test match out of my mind. I had been a Test player on the previous tour and I desperately wanted to be involved again. Making the Test team and winning the series had been my goals for the tour. Being captain never entered my head.

I was rooming with Mike Blair, the Scottish scrum-half. I told him about my conversation with Ian and he thought it was hilarious. In his mind the idea of playing on Saturday, Tuesday and Saturday was too far-fetched for words, but that was the hope I was clinging to. On that tour I would have played every day if they had asked me. I whole-heartedly believed that the Test team wasn't being picked until after the Tuesday night game. Paulie was captain of the Test team and he backed up what Ian had said. Paulie had no influence on team selection but he knew enough to know that the team hadn't been picked yet.

The match was in Port Elizabeth against the Southern Kings. I had two days to think about how I was going to handle the captaincy and I was glad I didn't have longer to dwell on it. Jim Williams' approach had always impressed me. He didn't say much before matches except to make promises to everybody in the dressing room about what he was going to do on the field. He was good to his word every time, and that made the rest of us desperate not to let him down.

I had played under other great captains too but I didn't want to be a clone of anybody. In this role I wanted to be myself. I decided that I wasn't going to talk for the sake of it and I would keep my points brief. The big thing I wanted to get across was that the Test team hadn't been picked yet. The other lads watching from the hotel would have believed that they were safely in the Test squad and we needed to make them sweat. That was my message. Was anybody buying it except me?

The atmosphere around the team was strange. Flat. For the first time on the tour not all of the management team had travelled to the game. It came out in little things like fellas not being ready for the warm-up in good time. Most of them probably believed that they had no chance of making the Test team now, whatever they did on the field or whatever assurances I tried to give them. Maybe they were right.

I wanted to make my pre-match speech without swearing, and I failed miserably. They made a DVD of the tour with full access to the dressing room and when I watched it later I was disgusted with myself. I counted nine or ten swear words. I'd desperately wanted the others to be as wound up for this match as I was. As captain, you feel a personal responsibility. You can feel the extra weight. I can remember being nervous about other big matches and about performing well but I can't remember being so nervous about winning. You look differently at fellas who give away penalties because you're wondering where the hell we're going to get those three points back. The glances that I got from Drico and Paulie over the years suddenly made a lot more sense.

I found the whole thing really challenging. You can't switch off for a second. Every time Nigel Owens blew his whistle there was a consequence that I had to think about. Did I need to speak to him? Did I need to speak to one of our lads? What were we going to do with this penalty?

Rog came off the bench early in the game which was a great help. He would have captained me with Munster and Ireland in the past but he didn't try to take over. At one stage in the first half we had a penalty inside their 22 and I asked him to kick to the corner. I could tell by his reaction that he wasn't sure it was the right call but I had a sense that they were about to break. From the line-out we got a scrum and forced a push-over try. For any pack that's a crushing moment.

They were mad keen to get a Super 15 franchise and

they wanted to make a name for themselves against us. They weren't much good, but they were filthy. Off the ball, all kinds of stuff went on. Nathan Hines was so furious at one stage that there was nothing I could say to calm him down. In the end we got out of it with a win. In the context of the tour it probably didn't count for a hill of beans except that losing in the week of the first Test would have created extra pressure around the place. For me, the sense of relief was massive.

I wasn't named in the starting fifteen for the first Test, but I made the bench. It wasn't what I had hoped for but I can't say I'd been given false hope all along. I hadn't. It was the third match on tour before I was given a run, and for all the talk about building combinations and units on the field I'd only been given one run with Paulie – a partnership that in one jersey or another was ten years old.

I knew that Ian rated me, though, and valued what I brought to the squad. I didn't doubt that. When we assembled for our training camp before the tour he'd built me up straight away. 'Donncha, we need you to carry more ball. Get your hands on the ball on this tour.' He wouldn't have known what a joy it was for me to hear that. For years with Ireland I'd always got the impression from Eddie O'Sullivan that he would have put me in oven mitts if it made sure I wouldn't carry the ball. None of my coaches ever encouraged me to be a ball-carrier. To be frank, it's the only enjoyable part of the game. Doing the grind of hitting rucks and making tackles and shuttling up and down in the kick-chase line, there's no buzz in any of that. I do it because that's my job. I take pride in my work and I accept that I will be judged primarily on how I perform in all those tasks. But most of what I do is measured in stats, and the only person who really notices is the video analysis guy. The thought of a ball-carry, though, will get you through all the shit. Ian gave me that licence, it was up to me to use it.

Before my first Lions tour Donal Lenihan impressed on me the importance of training well. They'll notice if you do and they'll notice if you don't. Donal had toured with the Lions as a player and manager and he knew the culture of the Lions inside out. That advice was the easiest thing in the world for me to follow. I approached every training session like a Test match, and it was the same in 2009. The standards in training are through the roof. Great coaching, no dopey mistakes. The environment is designed to make you better. I embraced that, one hundred per cent.

I came off the bench with about ten minutes left in the first Test. We came storming back from nineteen points down but we had too much ground to make up and ended up losing by five. Everyone knew it was a lost opportunity. We had conceded too much ground in the first half and we had them stretched for most of the second half. Even though I hadn't much time on the field I felt I made an impact. Gethin Jenkins said it to me later, and he said that Rob Howley had mentioned it to him. You cling to feedback like that and take hope from it.

I was picked for the last mid-week game three days later, against the Emerging Springboks. Rog got the consolation prize of being captain, having played no part off the bench in the first Test. In the second half I thought I was being replaced. Normally that would be bad news but in the week of a Test match you want to be taken off in the mid-week game. The earlier the better. It had happened to me before the second Test on the 2005 tour and I was in the starting fifteen the following Saturday. Number four was flashed up on the board, but when I reached the touchline it turned out that they had cocked up with the numbers and I was staying put. I was mortified. Alain Rolland was the referee and he could see from my face that I was nearly a broken man returning to the play. He nearly apologised and said they had definitely flashed my number on the board.

The Test team and replacements were named in a squad meeting the following day. Nobody from the management team had approached me beforehand, and in that case you assume that nothing has changed: you haven't been promoted to the team and you haven't been cut from the match-day squad. But the names were called out and mine wasn't there. I had come on for Alun Wyn Jones in the first Test and he was dropped to the bench, but Simon Shaw had leapfrogged over the two of us to make the starting fifteen.

Sitting in the meeting, I felt like I'd been kicked in the gut. Drico was next to me. He said 'hard luck' or something. I told him I hadn't been given a heads up and he couldn't believe it. It was basic decency and common practice at every level of the game to give a player advance notice of being left out. This was the highest level of the game, and they hadn't done it.

Graham Rowntree from the management team approached me at dinner later. David Wallace got up for a minute and Graham bolted into his seat.

'I was meant to get to you before that meeting,' he said. 'Sorry about that . . .'

I didn't want to hear it. Not now. Not in front of the others at the dinner table and not in the mood I was in. I cut him off before he could get going.

'Fuck off, I have no interest in chatting to you now.'

Before training the following day I went over and apologised to Graham for swearing at him. I explained the reason for my anger and he agreed that I had a good reason to be annoyed.

'We've gone with Shaw,' he said, 'because we think he brings physicality to the maul and the breakdown.'

'And you don't think I would have brought that?'

I had no problem with Simon Shaw being picked. I liked him and admired him. But I was owed an explanation in advance and I wasn't given one. Maybe they felt that Alun Wyn Jones gave them better cover on the bench for the front and middle of the line-out. I don't know. They didn't say. Warren Gatland was the forwards coach but he was also the Wales coach and that might have influenced Jones' selection. If an Irishman had been the forwards coach I might have expected a similar advantage.

Warren and I had known each other a long time. We didn't have a close relationship but I always thought we got on well. At one stage on the tour I asked him for a chat and he agreed to do it later. When I approached him again he was too busy. The next time I saw him he took evasive action in the corridor. After the episode with Rowntree, Warren didn't talk to me for the rest of the trip. I left the tour with a bad taste in my mouth about him.

That's the thing about Lions tours, though: a certain number of people are always going to be unhappy. Everyone dreams of being in the Test team, even those who only dreamed of making the squad in the first place.

There were no mid-week games for the last ten days of the tour and some fellas went on the piss every night. They still showed up for training the following day but they were reeking of drink. Probably because I was a teetotaller Ian asked me to keep an eye on the lads that were going bananas, but what could I do to stop them? I didn't get involved.

I promised myself that I wouldn't go off tour. I gave my best at training every day. On the final Tuesday I went so hard in a mauling session that I hurt my neck and I was in agony. I was saying to myself, 'Why did you have to go full gun at it?' But it's the only way I can go about my business. If I did anything else I would feel like a fraud.

I was determined not to drag my arse around the place and be a dead weight. At times I found it stressful. Inside my head I wanted to explode on somebody and let out my frustrations. Rowntree got a tiny taste of it but nobody else did. I wanted to be respectful to Paulie too. The series was lost with a narrow defeat in the second Test and as captain he had enough on his plate without having to look at my sour puss.

People probably looked at me and thought that I was coping just fine with the disappointment. Maybe they thought I didn't care as much as the others. Maybe that's how it looked. That's not how it felt.

18
Jenny and Sophie

It started with a photograph, like every charity we're asked to support. Before the Lions tour in 2009 I was approached by Mick Kearney, a great friend of mine, to help a UNICEF campaign. Rog and Tomás O'Leary were asked too, and we went through the usual drill: stood with the props, smiled for the camera, did what we were told. We knew it wouldn't take long and we were happy to do it. In and out.

When the shoot was finished, though, the UNICEF representative, Julianne Savage, wondered if any of us would stay on for a few days after the tour and help with another campaign in South Africa. Instinctively, we brushed it off. More than that, we laughed it off. Once the Lions tour was over we would be on our summer holidays. At that stage we'd have spent over six weeks in South Africa and we'd be looking to get out of the place.

It was unusual because we're never really asked to do more. On request, we turn up at launches or lunches or photo shoots and the charities use our public profiles in whatever way they can. All we give is a little of our time.

When I went home, though, I thought about it. In the course of the year my face turned up in any number of publicity photographs supporting one charity or another. The request usually came through Pat Geraghty, Munster's media manager. Pat and I get on really well and he probably knows I'm not going to turn him down. But what was I actually doing for any of these charities? Next to nothing. It might have made me look good but the whole thing seemed false. I needed to jump in somewhere and make a meaningful contribution. I wanted to work with a charity that helped children, and UNICEF was perfect.

I emailed them to say that I was willing to help once the tour was over and sent them my itinerary. We finished in Johannesburg, staying in the most luxurious hotel in the city. When you visit South Africa you're aware of the townships and the poverty and the crime but on a rugby tour you can spend your time in a comfortable bubble and not think about it.

The UNICEF team took me and Jenny away from that cosy environment to a place about two hours' drive from Johannesburg. It was a school run by a Protestant bishop that was trying to cope with refugees fleeing from Zimbabwe. Many of the children had come on their own, sent by their parents, in search of an education. I can't imagine the courage it took for these children to make that journey. Not knowing if they would be caught, not knowing if they would see their families again, not really knowing where they were going. The children that arrived were the lucky ones. Nobody knew how many kids had failed to make it, and Lord knows what happened to them.

In the beginning the school was dealing with about a dozen kids but the numbers had swollen to hundreds. UNICEF had intervened to fund the school but accommodation was a huge problem. The church had basically been turned into a hostel. Some parents had come to this place with small children and while they looked for work during the day their kids were minded in the cellar of the church. You couldn't call it a crèche, even though that was the purpose it served.

On the day of our visit a pipe had burst and little children were sleeping and playing just a few feet away from raw sewage. Other kids were taking a nap on the steps going down to the cellar. One baby was sitting alone on one of the steps. He can't have been more than ten or twelve months old but he'd been left to his own devices. They simply couldn't pay attention to every child. There was a lot of kindness and humanity in the chaos but the biggest thing of all was the chaos. I looked at all these kids and thought of my own nephews and nieces at home, imagining them being forced to live in these circumstances. I thought of the sacrifices a lot of these kids had made to come to this school and the risks they had taken, and I thought of myself in my own school days, running out of the place as soon as the bell rang, not appreciating for a second how lucky I was.

We went into the classroom to meet the children and chat to them. Some of them were incredibly warm and friendly. A few of them came up to Jenny and gave her a hug. Other kids, though, were suspicious when they saw that a television camera crew was following us. They covered their faces and hid behind their school-bags. It was like they were still afraid of being sent back to Zimbabwe and didn't want to be discovered.

It was humbling to sit and talk to them. One girl told me that she wanted to be a commercial solicitor. I guess she was only about fourteen but she had the whole thing mapped out in her head. She was living and learn-ing in circumstances that were unimaginable to me and Jenny but not only was she full of hope, she was full of ambition. She explained what a lucrative profession it was in South Africa and how she would eventually return home and make things better for her family.

On the following Friday night I appeared on a rugby programme on South African television where they showed footage of our visit to the church and school. I was incredibly nervous talking about the UNICEF visit because I didn't want to cock it up. The purpose of ask-ing me to make the visit in the first place was so that they could command a few minutes of air time on a mass-audience television programme. This was an opportunity to raise awareness about something that had a huge impact on the day-to-day lives of a lot of people. I felt a massive responsibility to do my best.

It wasn't like standing in Musgrave Park and posing for a promotional photograph and, basically, putting it behind me once I left the car park. I had seen this project, I knew how much help they needed, and my job for those couple of minutes was to help make a difference. Whatever profile I had as a rugby player was more useful in those couple of minutes than it had ever been in my life.

By then, the summer of 2009, Jenny and I were engaged to be married. Our relationship is a long story. You don't need to hear all of it. When we first met I wasn't particularly interested in having a relationship. It's not that I wasn't interested in girls, and it's not that I wasn't interested in Jenny, but I was more interested in rugby. I thought that being in a relationship would be a distraction, and at the time my only focus was making a breakthrough with Munster.

Jenny knew nothing about rugby and in those days couldn't have cared less. She says that she spotted me one day in A-Wear, clothes shopping with my sister Emer. Her friend Alice was going out with Mick O'Driscoll and they hatched a set-up one night after a Cork Con match. We were in a nightclub in town, Jenny just happened to be there too, and Micko just happened to spot her.

That was January 2002. We met once a month for about the next six months before Jenny did her final college exams and went to France for the summer. France wasn't outer space, but for a few weeks I didn't get in touch. Then one night I bumped into Jenny's friend Rita in town. She ate the head off me for not ringing Jenny. 'She's a nice girl and she's going to walk away from you and she'd be dead right.'

Rita brought me to my senses. Even though I hadn't known Jenny long and I didn't know her that well really, I knew I had strong feelings for her. She was warm, good-hearted, great fun, and I felt completely comfortable in her company. I had met a very special person and I needed to get my act together.

After the bollicking from Rita I called Jenny in France and we arranged to meet again when she came home. We went for a walk down by the Atlantic Pond, behind Páirc Uí Chaoimh, and I asked her to go out with me. After you couldn't say it was a whirlwind romance. We didn't move in together for another three or four years and I didn't propose until the end of March 2009.

It was actually the last day of March. For a laugh I had it in my mind to wait until April Fool's Day but that would have been a cheap gag. I suggested to Jenny that we go for a walk at the Atlantic Pond. It wasn't Paris and people slagged us about our affection for that place but both of us liked it and I wanted to propose in the place where we'd had our first date. I tried to get Jenny to sit down on the spot where I first asked her to go out with me, but the grass was wet. I think Jenny suspected that something was up.

Eventually I got her to sit on a bench, and I popped the question.

Having lived together for a few years it didn't make sense to have a long engagement. We set our wedding day for 23 December 2009, a few days after Munster's pool match away to Perpignan. Jenny never fusses over me or plays the nurse with all my bangs and bruises – it would wreck my head if she did. But I know she was worried that week about the state of my face coming back from France. Luckily, I didn't look like somebody that had been fed through a blender.

I guess when you have a wedding in December you're taking a big chance with the weather. As it happened, Ireland was in the grip of its worst cold spell for decades. But people made a huge effort to make it and we had the day of our lives.

Jenny basically organised the whole thing. She even went to the bother of booking a dancing class to try to knock me into shape for the first dance. I broke the instructor's heart and probably a couple of her toes. After two hours she gave up and wished Jenny the best of luck. It was the toughest €80 she ever earned.

I prepared my speech with the words of John Hayes ringing in my ears. I'd sat next to him on the plane home from Perpignan and, as ever, he'd called it straight.

'O'Callaghan,' he said, 'just remember, you're only an accessory in this wedding. We're all there to see Jenny. When it comes to your turn, stand up, speak up, and then shut up.'

He was right, as usual.

All I really wanted to say was that I'm a happier person around Jenny. She understands me like nobody else and brings out the best in me. The longer we've been together the stronger our relationship has become. She's an amazing person and I'm a lucky man.

After the trip to South Africa UNICEF asked me to be one of their ambassadors. I was thrilled to be asked and honoured to accept. They kept me busy with various bits and pieces in Ireland, but they also said they'd like me to take on another field trip. They warned me, too, that my South African experience was a gentle introduction.

During the 2010 Six Nations they asked me if I would visit Haiti. The earthquake had struck in the middle of January and the scale of the crisis was staggering: about 220,000 people were dead, 1.5 million people were homeless. The response in Ireland to the UNICEF aid appeal had been among the best in the world per head of population. The purpose of my visit was to maintain the profile of the appeal and to give people an idea of where their money was going. Jenny was expecting our first child late in the summer so I agreed to go for a week in July, five weeks before her due date.

Nothing could have prepared me for what I witnessed. It doesn't matter how many reports you watch on the television news or how many accounts you read in the newspapers, the reality is indescribable. They planned my itinerary carefully, exposing me to the worst sights later in the week – when I had built up a little bit of resistance, I suppose.

Camp Charlie was the UNICEF headquarters, and that's where I was put up for the week. All of the aid workers slept in a big dormitory tent. Each bed was two metres wide by two metres long which meant that I literally had a millimetre to spare at either end. Like all camp beds it wasn't very sturdy and it collapsed under me when I sat down. It wasn't designed for eighteen stones of lock-forward. I was mortified. I was thinking, 'How can I tell them I've broken their bed?'

I slept on the mattress for the week and every night I was so worn out by the day and what I'd seen that I was hugely grateful for it. I thought of the times that I'd complained about hotel rooms with Ireland and Munster and couldn't get over how petty I'd been.

They took me on a tour of Port au Prince on the first day. It's my nature to be chatty but I spent most of that day in silence. All I could see was destruction and devastation. Six months after the earthquake the rubble of some buildings had been left untouched. After a while I wondered about that. The terrible explanation was that there were bodies still entombed in the rubble. For now, that was their graveyard.

I was brought to a Mother and Baby tent where new mothers had a bit of time to themselves with their newborns. To me it didn't look like they had much peace in there, but I guess everything is relative. We were invited back to a tent where one of the mothers lived. It was just a temporary structure, not designed to cope with the torrential rain that typically fell for an hour or two in the afternoons. It wasn't really a tent either, even though that's what people called them. It was more like a lean-to pulled together from sheets of plastic.

One of her other children saw us coming and he ran inside, trying to shift the rain water that had poured through a leak in the roof. Then he took out a cloth and started cleaning. These poor people were living in the most appalling conditions but it was still home to them and this young boy was trying to make his home presentable for visitors. They had guests and they wanted to make us feel welcome. It might seem like a small thing but it showed their incredible dignity and spirit.

Those qualities were visible all over the place. Unlike other disaster scenes around the world, there hadn't been any looting. Everyone was trying to make the best of a desperate situation. You could see women and men with buckets of water cleaning the portaloos. There weren't nearly enough portaloos for everyone's needs and to prevent the spread of diseases it was vital that they were kept as clean as possible. It was a dirty, thankless job but these people were prepared to do it for the benefit of their community.

On another day I was brought to a school. The building had been destroyed in the earthquake but classes continued. The UNICEF workers handed out something that they called School in a Box, which had been funded directly from Irish donations. Inside the boxes were paper, pencils, sharpeners, all the bits and pieces you need for a day at school that our kids take for granted. The Haitian kids were so excited to get this stuff.

The school was broken up into two classes of smaller kids and older kids. We sat down with the younger kids first and they asked me about Ireland and about rugby, simple questions that they were probably prompted to ask. Then we moved on to the older kids, teenagers. One of them got up and asked why I was there. I thought it was a straightforward question, but I didn't see what was coming. I explained that I was in Haiti to see the good work that was being done with the money donated by Irish people.

Then he started telling me his story. His father had been killed in the earthquake, leaving his mother to raise five kids. It didn't cost much to send a child to school in Haiti but a school uniform was compulsory and she could only afford one. He might have been the oldest kid or the brightest kid, but anyway he was chosen to go to school. When he went home he had to teach the others what he had learned that day.

'What hope do I have?' he continued. 'After I finish

my exams, what will I do? There is nothing for me here. You've come over here for a few days and you'll go home feeling better about yourself. But I'll still be living here.'

I couldn't answer him. I didn't know what hope there was for him. What practical difference did my trip make to his life? How could I say that it made any difference? The last thing I'd expected was to be challenged.

One of the UNICEF people could see that I was in trouble and she intervened. She told him that, for a start, he could get a good education and if he got his exams there was the chance for further education. She asked him what he wanted to be, and he said a doctor.

'Great,' she said, 'then you can help the rest of your community.'

She completely changed the tone of the conversation. I was hugely grateful because I was lost for words. I admire people who are honest and speak directly, which is what that boy had done. He didn't wait until I left, he said what he thought to my face. He put me in my box, and he was right. At the end of the week I was getting on a plane home. He had to deal with a nightmare reality that I couldn't imagine.

I was rocked by the whole thing. If I had been hit with that on the first day I don't know how I would have coped for the week. Driving back in the car, it was pelting down with rain again and I couldn't get his words out of my mind. None of this was fair. He was caught in circumstances that weren't of his making. There was nothing that UNICEF or anybody else could do about that except try to create an environment in which his life could be better. At some point, it was up to him.

When I thought about it, I didn't doubt the value of my trip or the work that UNICEF was doing. I could see how brilliant they were at targeting the aid money and getting things done. They needed more money and more awareness of the ongoing struggle. Whatever coverage my trip generated in the media back home was going to help. My contribution wasn't going to change that boy's life, but the direct impact of UNICEF in his school gave him a fighting chance, and that's as much as could be done.

On the last day I was taken to another camp. I met mothers who handed you their baby and didn't want to take it back. They saw me as their child's ticket to a better life. It was an incredibly selfless thing to do: they were prepared to part with their baby if it meant he or she could get away from this nightmare. I saw a lot of resilience and hope in the Haitian people but in that gesture there was a certain amount of hopelessness. In that situation there's nothing you can say or do. My heart went out to them.

We flew home via New York. When I turned on my phone in JFK there were four missed calls from Jenny and a text asking me to ring. She was in hospital. Her waters had broken, and because there was a minor infection they were going to induce her.

The flight home was a nightmare. Every minute was like an hour. When we arrived in Dublin Paul Connolly of UNICEF had organised a spin for me to Cork. Manus Duff was the driver's name; he put his foot to the board and dropped me at the door of the Cork University Hospital. I legged it to Jenny's ward, worried that I might be too late. She was lying there as if everything was completely under control. I was sent home for a shower with a list of things she hadn't had time to pack before she left for the hospital.

Sophie was born later that evening. She was absolutely beautiful, and after a few tricky days in hospital she was strong enough to come home. I felt blessed. As a family I thought of all the things we could provide for Sophie. How much security and comfort we could give her. The things we take for granted. I had felt lucky at other times in my life, but maybe for the first time I knew what that really meant.

Epilogue

6 October 2011, Wellington

I sent Ultan a text about Nan. Emer had been to see her in hospital and things weren't great. I'd called down to her a couple of days before we left for the World Cup and she was in good spirits. Her lungs were the problem. At eighty-five years of age they were starting to give up. Nan was always a positive person, though, full of fun and full of life. Leaving her house that day I wasn't worried that she wouldn't be there when I returned from New Zealand. I knew Emer was concerned, though, when we spoke. The woman she'd seen lying in the hospital bed wasn't the Nan we knew.

In my text to Ultan I asked him to put Nan on the phone to me the next time he saw her. I didn't get a response. A couple of hours later, Jenny rang. Nan had passed away during the night.

I rang Emer and my brothers but I didn't get upset until I called Mom. Nan was her mom. Marie is not someone who shows her emotions very much but she was close to Nan. On the other end of a phone on the other side of the world there's only so much you can say. At home, everyone knows how to deal with a family bereavement. It's instinctive, I suppose. We're a close family anyway and Mom would have had a lot of support.

When you're away, it's completely different. Two days before the quarter-final of the World Cup I had to control my grief. After a death or a tragedy you often hear people saying that it puts normal life in perspective. I couldn't afford to think like that. There was no comparison between the death of my nan and a rugby match. I had to separate them completely. It was like I had to put my heart into a freezer. I know they were worried about me at home because I was very close to Nan, but I got on top of it. I couldn't go on to the field dedicating this performance to her because that would have ramped up my emotions and I'd have been conceding penalties from the first minute.

Deccie is brilliant in situations like this. He's a compassionate man and he genuinely cares for us as people. He asked me if I wanted to go home, but that wasn't necessary. He offered to organise a mass, but I didn't want that fuss either. Before the captain's meeting on Friday I went to mass in a local church a couple of minutes from the hotel, and afterwards I asked Rala to find me a black armband. In that way I carried Nan on to the field with me.

Were we ready for the knockout stage? I thought so. On the Wednesday we'd had our best training session of the World Cup. There was a real edge. Denis Leamy was steamrolling fellas, Rob Kearney and Fergus McFadden had a bit of a row. No harm in that. Shane Jennings played the role of the Welsh flanker Sam Warburton and he was skulled at every breakdown. Most of our plays were executed perfectly and the ones that broke down were easily corrected. We were on fire.

With just a six-day turnaround from the Italy match everything was brought forward a day. On Tuesday we had our video meeting with Mervyn Murphy. Merv goes into incredible detail in his analysis but he only feeds us the bits we need to digest. In his mind, the match was going to hinge on controlling the gain line – if we win the gain line and play our pattern correctly, we'll win. We knew all Wales's threats. We didn't underestimate any of the players. We knew exactly where they could hurt us and we were satisfied that we could counter everything they had.

At a press conference I said that this was our chance to separate ourselves from every other Ireland team. We weren't alone in winning a Grand Slam but reaching the semi-final of the World Cup was something no Ireland team had ever done before. We all realised the opportunity without dwelling on it. It didn't feel like a weight on our shoulders.

One afternoon I went for a cup of tea with Conor Murray, Keith Earls and Mick Sherry, the young Munster hooker who had just flown in as emergency cover. They didn't have a care in the world. They weren't uptight, they weren't afraid. Earlsy had been on a Lions tour already but Conor was only three months into his international career. He was facing the biggest game of his life with total ease. Like a veteran? No, because veterans can see all the pitfalls. Looking at those lads reminded me what it was like to be young.

The only thing that bothered me a little was the captain's meeting on Friday night. It wasn't half as emotional as it had been before the other games. That wasn't Drico's fault. The captain's meeting is a forum where the players take ownership of the team. All of us are free to speak up. Whether it's a good meeting or a bad meeting is a collective issue. For some reason that meeting didn't catch fire. For most of the World Cup we'd had a private chip on our shoulder about something. We didn't speak about it in public but it was part of our build-up. For this game that was missing.

One of the lads said, 'We have to hate these fellas tomorrow . . .' It was an important point to make, but straight away I was thinking, 'I hope we hate them already!' Why were we waiting until the day of the match? I was rooming with Rog and I mentioned it to him afterwards. 'I hope we're not thinking one week ahead.' The conversation didn't go any further. He probably thought I was being paranoid. On the night before a Test match you're always going to be worried about something.

On match day I felt differently about everything. Our hotel was heaving with Irish supporters. I'd never experienced an atmosphere like it before an Ireland match. It reminded me of the bus trip through Cardiff before the 2006 Heineken Cup final with two police-men on horseback parting a sea of Munster supporters. Our hotel lobby in Wellington was like that. Kick-off was at six o'clock but they were in there all day, drink-ing, singing, having the craic, making a racket. We were on the third floor which was like a mezzanine floor so you could be seen from the lobby walking along the corridor. Any time an Ireland player was spotted a roar went up.

Deccie called a team meeting for four o'clock. Everyone was there a few minutes early. Deccie arrived exactly at the appointed time, same as always – not a minute early, not a minute late. He pitched his talk perfectly.

Leaving that meeting, we were ready.

1 September, Queenstown

Before we left home for New Zealand we met President Mary McAleese in the Áras. I love listening to her. Every time she speaks to us she hits the right note. She talked about the experience ahead of us and how it would be something we would treasure for the rest of our lives. She urged us to grasp the experience and enjoy it. In France four years earlier we hadn't done either of those things. President McAleese didn't mention that. Too polite. She also said that she'd looked up Moss Keane's autobiography to see what he thought of touring New Zealand. I know from reading Moss's book that he hated it, and that's exactly how I felt too. Part of it was the place itself and the weather during their winter in June and July. The biggest part of it, though, was that every tour of New Zealand involved playing the All Blacks. Those matches never turned out the way we hoped.

This time it was different. Our itinerary was perfect. When we landed our first camp was in Queenstown, otherwise known as the Adventure Sports Capital of the World. It was the ideal place to ease the jet lag out of our systems and get started. Every day was balanced between hard training and a leisure activity: water sports, bungee jumping, you name it. The hotel was next to a lake, and after training we used to jump in off the pier. One of the locals offered us the use of his boat as an improvised diving board so some of the lads were bombing into the water from an even greater height. The water is very cold at this time of year and none of the locals would dream of swimming in it, but it was better than an ice bath for us. No matter how tough training was, there was something to look forward to later in the day.

Unlike the 2007 World Cup we brought our own chef, Sean Dempsey from the Killiney Castle Hotel in Dublin. Given our nightmare experience with the hotel food in Bordeaux it was a great call. After our first full day in Queenstown, though, the management allowed us to make our own dinner arrangements and eat outside the hotel. We were given a per diem of fifty dollars each and we could basically go where we liked. In that situation the risk is that players will go off with their own mates in little groups. In this case, that didn't happen. Going out for dinner turned into a social event for the whole squad and it created an extra buzz around the place. I imagine that's what the management hoped would happen.

We had spent a lot of time in camp in Carton House over the summer, but the atmosphere is different when you're in camp overseas. That's when you really need to come together, and we did. It wasn't forced or contrived. Every serious team in the world engages in team-bonding exercises. No matter how much thought or science is behind it, those exercises don't always work. They can't force it down your throat. Fellas must want to be part of it.

In Queenstown, the Irish management created the conditions where we could become even closer as a group. We trained hard together, we had fun together, we ate together in the evening. You could feel the group getting tighter. After about two weeks Marcus Horan rang me. 'Well, what's the craic?' Marcus has been on enough tours to know how things work. I'm sure after two weeks he thought there was bound to be a bit of bitching around the place. There wasn't. From the beginning, it was a happy camp. It stayed a happy camp. For the first time in my life, I enjoyed being in New Zealand.

We'd put the August warm-up games to bed before we left Dublin. Those matches hadn't gone well. The media and the public were up in arms. They were entitled to be frustrated but we couldn't afford to get dragged down by that. The last match against England at the Aviva was worrying for everyone. We had destroyed that England team in the Six Nations; five months later they came back to Dublin and beat us easily.

Deccie called a meeting. Among other things, he showed us six clips of English players stepping over the line with cheap shots. We'd let them get away with it. If it had been a Six Nations match or a Heineken Cup match we would have been in like a shot, laying down the law. His point was that England had come to play a Test match and we had turned up to play a friendly. That difference in mentality dictated how the match panned out.

It wasn't the last we heard of it. Before our opening

game in the pool against the USA, Gert Smal, our forwards coach, brought it up again. He said it was the first time he'd seen an Ireland pack playing without spirit. He said we'd been bullied. He said he'd been shocked by our performance. Gert has such a presence about him and speaks with such authority that every word he says carries weight. If those were his feelings, then we should be ashamed. Not one of us would argue with him.

The 22–10 win over the USA wasn't satisfactory. The pack did everything that was asked of it, more or less, and Gert seemed pleased enough. When he talked to us again a couple of days later he had reviewed the tape and had a few issues to raise with us, but by then he was thinking about Australia. The weather had been terrible, but that wasn't an excuse. It wasn't any worse than a bad winter's day at home. For a Test match it wasn't full-on international pace, which made our mistakes harder to excuse. We should have scored six tries but walked off with three. No bonus point.

Because it was the tenth anniversary of 9/11 it was an emotional day for the Americans. They were wound up. At one stage their number eight, Nic Johnson, pointed over at me and roared, 'I'm coming to get you!' He hadn't even picked up the ball and I'd nearly taken the head off him, conceding a penalty in the process. I know, stupid.

Afterwards, a few of us went into their dressing room to exchange jerseys. Not all of them wanted to swap. One of them said he was giving his to a soldier. I managed to do a swap with one of their second rows, John van der Giessen, but he made it clear that he was giving me something precious. 'This is a real important jersey to me. You take good care of it.' Message understood.

In our dressing room there were a few long faces. The players who went to the press conference had a flavour of what the coverage would be like back home. We didn't hear what went on in the RTE studio. Just as well. For us, though, it was nothing like the performances against Namibia or Georgia at the last World Cup. There was nothing like the same despair or confusion. We were disappointed, but it wasn't a crisis. Far from it.

After we left the stadium Phil Morrow, our fitness guy, took us to a gym he had booked nearby. It was ten o'clock on a Saturday night but he had arranged for them to open up especially for us. He put on a CD of up-tempo songs to set the mood – stuff by Oasis, Mumford and Sons, songs that everybody knew. Then for thirty minutes we went spinning on the exercise bikes. It was as much for our heads as our bodies. All of us left the gym in better form. Ready to move on.

17 September, Eden Park, Auckland – Ireland 15 Australia 6

On tour, the social committee plays a pivotal role in the day-to-day life of the squad. Everybody has a job: booking the cinema, finding restaurants, snitching on your team mates as an undercover agent. Myself, Drico and Geordan Murphy decided who would do what, and then I had the job of running the show from the top of the bus on the journeys home from training. It's also our job to issue fines for what we see as offences committed by members of the squad, or offences that are reported to us by busybodies. By the end of the World Cup we had gathered NZ$3,500 in fines. In the old days that would have been blown in a big session at the end of the trip, but those days are gone. This time the IRFU matched the figure and we gave all of it to charity.

Court sittings always generate a bit of fun. On this tour we added a twist. If you were found guilty of an offence you had the option of rolling the dice. If it landed on number one you didn't have to pay the fine. Number two meant that your fine was doubled. Three, your room mate pays it. Four gave you the option of nominating somebody else to pay your fine. Five was triple your fine, and six was a chance card where you dipped into a selection of forfeits dreamed up by every other member of the squad.

The week of the Australia match, Paul O'Connell rolled the dice and came up with a six. The chance card was a beauty – he had to draw a cat's nose and whiskers on his face and leave it there for twenty-four hours. In the middle of this we had our forwards' meeting. Paulie spoke for twenty minutes, and for as long as he spoke I never noticed the cat's nose and whiskers on his face. He was sitting there looking like something out of a pantomime with a tough audience in the palm of his hand, setting the tone for one of the biggest encounters of our career. Only O'Connell could have pulled it off.

The mood was good from early in the week. Deccie and the coaching staff rolled out a menu of plays and patterns that was more advanced than anything we had seen for the August matches or the USA game. They had been keeping stuff back specifically for Australia. Straight away, that gave us a lift.

After one of the squad meetings early in the week, Drico asked the players to stay behind when the coaches had finished. Shane Jennings and Geordan Murphy made two contributions that affected everybody. The back-row positions are a really competitive area on our team and Shane wasn't in the twenty-two for the Australia match. It was natural for him to be disappointed but he buried that. He said that his only purpose for the week was to help us win. He named out all the other back rows in the squad and he promised to do everything in his power to make sure they were properly prepared for the Australians. In training that week he played the role of David Pocock, the brilliant Australian flanker, which meant that he was smashed at every breakdown. He took unbelievable punishment, but he accepted it for the team. Without seeing a minute of action in the match, Shane was inspirational.

Geordie spoke about how we were going to beat

Australia and he reinforced a point Deccie had made earlier: England's record against them is far better than ours. Why? Because they run straight over the top of them. Their approach to playing Australia is the same as our approach to playing England: the first thing we do is smash them. Against Australia, we don't play like that. Having basically spent his whole career in England, Geordie knows how they perceive us. They see the aggression and lack of respect that we bring to games against England and wonder why we don't take that attitude into games against the Tri-Nations teams, especially when we play them in the southern hemisphere. We had to bring that mentality to this Test match.

Jerry Flannery was still with us but he was due to fly home. His calf had acted up again. It has haunted him, on and off, for about eighteen months. Fla has shown incredible perseverance and mental strength to keep on coming back but he can't buy a break. Normally your jersey is on a hook in the dressing room on match days. For this World Cup, Deccie had decided that the jerseys should be presented by a player for every match. For the Australia game, at the captain's meeting on Friday night Deccie asked Fla to do it.

It was one of the best things and one of the hardest things I ever witnessed in a team meeting. Fla was in bits. For the whole jersey ceremony he was in tears. Two days later he was leaving the World Cup, going home to an uncertain future. He's one of my oldest and closest friends in rugby. The respect I have for him as a person and as a player is through the roof. The pain he was feeling was written all over his face. When he presented me with my jersey we embraced. Receiving my jersey from him in those circumstances was one of the most emotional occasions in my rugby life.

I have goals for every match that I write down in my notebook. After that team meeting I wrote: wear your jersey like Fla would.

All of us were in a great state of mind: raw and bursting to get at them but clear about what we had to do. We always keep an eye on what the other team is saying in the media in case something slips out that we can use. This time it wasn't so much what they said but what they didn't say. Drico spotted it: they didn't know who the hell we were. It was obvious from their interviews that beyond a couple of names they couldn't tell you the rest of our team. We knew them inside out.

After eighty minutes they knew us.

The intensity was incredible. It was more stop-start than a normal Test, with breaks in play for all kinds of stuff, but when the game was on it was savage. It reminded me of NFL – a burst of mad action followed by a break. It felt like we were dictating the intensity. This was the kind of game we wanted.

The scrums were the key for us. They won a penalty off the first scrum and they were roaring and shouting. After that, we screwed them. The scrum is such a technical area but sometimes it works through sheer force of will, even when the mechanics are a little wrong. In the scrum I'm pushing behind Mike Ross, a brilliant prop. When Mike stays square, keeps his hips in and his legs short, my shove is more effective. Against Australia, Mike wasn't always able to get into that position but he was still beating his man. As an eight, we were finding a way to get on top. Greg Feek, our scrum coach, showed us later on the video how united we were, all eight forwards giving it everything. By comparison, their back row weren't even bound properly for some of the scrums.

With Greg, it's all about the details. He noticed that my right foot was pointing the wrong way in the scrum. It was at a wide angle, as if I was going to side-foot the ball. He said that was the reason why I was sometimes falling in on the hooker instead of staying on the tight head. He told me to straighten my leg, and I noticed a difference immediately. That kind of coaching is priceless.

When I got a chance to kick the ball early in the game, I couldn't tell you whether it was with the side of my foot or the top of my toe. It came loose outside their 22 and I hoofed it. To set up an attacking position, the ball needed to stop about five metres short of the Australian line, to give us a chance to grab one of them in possession and force a turnover scrum. I don't have that kind of control. I've come to the conclusion that I only have one kick in my repertoire and it goes about sixty metres. The ball went dead.

Kicking at goal was a more general problem. Johnny Sexton is a brilliant kicker but that day he missed shots at goal that he would normally get. We were level at half time when we should have been in front. In the dressing room, though, it was clear to us that Australia were there for the taking. The message was to go after it, not to wait and hope it fell into our lap. Seize it.

They didn't score in the second half. We squeezed the life out of them. We forced turnovers from the choke tackle that Les Kiss loves and they ran out of ideas. They went quiet too, which is always a good sign. A lot of the Australians are lippy, but when the game was going away from them they were in no mood for talking.

The crowd went ballistic. For atmosphere, it was like our best days in Croke Park. A lot of our crowd were young people who had emigrated to that part of the world, or backpackers travelling around Australia and New Zealand. Some of them, though, were locals who had adopted us as their second team. Willie Bennett, our masseur, was sitting in the stand next to an Irish supporter whose whole head was painted green, white and gold. He was jumping around and every now and then he'd turn to Willie.

'Who's the number ten?'

'Who's the number seven?'

Eventually Willie asked him if he was Irish. No, he was a Kiwi.

In the dressing room afterwards Gert let out the biggest roar I'd ever heard. It must have been so frustrating for him when we weren't performing. For a long time we'd been falling a million miles short of his standards. He couldn't have done any more for us.

After we beat Australia our popularity in New Zealand went off the scale. We're used to coming down here and being told we're useless by the locals. It was a pleasant change.

That night some of us stayed in the hotel, others went downtown to the bars. On the bus going back to the hotel Paul McNaughton, the team manager, had urged everyone to be careful and to look out for each other. A few of the England players had already been caught in compromising situations and the stories had been plastered all over the media. We didn't need an incident like that to spoil the biggest win in Ireland's World Cup history.

Regardless of our plans, Drico asked everyone to come to the team room for a drink. We spent an hour together, and the buzz was electric. Our World Cup had started. In our minds, everything was possible.

25 September, Rotorua International Stadium – Ireland 62 Russia 12

We're hard bastards to please. On our rest day, one of the options was whitewater rafting. There was also bungee jumping, not to mention golf for the faint-hearted. Seventeen of us signed up for whitewater rafting. It was a forty-five-minute bus journey to the location and the rafting took two hours. With our attention span, it was too long. We need to have our fun in short, sharp hits.

I was in a boat with Tommy Bowe, Jamie Heaslip, Keith Earls, Tony 'Mushy' Buckley and a photographer. There was an instructor too, but we thought it would be a laugh to leave without him while he was helping one of the other boats. We went back for him after a few minutes, but not before Mushy nearly lost his reason. We only went about eighty metres but that was enough to drive him crazy. I thought he was going to kill me.

'Stop it, man! That's fucking stupid! You can't leave him! You can't leave the fucking instructor! We know nothing about the river!'

'We'll be fine, Mushy, relax.'

Before then we'd thought it would be great craic to throw a few lads into the water. The problem was, all of us were wet after fifteen minutes, the water was cold, the air temperature was only about eight degrees and we still had two hours ahead of us paddling down the river. Not that myself and Tommy did much paddling. We were sitting at the back of the boat not doing a stroke.

On the bus back to the hotel I fined everyone for pretending to have a good time.

At home, Jenny and Sophie seemed to be doing fine. Jenny's sister, Caroline, moved in during the World Cup to keep them company, which was a comfort to me.

Skype was great for having face-to-face conversations, though I was worried that Sophie would think I only existed on a computer screen. A virtual dad. At Sophie's age kids develop quickly, learning new things all the time. Jenny was sending me little videos from her phone, which was great, but I couldn't help feeling that I was missing out.

My chats with Jenny were usually in the mornings, before I went training. Her form was always good – or at least she made sure it was while we were chatting. It could have been an act some days, but I never spotted that. I don't know if she realised how important that was for my morale. Knowing Jenny, I'm sure she did.

Deccie changed the team for the Russia match but I was still involved. I was delighted about that. I didn't want a rest. One match a week isn't a burden on anybody. I would play every week for the whole season.

In the build-up we gave Russia due respect. It was the same approach as every other match: detailed video work, special attention for their big players and momentum builders. We highlighted six of them, just as we had done against Australia. The big difference was that against Australia we were happy to go from set piece to set piece; against Russia we needed to play a phase game to get them blowing out of their arses. Without setting the world on fire, we achieved that. Job done. Move on.

The following Monday we flew to Dunedin. In the departure lounge we were greeted by a Maori singer with her guitar who was there to send us off with a few traditional songs. By then Damien Varley had joined the squad as Fla's replacement. Varls is a gifted musician and a brilliant singer so we put the arm on him to give us a song. He borrowed the guitar and sang the Christy Moore number 'North And South Of The River'. It was amazing. The Maori lady played another song, then Varls sang 'Ride On', followed by a few more numbers. People from all over the departure lounge had gathered around. It was such a simple thing, and such a magical thing. When the singing finished, the Maori lady took the ornate strap from her guitar and presented it to Varls.

2 October, Otago Stadium, Dunedin – Ireland 36 Italy 6

The scrum is a game within a game. Against Italy, it is where the game is won and lost. At a press conference, the Italy coach Nick Mallet said that his front row was superior to ours. I don't know what he thought he could gain by saying that. Maybe he was thinking back to the Six Nations in Rome where they had our scrum in trouble and we needed a drop goal from Rog in the last couple of minutes to win the match.

Our front row that day was the same as it is now: Cian Healy, Rory Best, Mike Ross. The big difference was that the game in Rome was the first time they had started together. Greg Feek showed us a clip from that match and a clip from the Australia match and highlighted all the improvements. There was no comparison. It looked like a totally different scrum.

From early in the week, we got our heads straight on what we needed to do. It was all about the scrum and breakdown. If we looked after that, everything else would take care of itself. Against Italy there's no point in playing around the edges, looking for a bit of space. As Eddie O'Sullivan used to say, it's got to be north and south – straight over the top of them. Direct.

Because we didn't get a bonus point against the USA we left ourselves open to the possibility of finishing third in the pool if we lost to Italy. That would have been an absolute disaster, but we didn't waste a minute thinking about it. We went out to put the Italians away.

They came out to start a row. They confused intensity and physicality with cheap shots. It was completely different to the game in Rome when their discipline was very good. They hit us hard that day, as they always do, but it was controlled aggression with no silly penalties. In Dunedin, it was more like the old Italy: eye-gouging, elbows in the face, holding you by the throat on the ground, looking for every opportunity to hit you a flake. It suited us fine because our discipline was never going to crack. Long before the end of the match, the ref was sick of them.

He penalised me for bringing down a line-out maul in the first half, but I had no choice. We were short of numbers and badly set up to defend it. The choice was three points or seven. In that situation you have to weigh up the consequences. At half time we made an adjustment to deal with it: in and around our 22 we weren't going to compete for their line-out ball in the air. Let them win it and we'll defend on the ground.

After half time, it wasn't an issue. They didn't get near our 22.

The scores were level at the break, but we knew they were on the point of cracking. Just before half time we were waiting for a scrum and three of them were on the ground looking for attention. The rest of them were sucking air. That gave us a huge lift.

In the second half, we murdered them. The brilliant thing was that we scored off moves we had practised. When you execute detail from the training pitch in a big match like that it's a massive thrill for everyone. They had some pressure at the end but even though we were three or four scores clear we defended like mad dogs to keep them out.

Earlsy's two tries were sweet, especially the one at the end. The Irish crowd went crazy again. It wasn't a typical rugby crowd but that didn't matter a damn to us. While Johnny Sexton was lining up the conversion for Keith's try they tried to start a Mexican Wave. It would never happen at Thomond Park or the Aviva but they were having a ball and all of us were being swept along on the same wave.

It was Earlsy's twenty-fourth birthday. In the hotel

later there was a cake for him and a big gathering of players' wives, girlfriends and parents. Keith made a brilliant speech about what this team means to him. Really raw and passionate, straight from the heart. Varley picked up a guitar and started a sing-song. There was good craic and a massive buzz and a serious feeling of togetherness. As a group, it was as tight as we've ever been.

Facing into one of the biggest weeks of our careers, we couldn't have been in a better place.

12 October, Cork, 4 a.m.

Wide awake. Jet lagged. I feel like having dinner even though it's the middle of the night. Salmon or bacon and cabbage. My stomach has no idea what's going on in the outside world. Make do with a protein shake followed by cottage cheese.

It's the Wednesday morning after the quarter-final of the World Cup. I've been home since Tuesday afternoon. The journey from our hotel in Wellington to my home outside Cork city took forty hours and forty minutes. The Wales defeat travelled with me every yard of the journey. Now it has settled into my home. Lord knows how long it will stay.

I sit down to watch it again – the second time I've faced it since the final whistle on Saturday. I don't know what I expect to find. Not consolation. On this tape, it doesn't exist.

How did it happen? How did we allow it to happen? If you'd told us six months ago that a quarter-final against Wales would be our route to a World Cup semi-final we would have been ecstatic. We knew they were good, we respected the improvement they had made, but we looked at the young Welsh players who had made a big impact at the tournament and we expected to beat them. As Les Kiss said, we had the right tools for every job. We absolutely believed we would win.

What happened? They outfoxed us. They won more collisions. They stopped our biggest ball-carriers. They beat us at the gain line. We missed too many tackles. We gifted them three tries. And in the end, we panicked. We didn't play like a team with hundreds of caps between us. On one of the biggest days in our rugby lives, we crashed.

We made poor decisions. Me? I tried to choke tackle Jamie Roberts after four minutes. Why? Because I wasn't just thinking of stopping him, I was thinking of a choke tackle and the turnover and the momentum shift. We put a big premium on preventing Roberts from getting over the gain line. In the very first tackle I was thinking beyond that. Crazy. The next thing I remember is somebody handing me my gum shield. I have no memory of being knocked down or getting up. Some of the lads were talking to me but I was in a world of my own. Concussed? Probably.

The Welsh weren't worried about turnovers in the

tackle. Their first thought was to stop us. Low tackle focus. Deny us go-forward ball. Their line speed was frightening. Our carriers were getting man and ball together.

Then our fundamentals started to crack. We were being penalised in the scrum, we lost a couple of line-outs, we were conceding turnovers at the breakdown. We'd talked about the breakdown all week. We knew all about Warburton. We'd discussed what we were going to do. We didn't do it.

What really killed us was our defence. It was the strongest part of our game throughout the tournament and it fell apart. The three tries we conceded were inexcusable.

I can only imagine how Les is feeling. Since he arrived at the end of 2008 he has transformed our defence. His defensive system was the biggest reason why we won the Grand Slam. We let him down. You can talk about Wales and their defensive coach Shaun Edwards, and how they worked us out and how cleverly they played. But all of their tries should have been prevented.

The Mike Phillips try started with a turnover at the line-out. My fault. My position was fractionally wrong for the jump. It was only out by six inches but that was the difference between getting the ball and not getting it. Paulie ate the head off me as we were running back. He was right. It was a small technical error that cost us possession and put us on the back foot.

The big problem was that it felt like we were on the

back foot all day. It felt like we were always chasing the game and never getting there. When we got it back to 10–10 after half time we needed to consolidate and drive on. Instead we conceded another bad try only a few minutes later. Over the years we'd always felt that there comes a point against Wales when they start playing as individuals, but you must force them into that situation. We never came close to achieving that.

We were the team that cracked. Trailing 15–10 shouldn't have been a big problem, but we made it look like it was. We kept trying the same things, obviously thinking that it's got to work some time. Stupid. Rory Best hit the nail on the head afterwards: we should have been able to adapt. A team with our experience should have been able to react on the hoof.

After the match our dressing room was silent. Words were pointless. Nobody would have listened. Down the corridor we could hear the Welsh players singing. They were living our dream.

In sport, the lows are always more intense than the highs. That's not what people think from the outside, that's not how it's packaged, but that's how it feels. It's not really about winning, it's about avoiding the feeling we had in that dressing room. The fear of experiencing that feeling is what drives you to win.

They beat us fair and square. Granted the chance of a lifetime, we underperformed. Maybe we could have lived with one of those realities if it hadn't been for the other. Not performing will haunt us.

Finish watching the match. Start unpacking. Jenny gets up. It's still early. Not even bright yet. Sophie will be up soon.

For three months, it feels like I've lived out of a suit-case. Monday 27 June was our first day of pre-season training in Carton House. On 24 July we went into camp. Of the next eighty nights, I spent only eight in my own bed. I feel like a visitor in my own home.

You do it without thinking. You don't question the sacrifices. You do it with all your heart.

This is the life I've made.

Part of me is dealing with the pain of losing. Part of me wishes we could play again tomorrow.

This is the life I love.

What next? Start again.

Start again.

Picture Acknowledgements

Every effort has been made to contact copyright holders. Those who have not been acknowledged are invited to get in touch with the publishers.

Photos not credited have kindly been supplied by Donncha O'Callaghan.

First section

Pages 6/7: AIL semi-final, Cork Con vs Young Munster 19/5/2001, Paul O'Connell of Young Munster jumps with Mick O'Driscoll and Donncha O'Callaghan of Con: © INPHO/Lorraine O'Sullivan, INPHO 00050518; European Cup semi-final, Munster 21/4/2001: © INPHO/Billy Stickland, INPHO 00048282; Heineken European Cup,

Munster 18/1/2003, (left to right) Alan Quinlan, Peter Stringer, Frankie Sheahan, Mick Galwey, John Hayes and Donncha O'Callaghan celebrate Munster's dramatic win: © INPHO/Morgan Treacy, INPHO 00086059.

Page 8: First cap for Ireland, RBS Six Nations 22/3/2003, Wales vs Ireland, Marcus Horan, Donncha O'Callaghan and John Hayes of Ireland face a Stephen Jones penalty: © INPHO/Patrick Bolger, INPHO 00089159; Irish rugby squad photo session before the departure to South Africa in June 2004: © Brendan Moran, Sportsfile, 141899.

Second section

Page 9: Paddy Wallace, Niall O'Donovan, Keith Wood, Donncha O'Callaghan, Marcus Horan and Arthur Tanner in the back of a van returning from training in Tonga, 2003: © INPHO/Billy Stickland, INPHO 00096042.

Pages 10/11: Celtic League Cup final, Munster vs Llanelli 14/5/2005, Munster's Donncha O'Callaghan beats Chris Wyatt of Llanelli in the line-out: © INPHO/Billy Stickland, INPHO 00147106; Celtic League rugby 5/9/2003, Munster's Donncha O'Callaghan with referee Paul Adams: © INPHO/Patrick Bolger, INPHO 00101827; 18/5/2004, Christian Cullen, Anthony Foley, Jim Williams, Donncha O'Callaghan and Paul O'Connell of Munster: © INPHO/ Billy Stickland, INPHO 00119128; Celtic League 7/1/2006, Edinburgh Gunners vs Munster, Donncha O'Callaghan shields the ball from Alastair Kellock: © INPHO/Dave Gibson, INPHO 00165885; Heineken Cup 22/10/2006, Munster, Marcus Horan congratulates Donncha O'Callaghan on scoring a try: © INPHO/Morgan Treacy, INPHO 00200557; 28/10/2006, Donncha O'Callaghan, Munster, scores his side's fourth try against Bourgoin, Heineken Cup 2006/7: © Kieran Clancy, Sportsfile, 226865.

Pages 12/13: Ronan O'Gara breaks through the Leinster defence to score in the Heineken Cup semi-final 23/4/2006: © Brendan Moran, Sportsfile, 207235; Donncha O'Callaghan celebrates Munster's victory over Biarritz in the Heineken Cup final at the Millennium Stadium, Cardiff 20/5/2006: © Brendan Moran, Sportsfile, 209756; Heineken Cup final 20/5/2006, Munster vs Biarritz, Donncha O'Callaghan offers a prayer in the changing room immediately after the match: © INPHO/Billy Stickland, INPHO 00201503; Heineken Cup final 20/5/2006, Munster vs Biarritz, some of the Munster players celebrate in the changing room after the victory against Biarritz: © INPHO/Billy Stickland, INPHO 00201502; Heineken Cup semi-final 2/5/2010, Biarritz Olympique vs Munster, Munster's Donncha O'Callaghan skips the tackle of Karmichael Hunt of Biarritz in the break that lead to Keith Earls' opening try: © INPHO/ James Crombie, INPHO 00427587; London Irish vs Munster, Heineken Cup 9/10/2010: © INPHO/Billy Stickland, INPHO 00464071.

Page 14: Heineken Cup final 24/5/2008, Munster, Alan Quinlan, Pat Geraghty and Donncha O'Callaghan in the changing room with the Heineken Cup trophy: © INPHO/ Billy Stickland, INPHO 00286358; Heineken Cup final 24/5/2008, Munster, Marcus Horan, John Hayes, Donncha O'Callaghan, Paul O'Connell, Rua Tipoki, Jerry Flannery, Denis Leamy and David Wallace in the changing room with the Heineken Cup trophy: © INPHO/Billy Stickland, INPHO 00286324; Munster homecoming celebrations in Limerick (Irish Independent 26/5/2008): © Emma Jervis, Press 22.

Page 16: Heineken Cup, Thomond Park, Limerick 16/10/2010, Munster vs Toulon, Donncha O'Callaghan and Jonny Wilkinson: © INPHO/Lorraine O'Sullivan, INPHO 00465327; Heineken Cup 16/1/2011, Toulon vs Munster, Donncha O'Callaghan watches the final few minutes of the game: © INPHO/Billy Stickland, INPHO 00480987; the Munster squad celebrate with the cup after victory over Leinster, Celtic League grand final, Munster vs Leinster, Thomond Park, Limerick 28/5/2011: © Diarmuid Greene, Sportsfile, 520301.

Third section

Page 17: Donncha O'Callaghan, Ireland, wins possession for his side in the line-out ahead of Julien Pierre, France, RBS Six Nations Rugby Championship, Ireland vs France 13/2/2011: © Brian Lawless, Sportsfile, 489528; Donncha O'Callaghan, Ireland, tackled by Alex Corbisiero, England, RBS Six Nations Rugby Championship, Ireland vs England 19/3/2011: © Stephen McCarthy, Sportsfile, ref. 499144.

Pages 18/19: Donncha O'Callaghan, Paul O'Connell, John Hayes and Alan Quinlan on top of Table Mountain, Capetown, Ireland rugby tour to South Africa 2004: © INPHO/Billy Stickland, INPHO 00123999; Donncha O'Callaghan and Paddy 'Rala' O'Reilly, British and Irish Lions training 18/6/2009: © INPHO/Billy Stickland, INPHO 00533999; British and Irish Lions safari trip 30/6/2009:

© INPHO/Dan Sheridan, INPHO 00353142; British
and Irish Lions tour to South Africa, Brian O'Driscoll and
Donncha O'Callaghan: © INPHO/Dan Sheridan, INPHO
00360671; Paul O'Connell and Donncha O'Callaghan,
British and Irish Lions tour 6/6/2009: © INPHO/Dan
Sheridan, INPHO 00348019; British and Irish Lions captain
Donncha O'Callaghan leads his side out onto the field,
Southern Kings XV vs British and Irish Lions, Nelson
Mandela Bay Stadium 16/6/2009: © Seconds Left, Sportsfile,
359373; British and Irish Lions tour to South Africa,
Donncha O'Callaghan and John Hayes: © INPHO/Dan
Sheridan, INPHO 00353459.

Page 21: RBS Six Nations 21/3/2009, Ireland celebrate
winning the Grand Slam: © INPHO/Morgan Treacy, INPHO
00331481; civic reception to honour the Grand-Slam
winning Ireland rugby team 7/5/2009, Donncha O'Callaghan
talks with the Queen: © INPHO/Dan Sheridan, INPHO
00343809; RBS Six Nations championship 21/3/2009, (left to
right) Paddy Wallace, Donncha O'Callaghan, Declan Kidney
and Brian O'Driscoll with the trophies after the game: ©
INPHO/Billy Stickland, INPHO 00534000; Ireland Rugby
Team visit Áras an Uachtaráin 20/4/2009, Donncha
O'Callaghan with President Mary McAleese and Martin
McAleese: © INPHO/Morgan Treacy, INPHO 00533998.

Page 23: Visiting a boys' school in South Africa after the 2009
Lions tour: courtesy UNICEF Ireland, © Rebecca Hearfield;
visiting a displaced family under canvas after the earthquake
in Haiti, 2010: courtesy UNICEF Ireland, © Mark Stedman,
Photocall Ireland.

Index

INDEX

INDEX

INDEX

INDEX

CONTENTS

INTRODUCTION

A cake is the most important part of any child's celebration and making your own cakes is such fun and so much more satisfying than buying one from a shop. This book gives you all the help you will need to make a kid's cake, with lots of new ideas to help make yours look really special.

Even if you are just starting out as a baker, you will find the recipes easy to follow. Each project is illustrated with a beautiful photograph to inspire you and full instructions are provided to help you through all the decorating. The front section of the book tells you everything you will need to know about basic recipes and equipment, how to master covering techniques, piping and making decorations for a professional finish. If you don't have special cutters, you will find templates and stencils included at the back of the book to help you, along with guides on how to cut the cakes into special shapes. Icing and making decorations takes time and patience and it is important to read through the instructions carefully and allow yourself plenty of time to complete all the stages of the chosen cake. If a cake looks a little difficult you can bake and freeze it already cut into pieces for up to 4 weeks ahead to help reduce the last-minute work involved.

This book tries to cover as many themes to interest children as possible. Some of the cakes are aimed at the very young, while others are aimed at older children. In the Seasonal & Celebration section you will find bright and colourful cakes for special ages. Fantasy & Adventure includes cakes with imaginative themes including pirates, dragons and a castle for a princess. There is a section that features favourite animals – bears, butterflies and even pigs in a muddy pool, which will bring delight to small faces. Hobbies & Interests are always a favourite subject for party cakes and boys will be delighted with football, cricket and rugby cakes, while girls will love a 'Teddies in Tutus' cake, fashion-themed cakes or a 'Disco Diva' cake.

These cakes show a variety of styles, but you can have fun adapting them yourself and creating your own unique designs. Whatever your level of skill, I'm sure you will find a cake in this book to delight your child.

Ann Nicol

KIDS' PARTY CAKES

GENERAL EDITOR: ANN NICOL

Quick & Easy

FLAME TREE PUBLISHING

Cake

Basics

❦

From the way they look to blowing out the candles, kids love everything about party cakes! To make sure they are not disappointed by the taste, brush up on your cake-baking basics by reading this chapter. Covering ingredients, equipment, basic cake recipes and decorating techniques to refer to later, you will soon be up to speed and baking expert cupcakes and sponges ready to customize with that creative touch.

INGREDIENTS

❖

*I*n baking, most cakes are made by mixing sugar, fats, flour and eggs together. During the mixing, air is incorporated into the mixture to greater or lesser degrees to make it rise during baking. As a cake mixture bakes, the strands of gluten in the flour are stretched and the heat hardens them to give a light, sponge-like texture.

SUGAR

Sugar is not just included to give sweetness to cakes, it also produces a structure and texture that make a cake tender, so always choose the correct type for your recipe.

- GRANULATED SUGAR This is the standard sugar that you add to your tea. It comes in white and golden unrefined varieties and is used for toppings. The coarseness of granulated sugar means that it does not dissolve easily and is not designed for most baking recipes, so is no good for the creaming method.

- CASTER SUGAR This is a fine-ground granulated sugar, which also comes in white and golden (or 'natural') unrefined varieties. It blends easily with butter and margarine when beaten or 'creamed' into light sponge mixtures.

- SOFT LIGHT AND DARK BROWN SUGARS These cream well and are usually used in richer cakes or spicy fruit mixtures such as carrot cake, and in recipes where rich colour and flavour are needed. Store this sugar in a tightly sealed container to prevent it from drying out. If it does become dry or lumpy, pound it back into crystals with the flat end of a rolling pin before you use it.

ⅅ MUSCOVADO SUGAR This sugar is natural and unrefined, with a deep brown colour and rich flavour that makes fruit cakes extra special. It comes in light and dark varieties.

EGGS

ⅅ STORING Always store eggs in the refrigerator, but remove them an hour or so before you start to bake, as better results will be achieved if you allow them to reach room temperature before using. This is because, at this temperature, eggs will whisk better and achieve more aeration.

This not only gives more volume to the mixture, but also allows the eggs to blend in more easily. Cold eggs used straight from the refrigerator can curdle or split a mixture.

ⅅ EGG TYPES Eggs sold as 'value' or 'economy' can be used for baking cakes and cupcakes, particularly if you are working to a budget (but do not forget the welfare issues involved in this choice). Also, do remember that these may be ungraded and of different sizes, so, for best results, buy eggs marked as 'medium' and 'large'. If you do use economy eggs, make sure to note the sizes you are using and try to even out the quantity by, say, using one large and two small eggs instead of three medium-size ones.

ⅅ EGG POWDER Dried egg-white powder gives good results and can be substituted in royal icing recipes, or in recipes where you are unsure about using raw egg whites in the case of pregnant women, the very young or the elderly.

Ingredients

FLOURS

Plain white flour provides the structure of a cake, but contains nothing to make it rise, so cakes that do not need raising agents are made with plain flour. Most recipes using plain flour have bicarbonate of soda or baking powder added to them to make the cakes rise. It is always advisable to sift this into the mixture to incorporate the raising agents evenly.

~ **SELF-RAISING FLOUR** This has raising agents already added, that will add air to make a cake rise, so is used for light sponge mixtures. If you have only plain flour available, add 2¹/₂ tsp baking powder to 225 g/8 oz plain flour to make it into a self-raising flour.

~ **STORING FLOUR** White flours should be stored in a cool, dry place for up to 6 months, but wholemeal flours will not keep as long, as they have a higher fat content, so check the use-by date on all packs. Flour is best stored in a sealed airtight container. Always wash and dry this thoroughly before refilling and never add new flour to old. Small micro-organisms will form in very old flour, from the protein, and these can be seen as tiny black specks that will spread into new flour. If you do not have a container, store the opened paper bag inside a large plastic bag and make sure all flour is kept dry. Damp flour weighs more and therefore alters the recipe, which could lead to heavy or flat cakes.

RAISING AGENTS

Raising agents are added to flour to make cakes rise and produce a light texture. It is important to be accurate when measuring these fine powders out, so always use a measuring spoon.

- BAKING POWDER This is a mixture of bicarbonate of soda and cream of tartar. When liquid is added, the powder fizzes and bubbles and produces carbon dioxide, which expands with heat during baking and gives an airy texture. Be careful not to use very hot or boiling liquid in mixtures, as these can reduce the power of baking powder.

- BICARBONATE OF SODA OR BAKING SODA This is a gentler raising agent and is often used to give melted or spicy mixtures a lift. Cakes will have a bitter flavour if too much is added, so measure this out carefully and accurately with a proper measuring spoon, not a domestic teaspoon.

FATS

Fat adds structure, texture and flavour to cakes and improves their keeping qualities. Always remove them from the refrigerator before using them – they are much easier to mix in when at room temperature.

- BUTTER AND HARD BLOCK MARGARINE Butter and hard margarine can be interchanged in a recipe, and the results will be the same. Butter, however, will always give a better flavour to cakes, so, if they are for a special occasion, is it well worth spending a little extra on this.

- SOFT MARGARINE Sold in tubs, this is wonderful for using in all-in-one sponge recipes where all the ingredients are quickly mixed together in one bowl. This fat always produces good results and is quick and easy to use because it does not have to be used at room temperature but can be taken straight from the refrigerator. Do not substitute soft margarine for butter or hard block margarine in a recipe, as it is a totally different kind of fat, which will not produce the same results. Cakes using soft margarine usually require extra raising agent, so do follow the recipe carefully and do not be tempted to overbeat the mixture, as it will become wet and the cakes may sink. Up to 2 minutes of whisking with an electric mixer is fine to make a smooth mixture.

Ingredients

SPICES

Most dried spices have a reasonably long shelf life, but will not keep indefinitely, and remember that they will gradually lose their aroma and flavour. It is a good idea to buy in small quantities only when you need them. You will find that both light and heat affect the power and flavour of spices, so, if stored in clear glass jars, keep them out of the light – the best place to store spices is in a dark, cool, dry place.

FLAVOURINGS

Flavouring extracts are very concentrated and usually sold in liquid form in small bottles. For example, a teaspoon measure will usually be enough to flavour a cake mixture for 12 cupcakes.

Vanilla and almond extracts are ideal to impart their delicate flavours into cake mixtures and you will find the more expensive extracts give a finer and more natural flavour. Rosewater can be used for flavouring both cake mixtures and icings and has a delicate, perfumed flavour. Fruit flavourings, such as lemon, lime, orange and raspberry, will give a fresh twist to mixtures and icings.

CHOCOLATE

Indulgent chocolate is a useful ingredient for any cake decorator, whether used just to make the cake itself or as a delicious icing too. For the best results and a professional finish and flavour, it is always advisable to buy the highest-quality chocolate you can find, although this will be more expensive. Better-quality chocolates contain a higher percentage of real cocoa fat, which gives a flavour and texture far superior to cheaper varieties.

Cheaper chocolate labelled as 'cooking' or 'baking' chocolate contains a much lower percentage of cocoa solids and is best avoided in favour of better-quality eating chocolate.

The amount of cocoa fat or solids contained in chocolate will be marked on the wrapper of any good-quality chocolate. Those marked as 70 per cent (or more) cocoa solids will give the best results and you will find that this chocolate is shiny and brittle and it should snap very easily.

- DARK CHOCOLATE Also known as 'plain' or 'plain dark' chocolate, this is the most useful all-purpose type of chocolate for baking, as it has a good strong flavour.

- MILK CHOCOLATE Milk chocolate has sugar added and is sweeter than dark, so is also good for melting for icings and decorations.

- WHITE CHOCOLATE This is not strictly chocolate, as it contains only cocoa butter, milk and sugar. It is expensive and the most difficult to work with, so must be used with care. It is best to grate it finely and keep the temperature very low when melting it.

- CHOCOLATE CAKE COVERING This is a cheaper substitute, which contains a minimum of 2.5 per cent cocoa solids and vegetable oil. It is considerably cheaper than real chocolate and the flavour is not as good, but it is easy to melt and sets quickly and well for a coating.

- COCOA POWDER Cocoa powder needs to be cooked to release the full flavour, so blend it with boiling water to make into a paste, then cool, before adding to a recipe, or sift it into the bowl with the flour.

- DRINKING CHOCOLATE Be aware that this is not the same as cocoa, as it contains milk powder and sugar. Some recipes may specify using drinking chocolate and these are successful, but do not substitute it for cocoa powder, as it will spoil the flavour of a cake.

Ingredients

KEY EQUIPMENT

BAKEWARE

It is worth investing in a selection of high-quality tins, which, if looked after properly, should last for many years. Choose heavy-duty metalware that will not buckle, or the new flexible silicone moulds – these are easy to turn out, most need very little greasing and they also wash and dry easily.

DEEP CAKE TINS With deep cake tins, you can buy both round or square tins, depending on preference. They vary in size from 12.5–35.5 cm/5–14 inches with a depth of between 12.5–15 cm/5–6 inches. A deep cake tin, for everyday fruit or Madeira cake, is a must, a useful size is 20 cm/8 inches.

METAL MUFFIN TRAYS Muffin trays come in different weights and sizes; they are generally available with six or 12 deep-set holes. When purchasing, buy the heaviest type you can – although these will be expensive, they produce the best results, as they have good heat distribution and do not buckle. Muffin trays can vary in the size and depth of hole, which obviously affects the eventual size of the muffin.

If using trays without a nonstick finish, it is advisable to give these a light greasing before use. To grease trays, apply a thin film of melted vegetable margarine with a pastry brush or rub round the tin with kitchen paper and a little softened butter or margarine. You will normally need to line metal muffin trays with deep paper muffin cases or strips of baking parchment.

SILICONE MUFFIN TRAYS AND CUPCAKE CASES These are flexible and produce very good results. Although they are sold as nonstick, it is still advisable to rub round each hole or case with a little oil on kitchen paper to prevent sticking. Silicone cupcake cases come in many bright colours and, unlike paper cases, are reusable. Simply wash out any crumbs after use in soapy water and leave them to dry, or clean them in the dishwasher.

PAPER CASES These come in many varieties, colours and shapes. It is advisable to buy the more expensive types, which are thicker and give a good shape to the cake as it rises. Oil and moisture are less likely to penetrate through the thicker cases, whereas it may show through the cheaper ones. Metallic gold, silver and coloured cupcake cases give good results and create a stunning effect for a special occasion. Cupcake cases also come in mini-muffin sizes. These may not be so easy to find, but can be bought from mail-order cake decoration suppliers.

CAKE POP BAKING MOULDS These are metal tins that come in two halves and have 12 small, round indentations for the cake mix. Fill one half of the tin and clamp the other tin on top and, as the mixture rises, it will form perfect round shapes. The round cakes are placed on thin lollipop sticks before decorating.

MINI CAKE TINS AND MOULDS These are small square or round domed cake tins that measure approximately 5 cm/2 inches across and make small individual cakes. You can buy mini cake pans using detachable grids that will make both square and round shapes.

BAKING PAPERS AND FOIL Nonstick baking 'parchment' or 'paper' is useful for lining the bases of small tins or for drying out chocolate and sugarpaste shapes.

Key Equipment

Greaseproof paper is needed for making triangular paper icing bags. Baking parchment can be used, but greaseproof paper is better, as it is thinner and more flexible.

A large sheet of kitchen foil is handy for wrapping cakes or for protecting wrapped cakes in the freezer.

USEFUL ITEMS

- **MIXING BOWLS** Three to four different sizes of mixing bowls are very useful for mixing and melting ingredients.

- **WIRE COOLING RACKS** Another vital piece of equipment is a wire cooling rack. It is essential when baking to allow cakes to cool after being removed from their tins.

A wire rack also protects your kitchen surfaces from the heat and allows air to circulate around the goodies, speeding cooling and preventing soggy bottoms.

- **MEASURING ITEMS** Baking needs 100 per cent accuracy to ensure a perfect result. Scales come in many shapes and sizes, both digital and with weights. Most have a weigh pan, although, with some, your own bowl is used. Measuring jugs and spoons are essential for accurate measuring of both your dry and wet ingredients.

MIXING SPOONS AND SIEVES Basic mixing cutlery is also essential, such as a wooden spoon (for mixing and creaming), a spatula (for transferring the mixture from the mixing bowl to the baking tins and spreading the mixture once it is in the tins) and a palette knife (to ease cakes out of their tins before placing them on the wire racks to cool). Also, do not forget a fine-mesh sieve, for sifting flour and powders.

CAKE TESTER OR SKEWER Use a small, thin metal skewer for inserting into the centre of a cake to test if the cake is ready. This is a handy piece of equipment, but, if you do not have one, a clean, thin metal knitting needle may be used instead.

PASTRY BRUSH A pastry brush is used for brushing glazes over cakes and melted butter round tins. As brushes tend to wear out regularly and shed their bristles, keep a spare new brush to hand.

PALETTE KNIVES A small and a large palette knife are ideal for many jobs, including loosening cakes from their tins, lifting cakes and swirling on buttercream icing. A palette knife with a cranked blade is useful for lifting small cakes or flat pieces of sugarpaste.

KITCHEN SCISSORS Scissors are essential for many small jobs, including cutting papers to size and snipping cherries, dried fruits or nuts into chunks.

GRATER A grater is useful for grating citrus zests, chocolate and marzipan/almond paste. Choose one with a fine and a coarse side.

Key Equipment

ELECTRICAL EQUIPMENT

Nowadays help from time-saving gadgets and electrical equipment makes baking far easier and quicker. There is a wide choice of machines available, from the most basic to the highly sophisticated.

FOOD PROCESSORS When choosing a machine, first decide what you need your processor to do. If you are a novice, it may be a waste to start with a machine which offers a wide range of implements and functions.

This can be off-putting and result in not using the machine to its ultimate potential. When buying a food processor, look for measurements on the sides of the processor bowl and machines with a removable feed tube, which allows food or liquid to be added while the motor is still running.

Look out for machines that have the facility to increase the capacity of the bowl and have a pulse button for controlled chopping.

For many, storage is an issue, so reversible discs and flex storage, or, on more advanced models, a blade storage compartment or box, can be advantageous.

Cakes

PREMIUM GOODS · HOMEMADE SPECIALITIES

It is also worth thinking about machines which offer optional extras which can be bought as your cooking requirements change. Mini chopping bowls are available for those wanting to chop small quantities of food. If time is an issue, dishwasher-friendly attachments may be vital. Citrus presses, liquidisers and whisks may all be useful attachments for the individual cook.

TABLE-TOP MIXERS Table-top mixers are freestanding and are capable of dealing with fairly large quantities of mixture. They are robust machines and good for heavy cake mixing as well as whipping cream, whisking egg whites or making one-stage cakes.

These mixers also offer a wide range of attachments ranging from liquidisers to mincers, juicers, can openers and many more and varied attachments.

HAND-HELD MIXERS A hand-held electric mixer makes quick work of whisking butter and sugar and is an invaluable aid for cake baking. They are smaller than freestanding mixers and often come with their own bowl and stand from which they can be lifted and used as hand-held devices. They have a motorised head with detachable twin whisks.

These mixers are versatile, as they do not need a specific bowl in which to whisk. Any suitable mixing bowl can be used. Do not be tempted to use a food processor for mixing small amounts, as it is easy to over-process and this may produce flat cakes.

Key Equipment

BASIC CAKE-MAKING TECHNIQUES

❦

LINING CAKE TINS

If a recipe states that the tin needs lining, do not be tempted to ignore this. Rich fruit cakes and other cakes that take a long time to cook benefit from the tin being lined so that the edges and base do not burn or dry out. Greaseproof paper or baking parchment is ideal for this. It is a good idea to have the paper at least double thickness, or preferably three or four thicknesses. Sponge cakes and other cakes that are cooked in 30 minutes or less are also better if the bases are lined, as it is far easier to remove them from the tin.

The best way to line a round or square tin is to lightly draw around the base and then cut just inside the markings, making it easy to sit in the tin. Next, lightly grease the paper so that it will easily peel away from the cake.

If the sides of the tin also need to be lined, then cut a strip of paper long enough for the tin. This can be measured by wrapping a piece of string around the rim of the tin. Once again, lightly grease the paper, push against the tin and oil once more, as this will hold the paper to the sides of the tin.

SEPARATING EGGS

When separating eggs (that is, separating the white from the yolk), crack an egg in half lightly and cleanly over a bowl, being careful not to break the yolk and keeping it in the shell. Then tip the yolk backwards and forwards between the two shell halves, allowing as much of the white as possible to spill out into the bowl. Keep or discard the yolk and/or the white as needed. Make sure that you do not get any yolk in your whites, as this will prevent successful whisking of the whites. It takes practice!

MAKING METHODS

- CREAMING Light cakes are made by the creaming method, which means that the butter and sugar are first beaten or 'creamed' together. A little care is needed for this method. Using a large mixing bowl, beat the fat and sugar together until pale and fluffy. The eggs are gradually beaten in to form a slackened batter and the flour is folded in last, to stiffen up the mixture. In some recipes, egg whites are whisked and added to the mixture separately for extra lightness.

When the eggs are added, they are best used at room temperature to prevent the mixture from splitting or 'curdling'. Adding a teaspoon of flour with each beaten egg will help to keep the mixture light and smooth and prevent the mixture from separating. A badly mixed, curdled batter will hold less air and be heavy or can cause a sunken cake.

- ALL-IN-ONE MIXTURES This 'one-stage' method is quick and easy and is perfect for those new to baking, as it does not involve any complicated techniques. It is ideal for making light sponges, but soft tub-type margarine or softened butter at room temperature must be used. There is no need for any creaming or rubbing in, as all the ingredients are simply placed in a large bowl and quickly beaten together for just a few minutes until smooth. Be careful not to overbeat, as this will make the mixture too wet. Self-raising flour with the addition of a little extra baking powder is vital for a good rise.

∾ FRUIT CAKES Rich fruit cakes are usually made by the creaming method, then dried fruits and nuts are folded into the mixture last.

CHECKING TO SEE IF THE CAKES ARE COOKED

For light sponge-type cakes, press the centre lightly with the fingertips and, if the cake is cooked, it should spring back easily. To test more thoroughly, insert a thin, warmed skewer into the deepest part of the centre.

If the cake is cooked, it will come out perfectly clean with no mixture sticking to it, but, if there is some mixture on the skewer, bake the cake for a little longer and test again.

Small cupcakes should be golden, risen and firm to the touch when pressed lightly in the centre. The last part of a cupcake to cook is the centre, so, after the baking time stated, check this area.

HOW TO PATCH UP MISTAKES

If the cakes are overcooked or are burnt on the outside, simply scrape this away with a serrated knife and cover the surface with buttercream. If the cakes are a little dry, sprinkle them with a few drops of sweet sherry or orange juice.

CUTTING THE TOPS LEVEL

Many cakes and cupcakes form a small peak while baking. However, some methods of decorating cakes require a flat surface, so, for these, trim the tops level with a knife. You can also coat cupcakes with apricot glaze and press on a disc of almond paste or sugarpaste to give a flat surface to decorate (*see* pages 40 and 46).

STORING CAKES

Chocolate and Madeira cakes can be made ahead of time and will store well for up to 5 days before decorating. Cover in fresh baking parchment, then wrap in foil and keep in a cool place, or, alternatively, freeze for up to 2 months.

Rich fruit cakes should be stored before cutting and need at least 1 month for the flavour to mature. Wedding cakes should be made 3 months ahead to give them a better flavour and enable the cake to become moist enough to cut cleanly into slices. Wrap rich fruit cakes in their baking papers, then overwrap in clean baking parchment, then a double layer of foil and seal with tape. Keep the cakes in a cool place until required.

COLOURING CAKE BATTERS

Brightly coloured layers of sponge cake are attractive and eye-catching for a children's party cake and are easily achieved. Add your choice of bright paste food colouring

Basic Cake-making Techniques

to the cake mix half a teaspoon at a time, remembering these colours can be quite strong, until you reach the desired colour. For a special effect, you can divide the cake mixture into two or three batches and colour each one of these differently.

It is advisable to only use paste colourings, as the liquid ones sold in bottles will tend to make the mixture go wet, and you will need a lot more of this type to achieve a deep colour.

CARVING CAKE INTO SHAPES

Once you have baked and cooled your cake, you may need to cut it into shapes to create a special novelty cake. It is a good idea to draw out the shapes on greaseproof paper with a pencil, then place this pattern on top of the cake, to cut around. This is an easy way to avoid making mistakes. If you make a mistake with the cutting,however, don't worry, you can stick pieces back together with a little buttercream.

FREEZING CAKES

If you are busy organising a children's party, it is a good idea to bake the cake bases ahead of time and either freeze them whole, or cut the pieces and freeze them separately. The cakes can be baked, cooled and stored in the freezer for up to 3 months ahead, then simply defrost them at room temperature for 2–3 hours.

It is easier to cut and decorate half-frozen cake, as it is firm and will not crumble easily. You can also cover the half-frozen pieces with buttercream easily, as the crumbs will not come off the solid pieces.

FREEZING FINISHED WHOLE CAKES Completed cakes covered in basic buttercream can be frozen whole without any extra decorations. Sugarpaste-covered cakes will not freeze well, however, as the sugarpaste will start to go wet and limp when it is defrosted. Avoid freezing cakes with any extra decorations such as granulated sugar, liquorice trimmings or sweets, as the colours from these will start to bleed into the buttercream.

BASIC RECIPES

RICH CHOCOLATE CAKE

Square Cake Size	13 cm/5 inch square	18 cm/7 inch square	23 cm/9 inch square
Round Cake Size	15 cm/6 inch round	20 cm/8 inch round	25 cm/10 inch round
plain chocolate	50 g/2 oz	125 g/4 oz	225 g/8 oz
soft dark brown sugar	150 g/5 oz	275 g/10 oz	575 g/1¹/₄ lb 3oz
milk	135 ml/4¹/₂ fl oz	200 ml/7 fl oz	500 ml/18 fl oz
butter, softened	50 g/2 oz	125 g/4 oz	225 g/8 oz
eggs, beaten	1	3	6
plain flour	125 g/4 oz	225 g/8 oz	450 g/1 lb
bicarbonate of soda	¹/₂ tsp	1 tsp	2 tsp
Cooking time	45 mins	1 hour	1¹/₂ hours

Preheat the oven to 180˚C/350˚F/Gas Mark 4. Grease and line the tin with nonstick baking parchment. Break the chocolate into small pieces and place in a heavy-based pan with one third of the sugar and all of the milk. Heat gently until the chocolate has melted, then remove from the heat and cool.

Beat the butter and remaining sugar together until fluffy, then beat in the eggs a little at a time. Gradually beat in the cold melted chocolate mixture. Sift the flour and bicarbonate of soda into the mixture and fold together with a large metal spoon until smooth. Bake for the time shown on the chart or until a skewer inserted into the centre comes out clean. Cool for 10 minutes, then turn out of the tin onto a wire rack to cool. Store wrapped in foil until needed, or freeze wrapped tightly in foil for up to 3 months.

MADEIRA CAKE

Square Cake Size	13 cm/5 inch square	16 cm/6 inch square	18 cm/7 inch square
Round Cake Size	15 cm/6 inch round	18 cm/7 inch round	20 cm/8 inch round
butter, softened	175 g/6 oz	225 g/8 oz	350 g/12 oz
caster sugar	175 g/6 oz	225 g/8 oz	350 g/12 oz
self-raising flour	175 g/6 oz	225 g/8 oz	350 g/12 oz
plain flour	75 g/3 oz	125 g/4 oz	175 g/6 oz
eggs	3	4	6
vanilla extract	$1/2$ tsp	1 tsp	1 tsp
glycerine	1 tsp	1 tsp	1 tsp
Cooking time	1 hour	1–$1^1/4$ hours	$1^1/4$–$1^1/2$ hours

Square Cake Size	20 cm/8 inch square	23 cm/9 inch square
Round Cake Size	23 cm/9 inch round	25 cm/10 inch round
butter, softened	450 g/1 lb	500 g/1 lb 2 oz
caster sugar	450 g/1 lb	500 g/1 lb 2 oz
self-raising flour	450 g/1 lb	500 g/1 lb 2 oz
plain flour	225 g/8 oz	250 g/9 oz
eggs	8	9
vanilla extract	2 tsp	1 tbsp
glycerine	2 tsp	1 tbsp
Cooking time	$1^1/2$ – $1^3/4$ hours	$1^1/2$ – $1^3/4$ hours

Preheat the oven to 160°C/325°F/Gas Mark 3. Grease and line the tin with nonstick baking parchment.

Cream the butter and caster sugar together in a large bowl until light and fluffy. Sift the flours together. Whisk the eggs into the mixture one at a time, adding a teaspoon of flour with each addition to prevent the mixture from curdling.

Add the remaining flour, the vanilla extract and glycerine to the mixture and fold together with a large metal spoon until the mixture is smooth.

Spoon into the tin and bake for the time shown on the chart until firm and well risen and a skewer inserted into the centre comes out clean.

Leave to cool in the tin for 10 minutes, then turn out onto a wire rack to cool. Wrap in foil and store for up to 3 days before decorating. Freeze wrapped in foil for up to 2 months.

- ∾ BOWL SHAPED To cook the cake in a 2 litre/3½ pint ovenproof bowl, grease the bowl well and use the amounts for the 13 cm/5 inch square cake, baking for 45 minutes–1 hour.

- ∾ LEMON VARIATION To make the lemon variation of the Madeira cake, you can simply omit the vanilla extract and add the same amount of finely grated lemon zest.

- ∾ ALMOND VARIATION To make the almond variation of the Madeira cake, you can simply omit the vanilla extract and add the same amount of almond extract.

ALL-IN-ONE QUICK-MIX SPONGE

To make sure you end up with the correct quantity of mixture for your tin when making an all-in-one sponge mix, use the guidelines below to select the ingredient quantities depending on tin size and shape.

Tin size and shape	Two 18 cm/7 inch sandwich tins	Two 20 cm/8 inch sandwich tins
Caster sugar	125 g/4 oz	175 g/6 oz
Soft tub margarine	125 g/4 oz	175 g/6 oz
Eggs	2	3
Self-raising flour	125 g/4 oz	175 g/6 oz
Baking powder	1 tsp	1 tsp
Vanilla extract	½ tsp	1 tsp
Baking time	25–30 mins	30–35 mins

Tin size and shape	13 cm/5 inch square	16 cm/6 inch square
Tin size and shape	15 cm/6 inch round	18 cm/7 inch round
Caster sugar	125 g/4 oz	175 g/6 oz
Soft tub margarine	125 g/4 oz	175 g/6 oz
Eggs	2	3
Self-raising flour	125 g/4 oz	175 g/6 oz
Baking powder	1 tsp	1 tsp
Vanilla extract	½ tsp	1 tsp
Baking time	30–35 mins	35–40 mins

Tin size and shape	18 cm/7 inch square	20 cm/8 inch square
Tin size and shape	20 cm/8 inch round	23 cm/9 inch round
Caster sugar	225 g/8 oz	350 g/12 oz
Soft tub margarine	225 g/8 oz	350 g/12 oz
Eggs	4	6
Self-raising flour	225 g/8 oz	350 g/12 oz
Baking powder	1½ tsp	2 tsp
Vanilla extract	1 tsp	2 tsp
Baking time	45–55 mins	50–60 mins

Tin size and shape	28 x 18 x 4 cm/11 x 7 x 1½ inch slab cake	30 x 25 x 5 cm/12 x 10 x 2 inch slab cake
Caster sugar	175 g/6 oz	275 g/10 oz
Soft tub margarine	175 g/6 oz	275 g/10 oz
Eggs	3	5
Self-raising flour	175 g/6 oz	275 g/10 oz
Baking powder	1 tsp	2 tsp
Vanilla extract	1 tsp	2 tsp
Baking time	30–40 mins	50–60 mins

Preheat the oven to 160°C/325°F/Gas Mark 3. Grease and line the tin with nonstick baking parchment, or butter the pudding basins well.

Place the sugar, margarine and eggs in a large mixing bowl. Sift in the flour and baking powder and add the vanilla extract.

Pudding basin size	900 ml/1½ pint	1.1 litre/2 pint
Caster sugar	125 g/4 oz	175 g/6 oz
Soft tub margarine	125 g/4 oz	175 g/6 oz
Eggs	2	3
Self-raising flour	125 g/ 4 oz	175 g/6 oz
Baking powder	1 tsp	1 tsp
Vanilla extract	½ tsp	1 tsp
Baking time	50 mins	1 hour

Beat the ingredients together with an electric mixer for 1–2 minutes until they are smooth and well combined. Spoon into the tins or basin and bake according to the time guideline above or until the cake appears well risen, just firm to the touch and is beginning to shrink away from the sides of the tin or basin.

Cool in the tin for 4 minutes, then turn out onto a wire rack to cool. Peel away the papers while still warm.

For variations:

∾ CHOCOLATE VARIATION Omit the vanilla extract and add 1 tbsp softened cocoa powder for the 2-egg mix, 1½ tbsp for the 3-egg mix, 2 tbsp for the 4-egg mix and 3 tbsp for the 5-egg mix.

∾ ORANGE OR LEMON VARIATION Omit the vanilla extract and add 2 tsp finely grated orange or lemon zest for the 2-egg mix, 3 tsp for the 3-egg mix, 4 tsp for the 4-egg mix and 2 tbsp for the 5-egg mix.

∾ COFFEE VARIATION Omit the vanilla extract and add 1 tbsp coffee essence for the 2-egg mix, 1½ tbsp for the 3-egg mix, 2 tbsp for the 4-egg mix and 2½ tbsp for the 5-egg mix.

BASIC VANILLA CUPCAKES

Makes 12–14

125 g/4 oz caster sugar
125 g/4 oz soft tub margarine
2 medium eggs
125 g/4 oz self-raising flour
½ tsp baking powder
½ tsp vanilla extract

Preheat the oven to 190°C/375°F/Gas Mark 5.
Line a bun tray with paper cases.

Place all the cupcake ingredients in a large bowl and beat
with an electric mixer for about 2 minutes until light and
smooth. Fill the paper cases halfway up with the mixture.
Bake for about 15 minutes until firm, risen and golden.

Remove to a wire rack to cool. Keep for 2–3 days in an
airtight container. Can be frozen for up to 2 months, but the
paper cases will come away when thawed and these will
need replacing.

∽ CHOCOLATE VARIATION Omit the caster sugar and use soft
light brown sugar instead. Sift 25 g/1 oz cocoa powder in
with the flour and baking powder. Omit the vanilla extract and add 2 tbsp milk instead.
Mix and bake as above.

∽ CHERRY & ALMOND VARIATION Add 50 g/2 oz finely chopped washed glacé
cherries. Omit the vanilla extract and use almond extract instead. Mix and bake as above.

SPECIAL REQUIREMENTS

❦

*I*f you have to cater for a child who has an allergy to wheat or dairy products, there are substitutes that can be baked into a cake for a special occasion.

❧ FLOUR Packs of both plain and self-raising wheat-free and gluten-free flours for baking can now be purchased in supermarkets and health-food stores. Make sure you check the sell-by dates on these flours, however, as they do not last as long as normal flours and will start to deteriorate.

❧ XANTHAN GUM This special ingredient is a natural product that is needed in gluten- and wheat-free baking to stabilise cakes and stop them from crumbling. Some flours contain a small amount of xanthan gum, but extra is needed, according to the recipe instructions, for success.

❧ FATS Dairy-free sunflower spread or soya spread can be used as a substitute for butter and margarine in baking.

❧ MILKS AND CREAMS Dairy-free milks can be used for baking, such as soya, almond and rice milk. Soya whipping cream, a blend of vegetable fat and soya beans, can also be used for baking. Coconut cream, sold in cartons, can be whipped to a texture similar to double cream and folded together with icing sugar to make an alternative frosting.

GLUTEN-FREE SPONGE

Serves 8–10

250 g/9oz dairy-free spread
250 g/9 oz golden caster sugar
4 large eggs
½ tsp vanilla extract
2 tbsp almond milk
225 g/8 oz gluten-free self-raising flour
1½ tsp gluten-free baking powder
1 tsp xanthan gum
40 g/1½ oz ground almonds

Preheat the oven to 190°C/375°F/Gas Mark 5. Grease two 20 cm/8 inch sandwich tins and line the bases with nonstick baking parchment.

Place the dairy-free spread in a bowl with the sugar and whisk with an electric mixer until light and fluffy. Whisk the eggs, vanilla and almond milk together, then gradually add to the mixture in the bowl and whisk until smooth.

Sift the flour, baking powder, xanthan gum and ground almonds together, then fold into the mixture in the bowl. Spoon into the tins and smooth the tops level. Bake for about 20 minutes until golden and the sides begin to shrink away from the tins.

Leave in the tins for 5 minutes, then turn out onto wire racks to cool. Sandwich together with frosting made with dairy-free spread and icing sugar or jam.

Basic Recipes

Decorating Basics

Giving cakes and cupcakes that all-important decorative touch is not always as easy as it looks! With key information on decorating ingredients, equipment and techniques, reading this section will help your masterpieces to look as good as possible. Also included are extremely useful icing recipes, including buttercream frosting, cream cheese frosting, sugarpaste icing and flower paste, which will feature in many of the projects throughout this book.

DECORATING INGREDIENTS

❧

*T*here are a multitude of ingredients you can use to decorate your cakes. Below, you will find reference to many of the icings, colourings and edible decorations you can buy, as well as, later, key icing recipes, which will show you how to whip up your own icings from scratch. The basic icing recipes will be referenced often throughout the main recipe chapters.

ᴗ ICING SUGAR Icing sugar is fine and powdery. It is usually sold plain and white, but can also be bought as an unrefined golden (or 'natural') variety. Use it for delicate icings, frostings and decorations. Store this sugar in a dry place, as it can absorb moisture and this will make it go hard and lumpy. Always sift this sugar at least once, or preferably twice, before you use it, to remove any hard lumps that would prevent icing from achieving a smooth texture – lumpy icing is impossible to pipe out.

ᴗ FONDANT ICING SUGAR This is sold in plain and flavoured varieties and gives a beautiful glossy finish to cake toppings. Just add a little boiled water to the sugar, according to the packet instructions, to make a shiny icing that can be poured or drizzled over cake tops to give a very professional finish. Colour the plain white icing with a few spots of paste food colouring to achieve your desired result.

Flavoured fondant icing sugar is sold in strawberry, raspberry, orange, lemon and blackcurrant flavours and also has colouring added. These sugars are ideal if you want to make a large batch of cakes with different-coloured and -flavoured toppings. Flavoured fondant sugars can also be whisked with softened unsalted butter and cream cheese to make delicious frostings in just a few moments.

ROYAL ICING SUGAR Royal icing sets to a classic, firm Christmas-cake-style covering or can be made to a softer consistency to give a glossy finish. Sold in packs as plain white sugar, this is whisked with cold water to give an instant royal icing. It has dried egg white included in the mixture, so does not need the long beating that traditional royal icing recipes require. It is also ideal to use for those who cannot eat raw egg whites.

TUBES OF WRITING ICING You can buy small tubes of ready-coloured royal icing or gel icing, usually in sets of black, red, yellow and blue, and these are ideal for small amounts of writing or for piping on dots or small decorations.

FOOD COLOURINGS You can buy food colourings in liquid, paste, gel and powder or dust forms in a great range of colours.

Paste food colourings are best for using with sugarpaste. These are sold in small tubs and are very concentrated, so should be added to the sugarpaste dot by dot on the end of a wooden cocktail stick. Knead the colouring in evenly, adding more until you get the colour you require.

Liquid and gel food colourings are ideal for adding to frostings. Add this cautiously, drop by drop, beating the frosting well until you reach the colour you require.

Dusts, sprays and lustre colourings should be lightly brushed onto dry sugarpaste with a paintbrush to form a delicate sheen to decorations such as flowers. Liquid paint and spray-on metallic colourings add a glossy sheen effect to decorations.

Coloured sugars can be made by adding a few dots of paste colouring to granulated sugar with a toothpick. Coloured sugars add sparkle to the sides of cakes and cupcakes. Coloured sugars can make up the background of a children's novelty cake, such the sand in a seaside cake, or a sparkly topping.

BOUGHT SUGAR DECORATIONS AND SPRINKLES A range of sprinkles can be bought in supermarkets or by mail order from specialist cake-decorating companies.

Decorating Ingredients.

APRICOT GLAZE & ALMOND PASTE

Makes 450 g/1 lb to cover 2 x 20 cm/8 inch, round cakes, or 24 small cakes

For the Apricot Glaze:

450 g/1 lb apricot jam
3 tbsp water
1 tsp lemon juice

For the Almond Paste:

125 g/4 oz sifted icing sugar
125 g/4 oz caster sugar
225 g/8 oz ground almonds
1 medium egg
1 tsp lemon juice

For the Apricot Glaze, place the jam, water and juice in a heavy-based saucepan and heat gently, stirring, until soft and melted. Boil rapidly for 1 minute, then press through a fine sieve with the back of a wooden spoon. Discard the pieces of fruit. Use immediately for glazing or sticking on almond paste, or pour into a clean jar or airtight plastic container and store in the refrigerator for up to 3 months.

For the Almond Paste, stir the sugars and ground almonds together in a bowl. Whisk the egg and lemon juice together and mix into the dry ingredients. Knead until the paste is smooth. Wrap tightly in clingfilm or foil to keep airtight and store in the refrigerator until needed. The paste can be made 2–3 days ahead of time, but, after that, it will start to dry out and become difficult to handle.

To use the paste, knead on a surface dusted with icing sugar. Brush the top of the cake(s) with apricot glaze. Roll out the paste to a circle large enough to cover the cake, or cut out discs large enough to cover the tops of the cupcakes. Press onto the cakes. To cover the sides of a large cake, cut out a strip long enough to go round the cake (work out the length by measuring the circumference with string). Roll the paste up into a coil and press one end onto the side of the cake. Unroll the paste, pressing into the cake as you go round. Press the top and sides together to join. Smooth the top and sides and leave to dry out for 24 hours before icing.

BASIC BUTTERCREAM FROSTING

❦

Covers a 20 cm/8 inch, round cake, or 12 small cakes

Ingredients

150 g/5 oz unsalted butter, softened at room temperature
225 g/8 oz icing sugar, sifted
2 tbsp hot milk or water
1 tsp vanilla extract
food colourings of choice

Beat the butter until light and fluffy, then beat in the sifted icing sugar and hot milk or water in two batches.

Add the vanilla extract and any colourings. Store chilled for up to 2 days in an airtight container.

Variations
Omit the vanilla extract and instead:

- COFFEE Blend 2 tsp coffee extract with the milk.

- CHOCOLATE Blend 2 tbsp cocoa powder to a paste with 2 tbsp boiling water and use instead of the hot milk or water.

- LEMON Beat in 1 tbsp fresh lemon juice, sieved.

CREAM CHEESE FROSTING

✧

**Covers a 20 cm/8 inch,
round cake,
or 12 small cakes**

Ingredients

50 g/2 oz unsalted butter, softened
at room temperature
300 g/11 oz icing sugar, sifted
flavourings of choice
food colourings of choice
125 g/4 oz full-fat cream cheese

Beat the butter and icing sugar together until light
and fluffy.

Add flavourings and colourings of choice and
beat again.

Add the cream cheese and whisk until light and fluffy.

Do not overbeat, however, as the mixture can
become runny.

SUGARPASTE ICING
(A.K.A. FONDANT FOR ROLLING OR MODELLING)

❦

Makes 350 g/12 oz to cover a 20 cm/8 inch, round cake, or 12 small cakes, or use for decorations

Ingredients

1 medium egg white
1 tbsp liquid glucose
350 g/12 oz icing sugar, sifted, plus extra for dusting

Place the egg white and liquid glucose in a large mixing bowl and stir together, breaking up the egg white.

Add the icing sugar gradually, mixing in until the mixture binds together and forms a ball.

Turn the ball of icing out onto a clean surface dusted with icing sugar and knead for 5 minutes until soft but firm enough to roll out.

If the icing is too soft, knead in a little more icing sugar until the mixture is pliable.

To colour, knead in paste food colouring. Do not use liquid food colouring, as this is not suitable and will make the sugarpaste limp.

To use, roll out thinly on a clean surface dusted with icing sugar to a circle large enough to cover a cake, or cut out discs large enough to cover the top of each cupcake.

FLOWER PASTE

Ingredients

2 tsp powdered gelatine
2 tsp liquid glucose
2 tsp white vegetable fat
450 g/1 lb sifted icing sugar
1 tsp gum tragacanth powder
1 egg white
icing sugar, for dusting

Flower, petal or 'gum' paste is used for making very thin, delicate flowers and decorations, which set hard so that they can be handled easily.

Flower paste will roll out much more thinly than sugarpaste and is worth using for wedding cakes, as it gives a realistic finish to flowers, and these can be made ahead of time and easily stored. It can be bought from cake decorating suppliers or by mail order in small, ready-made slabs in different colours or as a powder that can be reconstituted with a little cold water and made into a paste.

To make your own, follow the recipe and store the paste in the refrigerator, tightly wrapped in strong plastic until needed.

Place 1 1/2 tsp cold water in a heatproof bowl. Sprinkle over the gelatine and add the liquid glucose and white fat. Place the bowl over a saucepan of hot water and heat until melted, stirring occasionally. Cool slightly.

Sift the icing sugar and gum tragacanth powder into a bowl, make a well in the centre and add the egg white and the cooled gelatine mixture. Mix together to make a soft paste.

Knead the paste on a surface dusted with icing sugar until smooth, then wrap in clingfilm to exclude all air. Leave for 2 hours, then break off small pieces and use to make fine flowers and petals.

SMILING PUMPKIN CAKE

⟶ ⟵

Serves 10–12

For the cake base:

1 batch 13 cm/5 inch square
Madeira cake mixture baked in a
2 litre/4 pint bowl (see page 28)
4 tbsp apricot glaze

To decorate:

1.1 kg/2¹/₂ lb ready-to-roll
sugarpaste
orange, green and black paste
food colourings
icing sugar, for dusting

Trim the top of the cake level if it has peaked, then brush the apricot glaze over the domed side of the cake.

Colour 900 g/2 lb sugarpaste orange, roll it out on a board dusted with icing sugar to a round large enough to cover the cake. Using both hands, carefully lift it over the cake and smooth down. Trim the bottom edge level.

Colour half the remaining sugarpaste green and shape it into a stalk to sit on top of the pumpkin. Colour the rest of the sugarpaste black.

Roll six very thin sausages of black sugarpaste long enough to fit over the cake. Brush the sausages with a little cold boiled water and position them at regular intervals over the cake. Press them gently into place and trim the bottom edges neatly.

Roll out the rest of the black sugarpaste, and cut out three small triangles for eyes and a nose. Cut out a wide, smiley mouth (perhaps with a tooth missing!) that will stretch between two of the black sausages. Dampen the triangles and the pumpkin mouth and gently press into place. Finally, dampen the underside of the stalk and press this on top of the cake.

STARBRIGHT FIREWORKS CUPCAKES

✿

Makes 12

125 g/4 oz butter, softened
125 g/4 oz caster sugar
125 g/4 oz self-raising flour
2 medium eggs
1 tsp vanilla extract

To decorate

icing sugar, for dusting
225 g/8 oz ready-to-roll sugarpaste
dust or paste food colourings
1 batch cream cheese frosting
(*see* page 44)
edible silver balls (optional)
small candles

Preheat the oven to 180°C/350°F/Gas Mark 4. Line a 12-hole tray with deep paper cases.

Place the butter and sugar in a bowl, then sift in the flour. In another bowl, beat the eggs with the vanilla extract, then add to the flour mixture. Beat until smooth, then spoon into the cases, filling them three-quarters full.

Bake for about 18 minutes until firm to the touch in the centre. Turn out to cool on a wire rack.

To decorate the cupcakes, dust a clean, flat surface with icing sugar. Colour the sugarpaste in batches of bright colours, such as blue, yellow and orange. Roll each out thinly and cut out stars with a cutter or follow the pattern on page 253. Leave to dry out for 2 hours until firm. Place the frosting in a piping bag fitted with a star nozzle and pipe large swirls on top of each cupcake. Decorate each cupcake with stars, edible silver balls, if using, and small candles. Keep for 2 days in an airtight container in a cool place.

SNOWMAN CAKE

⸎

Serves 16–20

For the cake:

1 x 23 cm/9 inch, round
all-in-one quick-mix sponge cake
(*see* page 30)
1 x 15 cm/6 inch square, all-in-one
quick-mix sponge cake

To decorate:

1 batch royal icing (*see* page 50)
blue, red, black and green paste
food colourings
2¹/₂ batches vanilla buttercream
large round cardboard, measuring
about 51 cm/20 inches in diameter

Trim the top of the round cake with a sharp knife into a rounded shape for the snowman's body. Carve the sides to shape the arms and the bottom of the body. Trim the top of the square cake to a rounded shape for the snowman's head and carve two thirds of the sides to shape his round face and the last third for the hat, leaving the top straight.

Colour three quarters of the royal icing blue and spread over the top three quarters of the board. Spread white royal icing over the bottom quarter (reserving a little), roughing it up a little with a round-bladed knife to resemble snow. Before the icing has set, position the body and head on the board, pressing both into the royal icing. Leave until the icing has set, then spoon the reserved white royal icing into a piping bag fitted with a small star nozzle and pipe tiny 'snowflakes' over the blue icing. Leave to set.

Reserve 1¹/₂ batches of the buttercream, divide the rest equally between three bowls and colour one red, one black and one green. Spoon the coloured buttercreams into large piping bags, each fitted with a star nozzle, and pipe stars and lines over the cakes using the three colours for the hat, scarf, buttons, eyes and mouth of the snowman. You can follow the design in the picture or create your own patterns if you prefer. Pipe or spoon a flat circle of red buttercream for the nose. Spoon the reserved vanilla buttercream into a large piping bag fitted with a star nozzle and pipe stars over the rest of the snowman to cover him completely, working around what you have already piped, taking care not to smudge or pipe over your work.

SNOWMEN CUPCAKES

Makes 12

For the cakes:

2 egg whites
125 g/4 oz caster sugar
1 batch vanilla cupcakes
(*see* page 33)

To decorate:

450 g/1 lb ready-to-roll sugarpaste
orange, pink, blue and green paste
food colourings
1 batch vanilla buttercream
125 g/4 oz shredded soft coconut
small and large chocolate chips

Preheat the oven to 140°C/275°F/Gas Mark 1. Place the egg whites in a clean, dry bowl and whisk with an electric mixer until stiff. Whisk in the caster sugar gradually, whisking constantly, until stiff glossy peaks form. Spoon the meringue into a large piping bag fitted with a large plain nozzle. On a baking sheet lined with nonstick baking parchment, pipe 12 circles about 6 cm/2¹/₂ inches across. Pipe a small ball on top of each one to make a snowman shape and bake for about 45 minutes until pale and crisp. Leave to cool on a wire rack.

Colour the sugarpaste in four batches, one orange, one pink, one blue and one green. Trim the tops of the cakes flat if they have peaked.

Spread a little buttercream on top of each cake, then stick a meringue snowman firmly on top. Spread each snowman all over with buttercream, then press the shredded coconut onto this. Repeat with the remaining cakes.

Model the coloured sugarpastes into hats and scarves and mark indentations onto the scarves with a pasta wheel to represent knitting. Place the hats and scarves onto the snowmen. Make carrot noses out of orange scraps and place on the faces. Make eyes with the larger chocolate chips and use the smaller ones to make a mouth.

Animals

From the tiny bumblebee to the giant elephant, animals make a fun and bright theme for children's cakes and cupcakes. Roll out some sugarpaste and get inspired by these exciting projects. If you've got a cheeky monkey in your midst, the Monkey Island Cake is bound to go down a treat, whilst young horse lovers will be delighted by the Ponies in their Stable Cake.

FUZZY BEAR CAKE

❦

Serves 30

For the cake base:

1 x all-in-one quick-mix sponge
baked in a 900 ml/1 $1/2$ pint
pudding basin (*see* page 32)
1 x all-in-one quick-mix sponge
baked in a 1.1 litre/2 pint
pudding basin
1 x all-in-one quick-mix sponge
baked in an 18 cm/7 inch,
round cake tin

To decorate:

chocolate mint stick sweets
2 batches vanilla buttercream
brown paste food colouring
2 chocolate bean sweets
1 soft prune
candles

Cut the top of the larger cake flat and place upside down on a
cake board with the dome shape uppermost. Cut a thin slice
from one side of the smaller cake. Cut the smaller round cake
into ears, arms and legs as shown in the diagram on page 245.
Assemble the pieces as shown in the diagram using chocolate
stick sweets to secure the pieces to each other.

Colour the buttercream light brown and use a little to stick the
pieces of the bear together. Place the remaining buttercream in
a large piping bag fitted with a star nozzle and pipe stars all over
the bear, making sure to cover the whole cake. Press 2 chocolate
beans into the face for eyes and a prune for his nose, then
arrange candles in front of the bear to finish.

HAPPY PIG CUPCAKES

Makes 12

For the cake base:

1 batch chocolate cupcakes
(*see* page 33)

To decorate:

1¹/₂ batches vanilla buttercream
green, brown and pink paste
food colourings
200 g/7 oz ready-to-roll sugarpaste
small amount of royal icing (optional)

Trim the tops of the cupcakes if they have peaked. Colour two thirds of the buttercream green and spoon into a large piping bag fitted with a medium plain nozzle. Pipe random lines and swirls backwards and forwards over the cupcakes to cover the tops right to the edge.

Colour the remaining buttercream dark brown and spoon into a piping bag fitted with a large plain nozzle. Pipe a wide swirl in the centre of each cupcake, leaving half the green buttercream visible. Gently rough up the brown buttercream with a knife, hollowing out the centre a little, without disturbing the green buttercream swirls.

Cut off a tiny piece of the sugarpaste and colour this dark brown to make the pigs' features. Colour the remainder pink. For the pigs, shape the pink sugarpaste into 12 circles, about 3 cm/1¹/₄ inches in diameter. Roll 12 small pieces of pink sugarpaste into balls, flatten, dampen and press into place for the pigs' snouts. Shape 24 ears from the remaining pink sugarpaste, dampen and press two onto each pig's head.

Roll tiny pieces of dark brown sugarpaste into 24 circles, dampen and press two on each pig's head for eyes. Shape 24 tiny sausages from dark brown sugarpaste, flatten, dampen and press two on each pig's snout for nostrils. Alternatively, use piped brown royal icing for these features. Carefully position a pig in the centre of each cupcake, pressing down gently into the brown buttercream.

TEDDIES` PARTY CAKE

Serves 10–12

For the cake base:

1 x 20 cm/8 inch Madeira cake
(see page 28)
6 tbsp apricot glaze

To decorate:

575 g/1¼ lb white marzipan
green, brown, pink, yellow, red
and black paste food colourings
cake varnishing gloss (optional)
350 kg/12 oz ready-to-roll
sugarpaste
icing sugar, for dusting
red royal icing tube
edible gold balls

Cut the top of the cake level and brush the cake with apricot glaze. Colour the marzipan light green and use to cover the cake (see page 62). Flute the base up, pinching between your thumb and forefinger. Brush on cake varnishing gloss, if liked, to give a shiny finish.

Roll out 125 g/4 oz sugarpaste thinly on a surface dusted with icing sugar and use to cover a 25 cm/10 inch cake board. Trim the edges then place the cake onto the covered board.

Colour 250 g/9 oz sugarpaste light brown, 25 g/1 oz pink, 25 g/1 oz yellow, 25 g/1 oz red and 25 g/1 oz black. Model the light brown sugarpaste into two bears and make pink faces and paws. Roll small black balls and press on for noses. Make white balls with small black dots for eyes.

Arrange one bear to be 'climbing' onto the cake and sit the other on top. Mould a brown barrel with scraps and mark with a skewer. Roll out white sugarpaste thinly, cut into a strip and position slightly 'ruffled' as shown.

Roll out the pink and white sugarpastes and stamp into daisies and circles. Stick to the sides of the cake, then roll small yellow balls for daisy centres and press onto the flowers. Mould the red sugarpaste into small cups and make tongues for the bears. Write your message on the white strip with red royal icing. Sprinkle the top of the cake with gold balls to finish.

FARMYARD CAROUSEL CAKE

❧

Serves 12–14

For the cake base:

1 x 20 cm/8 inch, round Madeira
cake (see page 28)
1 x 20 cm/8 inch, all-in-one quick-
mix sandwich layer (see page 30)

To decorate:

strong glue
1 piece 20 cm/8 inch long thick
wooden dowelling
white paper
thin red ribbon trim
^{1}/2 batch vanilla buttercream
1.75 kg/3^1/2 lb ready-to-roll
sugarpaste
green, blue, brown, yellow, red,
grey, pink and orange
paste food colourings
icing sugar, for dusting

Using strong glue, stick a 20 cm/8 inch thin cake board onto the length of thick wooden dowelling and leave until firmly set. Glue a strip of white paper round the dowelling, then stick round a piece of thin red ribbon. Cut the top of the large cake completely flat, spread the top and sides with buttercream and place on a thin, 30 cm/12 inch, round cake board. Trim the sandwich cake to give a sloping effect and coat with buttercream. Colour 700 g/1^1/2 lb sugarpaste green, 125 g/4 oz blue, 125 g/4 oz brown, 350 g/12 oz yellow, 125 g/4 oz red, 25 g/1 oz grey, 50 g/2 oz pink and 25 g/1 oz orange, leaving the rest white. Use the green sugarpaste to cover the large cake (see page 62). Use the trimmings to cover the edge of the cake board. Roll a thick blue sugarpaste strip to go round the cake, dampen lightly and stick in place. Roll the brown sugarpaste into thin strips and stick over the blue to form a fence. Mark with a knife for a wooden effect. Use green trimmings to make strands of grass and foliage as shown. Mould appropriately coloured sugarpastes into animals and use trimmings to make the details, as shown. Use scraps and a small daisy cutter to stamp out flowers; decorate as shown.

Stand the sandwich cake on the pole between two suitable supports, such as pudding basins, to hold it upright whilst decorating. Use the yellow sugarpaste to cover the cake. Cut out a yellow strip, 2 cm/^{3}/4 inch wide, with a fluted pasta wheel. Roll out the red sugarpaste and cut out tapering strips as shown. Stick the red and yellow strips over and around the cake with a little cold boiled water. Make a red ball for the centre and stick down. Press the cake on the pole down into the green cake, making sure it is firmly wedged, and decorate the join with green trimmings. Place the animals round the cake as shown.

KITTY FACES CUPCAKES

Makes 14–16

125 g/4 oz self-raising flour
125 g/4 oz caster sugar
125 g/4 oz soft margarine
2 medium eggs, beaten
1 tsp vanilla extract

To decorate:

1 batch buttercream
(see page 42)
pink paste food colouring
50 g/2 oz desiccated coconut
liquorice all-sorts sweets
red gel writing icing tube

Preheat the oven to 180°C/350°F/Gas Mark 4. Line two 12-hole bun trays with 12–14 paper fairy-cake cases or silicone moulds, depending on the depth of the holes.

Sift the flour into a bowl and stir together with the caster sugar. Add the margarine, eggs and vanilla extract and beat together for about 2 minutes until smooth.

Spoon into the cases and bake for 15–20 minutes until golden and firm to the touch. Turn out on a wire rack. When cool, trim the tops flat if they have peaked slightly.

Colour the buttercream pink and spread over the top of each cake. Pour the coconut onto a shallow dish. Press the top of each iced cupcake into the coconut. Cut the sweets to form pink ears, eyes, a jelly nose and whiskers and pipe on a red mouth in red gel icing. Keep in an airtight container in a cool place for 2 days.

PIGGIES IN THE MUD CAKE

Serves 14–18

For the cake base:

1 x 20 cm/8 inch, round chocolate cake (see page 27)

To decorate:

1/2 batch vanilla buttercream
450 g/1 lb ready-to-roll chocolate sugarpaste
icing sugar, for dusting
450 g/1 lb ready-to-roll white sugarpaste
green, pink and yellow paste food colourings
400 g/14 oz milk chocolate, broken into squares
28 chocolate wafer finger biscuits

Cut the cake in half, spread the bottom layer with buttercream, then sandwich the cakes back together. Spread the top and sides of the cake with buttercream. Roll out the chocolate sugarpaste on a surface dusted with icing sugar to a circle large enough to cover the top and sides of the cake. Drape the icing over, smooth down and trim the edges.

Colour 225 g/8 oz white sugarpaste light green and roll out thinly. Cover a thin cake board with the green paste, then mark with the tines of a fork to represent grass. Place the cake on the board. Colour 125 g/4 oz sugarpaste pink and model into pigs' bodies, heads and arms, and bottoms.

Melt the chocolate in a heatproof bowl standing over a pan of simmering water. Dip each chocolate wafer biscuit in the chocolate to cover, remove from the bowl and stick onto the sides of the cake. Make a rough pattern with the tines of a fork to represent wood bark while the chocolate is still wet. Repeat with the remaining biscuits. Place the pigs' bodies on top of the cake as shown. Pour the remaining melted chocolate round them to form their muddy pool.

Roll out green sugarpaste scraps to make trailing plants and leaves and stick round the sides of the pool. Roll out the remaining scraps of sugarpaste, then stamp out small coloured daisies and place on the grass. Make yellow centres for the flowers and stick in place to finish.

DUCKY DUCK CAKE

⋘⋙

Serves 10–12

For the cake base:

1 x all-in-one quick-mix sponge
baked in two 20 cm/8 inch
sandwich tins (*see* page 30)
1 x all-in-one quick-mix sponge
baked in a 15 cm/6 inch, round
tin (*see* page 30)

To decorate:

1¹/₂ batches vanilla buttercream
yellow and orange paste
food colourings
125 g/4 oz ready-to-roll sugarpaste
75 g/3 oz shredded soft coconut
thin chocolate mint stick sweets
2 white marshmallows
2 black fruit pastille sweets

Cut the large cake in half lengthways to form two half-moon shapes, sandwich together with a little buttercream and stand with the flat side uppermost. Cut the small cake as shown on page 244, and stick the head, back and tail together with buttercream as in the diagram.

Colour the remaining buttercream yellow and the sugarpaste orange. Spread the yellow buttercream over the duck to cover completely, flicking up occasionally with a palette knife to represent feathers. Toss the coconut in a little yellow food colouring, then press onto the buttercream.

Mould the orange sugarpaste into a beak shape. Press 4 chocolate stick sweets into the front of the duck's head, then press the beak onto these. Decorate the face; make two eyes with white marshmallows, then dab 2 black sweets with buttercream and stick onto the white marshmallows as shown to finish.

PONIES IN THEIR STABLE CAKE

✼

Serves 12–14

For the cake base:

1 x 20 cm/8 inch, square Madeira
cake (see page 28)

To decorate:

1.2 kg/2¹/₂ lb ready-to-roll
sugarpaste
black, brown, green, lilac,
pink and yellow paste food
colourings
¹/₂ batch vanilla buttercream
icing sugar, for dusting
cocktail sticks

Colour 700 g/1¹/₂ lb sugarpaste light grey with a little black food colouring, then colour 225 g/8 oz dark grey, 75 g/3 oz brown, 50 g/2 oz black, 25 g/1 oz green, and 15 g/¹/₂ oz each lilac, pink and yellow. Reserve a tiny amount of white. Cut the top of the cake flat if it has peaked. Cut the cake in half down the middle. Spread one half with buttercream, then sandwich one half on top of the other. Spread all over with buttercream. Spread a 25 cm/10 inch cake board thinly with a little buttercream. Thinly roll out the dark grey sugarpaste on a surface dusted with icing sugar and cover the board, trim, then mark on a tiled pattern. Use the light grey sugarpaste to thinly cover the cake (see page 62). Place the cake on the covered board. Using a round-bladed knife, mark on a wooden effect. Cut out three 'windows' at the front. Use the black sugarpaste to fill in the spaces.

Make the ponies' heads. Roll 15 g/¹/₂ oz each of black, brown and grey sugarpaste into three balls. Press the front of each ball down to elongate into a muzzle shape, then make ears from the scraps. Place each on a cocktail stick and stick into a stable window. Roll strands of contrasting sugarpaste thinly to make the manes and mark on nostrils with a skewer. Use white sugarpaste to fashion eyes and extra markings, if liked.

Roll the remaining brown sugarpaste into thin sausages and decorate the sides and roof, sticking on with a little cold boiled water. Using small cutters, make ivy leaves with the green sugarpaste and pink, yellow and lilac daisies, and decorate as shown. Press green scraps round the base of the cake and mark with a skewer for grass. Add a few small daisies to finish.

IN THE JUNGLE CAKE

Serves 10–12

For the cake base:

1 x 20 cm/8 inch Madeira cake
(see page 28)

To decorate:

1 batch vanilla buttercream
green, grey, yellow,
brown, pink and black
paste food colourings
1.25 kg/2¹/₄ lb ready-to-roll
sugarpaste
icing sugar, for dusting

Colour a quarter of the buttercream green, place in a piping bag fitted with a star nozzle and reserve. Cut the top of the cake level and spread with a little buttercream, then spread the remainder over the sides.

Colour 575 g/1¹/₄ lb sugarpaste light green and use to cover the cake (see page 62). Roll out 125 g/4 oz white sugarpaste thinly and use to cover a 25 cm/10 inch cake board. Trim, then place the cake onto the covered board. Pipe a shell border round the base of the cake with the green buttercream.

Colour 125 g/4 oz sugarpaste grey, 75 g/3 oz yellow, 50 g/2 oz brown, 25 g/1 oz dark green, 15 g/¹/₂ oz pink and 50 g/2 oz black. Model the grey sugarpaste into a round for the elephant's head, then pull out into a trunk shape. Make an oval-shaped body, short arms and legs, and flat ears. Stick the pieces together with a little cold boiled water and mark details with a skewer. Model white tusks and eyes and stick onto the elephant. Model the yellow sugarpaste into a round for the giraffe's body, then pull out to make a long neck. Make legs, ears and horns as shown. Paint the giraffe with brown dots. Make a black coil and place by the side of the cake for a snake, adding white eyes and a pink tongue. Make a zebra's head from the remaining white sugarpaste. Roll black scraps into thin sausages and place on the head for stripes, then stick on a black nose and white balls for eyes. Roll the brown sugarpaste into long, thin sausages and stick to the cake. Make small green leaves and stick near to the brown vines as shown.

PINK BUTTERFLY CAKES

❧

Makes 12

150 g/5 oz butter,
softened at room temperature
150 g/5 oz caster sugar
3 medium eggs, beaten
1 tsp vanilla extract
150 g/5 oz self-raising flour
$^{1}/_{2}$ tsp baking powder

To decorate

225 g/8 oz ready-to-roll
sugarpaste
pink and brown paste
food colourings
1 batch cream cheese frosting
(see page 44)
gel writing icing tubes

Preheat the oven to 180°C/350°F/Gas Mark 4 and line a 12-hole tray with deep paper cases.

Place the butter, sugar, eggs and vanilla extract in a bowl and then sift in the flour and baking powder. Beat together with an electric hand-mixer for about 2 minutes until pale and fluffy. Spoon into the paper cases and bake for 20–25 minutes until firm and golden. Cool on a wire rack.

To decorate, take the sugarpaste and colour 200 g/7 oz pale pink and the remainder brown. Roll out the sugarpaste thinly and, using a cutter or freehand, cut out four petal shapes for the wings for each cupcake and set them on nonstick baking parchment or clingfilm. Cut out 48 shapes altogether and leave to dry flat until firm (about 2 hours). Colour the cream cheese frosting bright pink and place in a piping bag fitted with a star nozzle.

Swirl pink icing on top of each cupcake, then press four wings on top of each. Mould the brown icing into body shapes and place on each cupcake. Pipe dots on the wings with tubes of gel writing icing. Keep for 2 days in an airtight container in a cool place.

UNDER THE SEA CAKE

Serves 12–14

For the cake base:

1 x 20 cm/8 inch, round Madeira
cake (see page 28)

To decorate:

1 batch vanilla buttercream
1.25 kg/2¹/₂ lb ready-to roll
sugarpaste
turquoise, light blue, green,
orange, pink, yellow and black
paste food colourings
icing sugar, for dusting
gold lustre powder
small birthday candles

Cut the top of the cake level, then cut in half and spread one half with a little buttercream. Sandwich the cake back together. Colour 575 g/1¹/₄ lb sugarpaste turquoise, 50 g/2 oz pale blue, 225 g/8 oz lime green, 75 g/3 oz orange, 50 g/2 oz bright pink, 25 g/1 oz yellow and 25 g/1 oz black and leave the remainder white. Use the turquoise sugarpaste to thinly cover the cake (see page 62). Roll 125 g/4 oz white sugarpaste into a thin sausage and press round the base of the cake. Mark on shell shapes with a clean, small, ridged bottle cap. Roll out a thin strip of white sugarpaste and place across the front of the cake.

Roll 25 g/1 oz blue sugarpaste into a ball. Roll the remaining blue sugarpaste into eight thin sausages, tapering the ends to a point, and mark on small circles. Place the tentacles onto the cake as shown, then place the octopus's head on top. Model a cylindrical shape for a clownfish from 25 g/1 oz orange sugarpaste. Shape flat orange fins, outlined with strips of black and white sugarpaste, mark with a knife and press in place. Make black and white eyes for the clownfish and octopus and press in place, then mark on mouths with a skewer. Cut out stars and mark on dots with a skewer to make starfish and model seashells from the white and orange sugarpastes, and dust lightly with gold lustre powder. Roll the green sugarpaste into thin strips and twist for seaweed. Roll out the pink sugarpaste and cut out holes with the top of an icing nozzle or a small, clean bottle cap for coral. Re-roll the scraps and make small coloured cones. Stick everything in place and finish with small candles pushed into scraps of pink sugarpaste.

SMILING CROCODILE

◌֍◌

Serves 25

For the cake base:

1 x 30 x 25 cm/12 x 10 inch all-in-one
quick-mix slab cake (see page 31)
2 bought mini Swiss rolls

To decorate:

chocolate mint stick sweets
2¹/₂ batches vanilla buttercream
25 g/1 oz red and 50 g/2 oz black
ready-to roll sugarpaste
icing sugar, for dusting
emerald green and leaf green paste
food colourings
2 large and 2 mini white
marshmallows
3 tbsp white royal icing (see page 50)
or 1 small tube white royal icing
125 g/4 oz golden granulated sugar
18 green jelly sweets

Cut the cake into a body, tail and four leg pieces, following the pattern on page 245. Assemble the pieces on a large board or tray, then secure the pieces together with chocolate stick sweets. Place the mini Swiss rolls in the centre of the head and stick on with a little buttercream. Roll out the black and red sugarpastes on a surface dusted with icing sugar to two thin strips, long enough to go round the mouth of the crocodile. Stick the black one round the mouth and the red one on top, as shown, with a little buttercream.

Colour three quarters of the buttercream emerald green and the remainder leaf green. Place the leaf green buttercream in a large piping bag fitted with a star nozzle and pipe stars onto the back of the body and tail filling in all the spaces. Fill the bag with the emerald green buttercream and pipe stripes around all the edges and all over the rest of the body as shown.

Position the 2 large marshmallows in front of the Swiss rolls and the 2 smaller ones at the front of the head for nostrils, then stick black sugarpaste circles onto them as shown. Place the royal icing in a small paper icing bag fitted with a straight nozzle or pipe from the tube onto the mouth area to make triangular pointed teeth. Pipe white dots onto the eyes.

Scatter the granulated sugar round the animal for sand, then stick the green jelly sweets in place for claws by the feet and onto the back of the body and tail for spines. Finish by piping over any areas that need an extra layer of green buttercream.

FRIENDLY OCTOPUS CAKE

Serves 12

For the cake base:

1 x 20 cm/8 inch, all-in-one quick-mix
sponge cake (*see* page 30)

To decorate:

1 batch vanilla buttercream
blue, orange, yellow, green, pink and
red paste food colourings
350 g/12 oz ready-to-roll sugarpaste
black food colouring pen

Trim the top of the cake level if it has peaked. Brush away any loose crumbs, then place in the freezer for 30 minutes – this will make it easier to spread with the buttercream. Colour the buttercream bright blue and, using a palette knife, spread it over the cake in an even layer. You may find it easier to spread the cake with a thin layer to begin with, then cover this with a second, thicker layer. Smooth as neatly as you can.

Colour 125 g/4 oz sugarpaste bright blue and roll a piece into a walnut-size ball to make the head of the octopus, flattening it slightly. Shape eight legs, rolling thin sausages about 4 cm/1½ inches long. Reserve the remaining blue sugarpaste. Shape two tiny pieces of white sugarpaste into circles for the eyes, mark a black pupil on each with the black food colouring pen, dampen and press into place on the head. Position the head in the centre of the cake and arrange the legs on either side, twisting them as you press them into position.

Divide the remaining sugarpaste into five equal pieces and colour the pieces orange, yellow, green, pink and red. Pull off small pieces of each, including the reserved blue, and shape or stamp into thin circles measuring about 1 cm/½ inch across – you need about 16 circles in total. Press these over the top and sides of the cake. Roll the remaining pieces of coloured sugarpaste into balls about the size of a large pea, dampen and press them around the base of the cake so they are touching.

LADYBIRD CAKE

❀

Serves 20

For the cake base:

1 x 23 cm/9 inch, all-in-one quick-mix sponge (*see* page 30)
450 g/1 lb apricot glaze
1 x 15 cm/6 inch, round all-in-one quick-mix sponge

To decorate:

1.7 kg/3³/₄ lb ready-to-roll sugarpaste
blue, red, black and green paste food colourings
icing sugar, for dusting
¹/₂ batch vanilla buttercream
confectioner's glaze

Trim the top of the large cake level if it has peaked, then brush half the apricot glaze over the top and sides of the cake. Colour 900 g/2 lb of the sugarpaste pale blue and use to cover the large cake (*see* page 62). Transfer to a cake board or plate. Trim the smaller cake into a dome shape, then cut a ridge down the centre for the ladybird's body. Brush the remaining apricot glaze over the cake. Colour 400 g/14 oz sugarpaste red and use to cover the smaller cake. Spread the centre of the larger cake with buttercream and lift the smaller cake on top. Reserve a very small amount of the remaining sugarpaste and colour half of the rest black and half green.

Roll out the green sugarpaste and cut out blades of grass with a sharp knife. Dampen and press them around the bottom edge of the larger cake. Shape the ladybird's head from a ball of black sugarpaste. Shape two antennae, stick onto the head with edible glue and leave to set. Shape six legs and brush these and the head and antennae with confectioner's glaze. Cut out about 12 thin circles from black sugarpaste, 1 cm/¹/₂ inch in diameter. Dampen and press over the body. Shape two small pieces of white sugarpaste into circles for eyes, with smaller black pieces for pupils, dampen and press into place. Shape a mouth from a small sausage of white sugarpaste. Colour a tiny amount of white sugarpaste pink using just a dot of red colouring and roll into two balls. Dampen the mouth and press into place with the two small balls of pink sugarpaste at each end. Fix the head and legs in place with a little cold boiled water. Colour the remaining buttercream green, spoon it into a piping bag fitted with a fine plain nozzle and pipe wiggly lines around the base of the ladybird for 'grass' to finish.

LAZY GIRAFFE CAKE

❧

Serves 16

For the cake base:

1 x 20 cm/8 inch, round, all-in-one
quick-mix sponge mixture baked
in an oval cake tin measuring
about 24 x 17 cm/9^1/$_2$ x 6^1/$_2$ inches
rectangular cake card measuring
about 33 x 23 cm/13 x 9 inches
6 tbsp apricot glaze

To decorate:

1.4 kg/3 lb ready-to-roll sugarpaste
icing sugar, for dusting
red, brown, blue and orange paste
food colourings
black sugarcraft pen
^{1}/$_2$ batch royal icing (see page 50)

Trim the top of the cake level if it has peaked. Lift it onto the cake card and brush the top and sides with the apricot glaze. Brush the board around the cake with a little water so the overlap of sugarpaste will stick to it. Roll out 900 g/2 lb of the sugarpaste on a board dusted with icing sugar and use to cover the cake (see page 62). Press down some overlap onto the board, trimming it neatly. Using a scroll-patterned embossing tool, mark a pattern all over the sugarpaste. Leave for 12 hours, or longer, until firm.

Colour a quarter of the remaining sugarpaste deep red, roll out and, using small cutters of different sizes, stamp out 20 flowers and 20 hearts. Press a cocktail stick in the centre of each flower and hollow out the centres of the hearts with a sugarcraft bone tool. Colour the remaining sugarpaste light brown and shape an oblong about 9 cm/3^1/$_2$ inches long for the giraffe's head. Shape as shown, smoothing a sugarcraft ball tool over it where necessary, and make a cut for the mouth. Once firm, use a small paintbrush and dark brown colouring to highlight the mouth, and lighter brown colour to paint on the nostrils. Shape two circles of white sugarpaste for the eyes, dampen and press in place. Draw on eyebrows, eyelashes and pupils using a black sugarcraft pen. Colour two pinhead-size pieces of sugarpaste blue and press onto each pupil. Shape two tiny horns and fix on the head with cold boiled water. Roll out the remaining light brown sugarpaste to a sausage about 23 cm/9 inches long for the neck and arrange it as shown. Fix the neck and head in place with royal icing. Shape two small ears, dampen and press on the sides of the head. Leave until the neck has set firm before painting on markings with orange colouring. Finally, fix the flowers and hearts in place with a little royal icing.

BUZZY BEE CUPCAKES

Makes 12

1 batch chocolate cupcakes
(*see* page 33)

To decorate:

1 batch vanilla buttercream
green, hot pink, pale lavender,
yellow and black paste food
colourings
200 g/7 oz ready-to-roll sugarpaste
icing sugar, for dusting

Trim the tops of the cupcakes if they have peaked during baking. Colour the buttercream green and spoon into a large piping bag fitted with a medium plain nozzle. Pipe random lines and swirls backwards and forwards over the cupcakes to cover the tops almost to the edge.

Reserve a small piece of the sugarpaste for the bees' wings. Divide the rest of the sugarpaste into four equal pieces and colour them hot pink, pale lavender, yellow anda black. Roll out the hot pink and lavender sugarpaste separately on a board dusted with icing sugar and cut out 12 blossoms from each, using a six-petal flower cutter, about 2.5 cm/ 1 inch across. Roll tiny pieces of yellow sugarpaste into balls, flatten them, dampen the base of each and press into the centre of the blossoms. Arrange a blossom of each colour on top of the cupcakes, pressing them down gently into the buttercream.

Shape 12 ovals, about 2.5 cm/1 inch long, from the yellow sugarpaste to make the bees' bodies. Wrap two strips of black sugarpaste around each, dampening the undersides to fix them in place. Roll 24 small rounds from black sugarpaste, dampen and press into place for eyes. Roll 12 small sausages of black sugarpaste, flatten, dampen and press into place for smiley mouths. Shape 24 wings from the reserved white sugarpaste, dampen and press two on the back of each bee. Brush the underside of each bee with water and position in the centre of the cupcakes, or fix in place with a dab of buttercream.

CHEEKY MICE CAKE

Serves 8–10

For the cake base:

1 x 18 cm/7 inch, square chocolate
sponge cake (*see* page 27)

To decorate:

1¹/₂ batches cream cheese frosting
(*see* page 44)
yellow, pink and purple paste
food colouring
225 g/8 oz ready-to-roll sugarpaste

Trim the top of the cake flat if it has peaked. Colour the cream cheese frosting yellow and liberally spread over the top and sides of the cake, making it as smooth as you can. Place on a flat plate or board and press a round item such as a plastic bottle top into the frosting a few times to give a holey effect.

Reserving a little white for the eyes, colour 75 g/3 oz sugarpaste pink and the rest purple. Take a small piece (less than one quarter) of each, colour a darker shade and reserve.

Model the mice as shown using a ball about two thirds of each lighter colour for the bodies, small flattened balls for the ears and the rest for the heads. Make the eyes from tiny balls of the reserved white sugarpaste, and pupils, noses, legs and tails made from sausages of the darker shade of sugarpaste attaching, them with a little cold boiled water.

Place the mice on the corner of the cake and press a scraping of cream cheese frosting in their paws to finish.

BEAUTIFUL BUTTERFLY CAKE

Serves 30
(including the cupcakes)

For the cupcakes:
1 batch vanilla cupcakes
(see page 33)

To decorate:
white paper
1 batch royal icing using packet mix
pink, yellow and blue paste food
colourings
1 batch vanilla buttercream

For the large cake:
1 x 30 x 25 x 5 cm/12 x 10 x 2 inch
all-in-one quick-mix sponge slab
cake (see page 31)

To decorate:
^{1}/$_2$ batch vanilla buttercream
900 g/2 lb light pink, 175 g/6 oz
dark pink, 125 g/4 oz light yellow,
175g/6 oz dark yellow and 125 g/
4 oz blue ready-to-roll sugarpaste
icing sugar, for dusting

To make the small butterflies, draw round the pattern on page 251 onto a sheet of white paper. Place the paper under a sheet of waxed paper. Divide the royal icing between four bowls, leave one white and colour the remaining icing pink, yellow and blue. Place the white icing in a paper icing bag fitted with a no 1 straight nozzle and carefully pipe round the outline of 12 sets of wings, making a neat join. Add a few drops of water to each of the colours to make a runny consistency. Place a no 2 straight nozzle in a small paper icing bag and fill with blue icing. Pipe the icing into the wings outline, flooding and spreading to the edges. Repeat with the pink and yellow icing, to make four of each. While the icing is still wet, pipe different-coloured dots onto the wings, then leave to dry for 3 hours. Colour the buttercream pink, place in a large piping bag fitted with a star nozzle and pipe onto the cupcakes in swirls. Peel away the waxed paper from the wings. Pipe a body onto each cupcake with the remaining white icing, then place two wings in each.

For the large cake, cut the cake into the shape illustrated on page 244. Spread all over with buttercream. Roll out the light pink sugarpaste on a surface dusted with icing sugar and use to cover the cake (see page 62). Place on a cake board. Following the design on page 244, roll and cut out the dark pink, yellow and blue sugarpastes to decorate the wings. Roll out all the remaining sugarpaste pieces thinly and stamp out large, medium and small daisies with a daisy stamp. Dampen all the shapes lightly with a little cold boiled water and press into position as shown.

MONKEY ISLAND CAKE

✦

Serves 30

For the cake base:

1 x 20 cm/8 inch, round
Madeira cake (see page 28)
1 x 15 cm/6 inch, round
Madeira cake

To decorate:

½ batch vanilla buttercream
1.2 kg/2½ lb ready-to-roll sugarpaste
green, brown, red and yellow paste
food colourings
icing sugar, for dusting
700 g/1½ lb marzipan
small tubes black and red
piping icing
thin liquorice sticks

Cut the tops of the cakes level if they have peaked, then cut each in half. Sandwich back together with a little buttercream, then spread the remaining buttercream thinly over the outsides. Colour all but a small piece of the sugarpaste bright green. Roll out 700 g/1½ lb on a surface dusted with icing sugar and use to cover the large cake (see page 62). Use 450 g/1 lb to cover the small cake. Place the small cake on a 15 cm/6 inch, thin cake board, place on top of the large cake and mark all over with the back of a fork. Push green scraps through a garlic press to make grass and press round the bases of both cakes.

Colour 350 g/12 oz of the marzipan brown, 125 g/4 oz beige, 50 g/2 oz red, 125 g/4 oz yellow and 50 g/2 oz green. Model the yellow into bunches of bananas, open banana skins and a snake. Use white sugarpaste or plain marzipan to fashion pieces of 'peeled' banana to stick onto open banana skins. Make two large and four small monkeys. Roll round body pieces and long, thin sausages for arms, legs and tails. Make beige ovals and stick to the body parts. Make brown and beige heads, beige ears and beige mouths and cut across to open them. Roll small white balls for eyes and red strips for tongues. Pipe small black dots on the eyes and mark nostrils on the faces with a skewer. Assemble as shown, then place on the cake with the bananas.

Roll the remaining brown marzipan into long, thin strips and wrap around the liquorice sticks to make tree trunks. Bend and place on the cake, securing with cocktail sticks. Make green marzipan palm leaves, snipping the edges with scissors, and press onto the trees. Roll long, thin, green sausages for vines and red and yellow scraps to stamp out thin daisies. Arrange all as shown.

FARMYARD FRIENDS CUPCAKES

✿

Makes 20

For the cakes:

1½ batches (to make 20 small)
chocolate cupcakes
(*see* page 33)
4 tbsp apricot glaze

To decorate:

1.1 kg/2 lb 6 oz ready-to-roll
sugarpaste
green, pink, yellow and brown
paste food colourings
icing sugar, for dusting
black sugarcraft pen

Trim the tops of the cupcakes if they have peaked, then brush over the apricot glaze. Colour 350 g/12 oz sugarpaste pale green and roll out on a board dusted with icing sugar. Using a fluted cutter slightly larger than the tops of the cupcakes, stamp out 12 circles and press into place.

To make the animal decorations, divide the remaining sugarpaste into four pieces (one of which is slightly bigger than the rest) and colour one pink, one yellow and one brown, leaving the bigger piece white.

Roll out all the sugarpastes thinly. Using the photograph as a guide for colours and the templates on page 249 as a guide for shapes, cut out four bodies and heads of each animal (pig, sheep, cow, horse and chicken), and the appropriate number of ears, snouts and beaks. Roll tiny sausages of brown sugarpaste for the chicken nests. Dampen the pieces with cold boiled water and press on top of the cupcakes.

Draw on facial features, body markings and hooves where appropriate with a black sugarcraft pen. Use a cocktail stick to mark nostrils and mane and tail textures.

Finish by adding tiny coloured dots of sugarpaste onto some of the animals, fixing them in place with a dab of water.

Fantasy & Adventure

Kids have boundless imaginations and an appetite for dreaming up all kinds of fantasy worlds and adventures; pirate ship missions and magic genies to angels and princesses and everything in between. With these fantastic projects, you can bring these imaginary worlds to life in cake form. The Colourful Candyland Cake is a dream come true for sweetie fans, whilst the Princess Castle Cake is the epitome of perfection for aspiring royalty.

REGAL ROSE CUPCAKES

Makes 12

For the cakes:

1 batch vanilla cupcakes
(*see* page 33)
4 tbsp apricot glaze

To decorate:

700 g/1¹/₂ lb ready-to-roll
sugarpaste
pink, green and yellow paste food
colourings
icing sugar, for dusting
edible glue
white and yellow sugar sprinkles

Trim the tops of the cupcakes level if they have peaked, then brush over the apricot glaze. Colour 500 g/1 lb 2 oz sugarpaste deep pink. Reserve 150 g/5 oz and roll out the rest on a board dusted with icing sugar. Using a plain cutter the same size as the tops of the cupcakes, stamp out 12 circles and press one circle on top of each cupcake, smoothing it down neatly.

Use the reserved pink sugarpaste to model six roses (*see* page 63). Colour half the remaining sugarpaste pale green, roll out and cut out 24 leaves with a cutter or small, sharp knife. Mark a vein down the centre of each leaf with a knife or cocktail stick, taking care not to cut the leaves in half.

Colour the rest of the sugarpaste yellow, roll out thinly and cut out six strips measuring about 6.5 cm/2¹/₂ inches long by 2 cm/³/₄ inch wide. Using a small, sharp knife, cut 'V' shapes into one long edge of each to make the tops of the crowns. Curl each strip round in a circle and stick the ends together with edible glue.

Brush the edges of the sugarpaste covering the cupcakes with edible glue and press on the sugar sprinkles. Stick the crowns in the centre of six cupcakes with edible glue, brush the bottom edges of the crowns with more glue and press sprinkles around each. Stick the roses and the leaves on top of the remaining cupcakes with edible glue to finish.

ONE-EYED PIRATE CAKE

❧

Serves 10–12

For the cake base:

1 x 13 cm/5 inch, square almond
Madeira cake baked in a 2 litre/
4 pint bowl (see page 28)
4 tbsp apricot glaze

To decorate:

1.3 kg/2³/₄ lb ready-to-roll
sugarpaste
flesh, red and black paste food
colourings
icing sugar, for dusting

Trim the top of the cake level if it has peaked, then brush the apricot glaze over the domed side of the cake. Colour 900 g/2 lb sugarpaste flesh toned, roll it out on a board dusted with icing sugar and use to cover the cake (see page 62). Gather up the trimmings and roll two small balls about 1 cm/¹/₂ inch in diameter. Flatten the balls with your fingers to make a nose and left ear, dampen the underside and side respectively and press in place.

Colour two thirds of the remaining sugarpaste red to make the headscarf and roll out very thinly to a semicircle large enough to fit over the top third of the cake. Trim the bottom edge of the semicircle straight, dampen the underside and lift into position, smoothing it down, then trim. Using the trimmings, roll a small ball about 1 cm/¹/₂ inch in diameter. Roll out a small piece of the paste and cut a strip, 2.5 cm/1 inch wide. Cut a 'V' shape into one end of the strip. Dampen both the ball and the strip and press into place to make the knot at the end of the pirate's scarf. Roll out half the remaining sugarpaste very thinly and cut out eight circles, 1.5 cm/³/₄ inch in diameter (if you don't have a cutter this size, use the base of a small icing nozzle). Dampen the undersides and press into position over the pirate's scarf.

Cut another slightly smaller round measuring about 1 cm/¹/₂ inch for the eye, dampen and fix into place. Colour the rest of the sugarpaste black and roll out very thinly. Cut out a long, thin strip and a round for the eye patch and a small, heart-shaped piece for the pupil, dampen and press into place. Using the tip of a sharp knife, mark the pirate's mouth to finish.

MAGIC GARDEN CAKE

༺ఞ༻

Serves 20

For the cake base:

1 x 15 cm/6 inch, round lemon
Madeira cake (*see* page 28)
1 x 23 cm/9 inch, round lemon
Madeira cake
6 tbsp apricot glaze

To decorate:

15 cm/6 inch, round cake board
1.8 kg/4 lb ready-to-roll sugarpaste
blue, green, pink, yellow and purple
paste food colourings
icing sugar, for dusting
edible silver balls
black and green sugarcraft pens

Trim the tops of the cakes level if they have peaked, then brush the apricot glaze over the cakes. Colour 450 g/1 lb sugarpaste pale blue and use to cover the small cake. Trim the bottom neatly and lift the cake onto the cake card. Colour 900 g/2 lb sugarpaste pale green and use to cover the larger cake. Transfer this to a board or plate and put the smaller cake on top. Colour the trimmings of pale blue sugarpaste a deeper shade of blue. Roll into balls, about the size of a small pea, dampen these with cold boiled water and press them around the base of the smaller cake. Colour the trimmings of pale green sugarpaste a deeper shade of green.

Colour half the remaining sugarpaste deep pink and roll out a strip 1 cm/ 1/2 inch wide and long enough to go around the large cake. Mark lines along the edges of the strip, dampen and press around the base of the cake. Colour small pieces of the remaining sugarpaste pale pink, yellow and pale purple, leaving one piece white. Cut leaves and flower stalks from the green sugarpaste, then cut flowers from the pink or white sugarpaste and butterflies from the purple sugarpaste using butterfly cutters. Dampen the cut-outs and position as shown. Add flower centres using white or pink sugarpaste and details on the butterflies using yellow, pink and blue sugarpaste. Shape bees from yellow and white sugarpastes and press around the sides of the larger cake. Draw antennae on the butterflies (with edible silver balls on the tips) using a black sugarcraft pen and small trails of dots around the butterflies with a green pen, and mark lines on the wings with a knife. Add details to the flowers with the black pen and on the leaves with the green pen to finish.

SLEEPING ANGEL CAKE

Serves 40

For the cake base:

1 x 23 cm/9 inch, square
Madeira cake (*see* page 28)
1 x 16 cm/6 inch, square
Madeira cake

To decorate:

1 batch vanilla buttercream
1.8 kg/4 lb ready-to-roll sugarpaste
pink, flesh and brown paste
food colourings
icing sugar, for dusting
2 tbsp royal icing (*see* page 50)

Trim the tops of the cakes if they have peaked. Cut each cake in half horizontally and spread one half with a little buttercream. Place the other layer on top and spread the remaining buttercream over the top and sides of the cakes.

Colour 1.25 kg/2½ lb sugarpaste light pink. Use 875 g/1¾ lb pink sugarpaste to cover the large cake (*see* page 62), then place on a 30 cm/12 inch cake board. Repeat to cover the small cake with the remaining pink sugarpaste and place on a thin cake board. Place the small cake on top of the larger one.

Colour 50 g/2 oz sugarpaste flesh toned. Roll half into a ball for the angel's head, two sausages for arms and two tiny balls for feet. Roll 50 g/2 oz white sugarpaste into a triangular shape for the body, then position the pieces onto the small cake as shown. Mark a face on the angel with a skewer, then colour the royal icing brown and place in a piping bag fitted with a no 1 straight nozzle. Pipe strands on the head for hair.

Roll the remaining white sugarpaste out thinly and cut into thin strips 2 cm/¾ inch wide. Dampen the underside of each strip with a little cold boiled water and press round the base of the large and small cakes. Make bows (*see* page 63) with trailing ribbons for each of the cake corners. Re-roll the trimmings and cut out small stars with a star cutter, along with two little wings. Stick the stars onto both the cakes as shown, in a cascade, one on top of the angel's head and the wings on her back.

FAIRY DUST FLOWER CUPCAKES

Makes 12

For the cakes:

1 batch vanilla cupcakes
(see page 33)

To decorate:

125 g/4 oz ready-to-roll sugarpaste
pink and blue paste food colourings
icing sugar, for dusting
1 batch vanilla buttercream
25 g/1 oz granulated sugar

Colour 25 g/1 oz sugarpaste deep pink and the remainder blue.
Roll out the blue sugarpaste on a board or surface dusted with
icing sugar and cut out 12 daisies using a medium daisy cutter.
Mould the pink sugarpaste into 12 small balls and mark the
centre of each with the tip of a small knife to represent the centre
of a flower. Press the petals upwards to curl them, then lightly
dampen the underside of each pink centre and press into the
daisies. Leave to dry for 1 hour on nonstick baking parchment.

Colour the buttercream pale pink and the granulated sugar
a deeper shade of pink with a little pink paste food colouring.

Place the pink buttercream in a large piping bag fitted with
a plain nozzle. Pipe a plain swirl round the outside of each
cupcake, then fill in the centre by piping a large round swirl.

Just before serving, spread the pink sugar out onto a saucer and
dip the outside of each cake in the sugar, lightly coating round
all the sides. Place a daisy in the centre of each cake to finish.

PRINCESS CASTLE CAKE

Serves 40–50

For the cake base:

2 x 12 cm/5 inch Madeira cakes
2 x 20 cm/8 inch Madeira cakes

To decorate:

hundreds and thousands
5 ice-cream cones
¹/₄ batch royal icing (see page 50)
3¹/₂ batches vanilla buttercream,
coloured pale pink
150 g/5 oz ready-to-roll sugarpaste
cream paste food colouring
Iced Gems
jelly sweets
50 g/2 oz desiccated coconut
green liquid food colouring
coloured paper and cocktail sticks,
for the flags

Pour the hundreds and thousands out on a sheet of nonstick baking parchment. Coat the ice-cream cones with royal icing and roll them in the hundreds and thousands to cover.

Trim the tops of the cakes flat if they have peaked and sandwich them together in pairs with a small amount of buttercream to make deep cakes. Cover both cakes with the remaining buttercream and mark lines in it with a fork as shown. Place the larger cake on a 30 cm/12 inch cake board and the smaller cake on a thin, 12 cm/5 inch, square cake board and place it on top of the larger cake.

Colour the sugarpaste cream, then roll long, thin sausages to go round the bases of the cakes and press into place. Roll out and cut out a square of sugarpaste for the gate. Press this into place and make the drawbridge from thin sausages of sugarpaste as shown.

Position the decorated ice-cream cones, Iced Gems and jelly sweets around the cake as shown.

Put the desiccated coconut in a bowl and, while stirring, add drops of green food colouring until the desired colour is achieved. Scatter the coconut around the edge of the board. Add flags made from coloured paper stuck on cocktail sticks – why not add a name or message on them too? Push the flags into the tops of the cones to finish.

COLOURFUL CANDYLAND CAKE

❧

Serves 80

For the cake base:

1 each 15 cm/6 inch, 20 cm/8 inch and 25 cm/10 inch, round Madeira cake (see page 28)

To decorate:

1½ batches vanilla buttercream
3 kg/6 lb 6 oz ready-to-roll sugarpaste
icing sugar, for dusting
yellow, pink, blue, purple, green and red paste food colourings
candles

Trim the top of the cakes flat if they have peaked and spread the buttercream over the top and sides. Colour 1.7 kg/3 lb 11 oz sugarpaste yellow and use to cover the cakes (see page 62). Place the small cake on a 15 cm/6 inch thin cake board, the medium cake on a 20 cm/8 inch thin cake board and stack the cakes on a large board (see page 69).

Colour 700 g/1½ lb sugarpaste pink, roll one third into a ball and roll out on a board dusted with icing sugar. Cut a circle slightly larger than the top cake and use fluted cutter or pastry wheel to cut semicircles from the edges as shown. Dampen the top of the cake with a cold boiled water and drape over the pink circle, easing it down the sides. Repeat with strips of pink sugarpaste to cover the visible top edges of each cake. Reserve the offcuts.

Use 150 g/5 oz white sugarpaste to model the two cats as shown (or use a mould if you have one). Keeping some of it white for details, colour the remaining sugarpaste in batches of blue, purple, green and a little red. Roll these out, then cut out the doors and windows on the castle as shown and attach with a little cold boiled water. Press markings into them with a knife and star stamps. Add coloured details to the cats.

Use up all the offcuts, creating spirals and balls topped with a white cut-out daisy and coloured centre. Press these onto wooden skewers and push into balls of green sugarpaste around the board. Add candles to finish.

PRINCESS & THE FROG CAKE

❧

Serves 10–12

For the cake base:

1 x 22 cm/9 inch, round all-in-one quick-mix sponge made in a pudding basin (see page 32)

To decorate:

1.25 kg/2 lb 13 oz ready-to-roll sugarpaste
green, pink, purple and yellow paste food colourings
1/2 batch vanilla buttercream

Colour 30 g/1 1/4 oz sugarpaste green and model a 4 cm/1 1/2 inch high frog, marking the features with a knife and adding tiny balls of white for the eyes. Colour 100 g/3 1/2 oz sugarpaste deep pink and 900 g/2 lb sugarpaste light purple. Make 12 tiny, 1 cm/1/2 inch pink roses (see page 63). Use the rest of the pink and a little of the purple to model the crowns as shown, supporting them with balls of clingfilm or cotton wool while drying.

Trim the top of the cake flat if it has peaked and turn upside down. Spread the buttercream over the top and sides. Place on a large cake board or flat plate. Roll 750 g/1 1/2 lb purple sugarpaste to a 40 cm/16 inch round and lift onto the cake loosely, lifting and crimping the paste to fall into gentle folds. Tuck and trim round the base. Take 100 g/3 1/2 oz of the purple sugarpaste and model it into the shape of the body. Attach two smaller balls on each side with a little cold boiled water and stick the torso on top of the cake.

Colour two thirds of the remaining sugarpaste pale pink and the rest yellow. Model the head and arms and stick these, together with the frog, into place. Model locks of yellow hair and paint features on the faces using the black and purple colourings and a very fine-tipped paintbrush.

Roll the remaining purple sugarpaste and offcuts into thin strands and, with a little water, stick them round the bottom of the dress in groups of three to create the swags. Add a sugar rose between each swag to finish.

DREAM CAROUSEL CAKE

❧

Serves 10–12

For the cake base:

1 x 22 cm/9 inch, round Madeira
cake (*see* page 28)

To decorate:

450 g/1 lb flower paste
1.1 kg/2 lb 6 oz ready-to-roll
sugarpaste
pink, green and brown paste
food colourings
stiff white card
icing sugar, for dusting
1/2 batch vanilla buttercream
3 white plastic cake dowels
1/2 batch royal icing (*see* page 50)
bought fabric flowers and ribbons

Using the flower paste and a silicon mould (*see* page 55) make three horses. Leave to dry. Colour the sugarpaste pink.

Cut a 25 cm/10 inch diameter circle out of stiff white card and cut a slit into the centre. Overlap the cut edges slightly and staple or stick together to create a shallow cone that will fit on a thin, 22 cm/9 inch cake board. Secure it to the board with a couple of balls of pink sugarpaste. Roll out 300 g/11 oz pink sugarpaste on a surface dusted with icing sugar and cover the cone and the edge of the board. Trim and crimp a pattern around the edge.

Trim the top of the cake flat if it has peaked and spread the buttercream over the top and sides. Use the remaining sugarpaste to cover the cake (*see* page 68). Place on a 28 cm/11 inch cake board and crimp a design to match the roof.

Make a cylinder of white card to fit in the centre of the cake and press this and three white plastic cake dowels into place onto the top of the cake.

Colour dessertspoonfuls of royal icing pale green, deep pink and brown and pipe the tiny leaves, deep pink swags (on the roof) and a message. Colour the remaining royal icing pink and add the pale swags, then attach all the ribbons and flowers with it as shown. Prop the horses in place, balance the roof on top and add a ribbon and bow around the base to finish.

SECRET GARDEN CUPCAKES

⊂⊛⊃

Makes 12

For the cakes:

! batch vanilla cupcakes
(*see* page 33)

To decorate:

75 g/3 oz ready-to-roll sugarpaste
pink and green paste food colourings
icing sugar, for dusting
1 batch vanilla buttercream
2 tbsp royal icing (*see* page 50)
coloured pink, or a small tube of
pink royal icing

Colour 25 g/1 oz sugarpaste deep pink, 25 g/1 oz light pink and leave the remainder white. Roll out the deep pink paste on a board or surface dusted with icing sugar and cut out 12 daisies using a medium daisy stamp. Press the petals upwards to curl them, then leave to dry for 1 hour on nonstick baking parchment.

Trim the tops of the cakes flat if they have peaked. Colour the buttercream bright green, then place in a paper piping bag fitted with a leaf nozzle and pipe small green leaves all over the top of each cake, carefully filling in all the spaces. Place a deep pink, light pink and white daisy in the centre of each cake.

To finish, place the royal icing in a small paper piping bag fitted with a plain nozzle, or use a piping tube, and pipe a small dot in the centre of each daisy.

GENIE LAMP CAKE

cԍ

Serves 18

For the cake base:

1 x 22 cm/8¹/₂ inch square
Madeira cake (*see* page 28)

To decorate:

¹/₂ batch vanilla buttercream
1.2 kg/2 lb 10 oz ready-to-roll
sugarpaste
pink, brown, blue and purple paste
food colourings
pink spray food colouring (optional)
icing sugar, for dusting
gold lustre powder
³/₄ batch royal icing (*see* page 50)
blue ribbon frill

Trim the top of the cake flat if it has peaked and spread with buttercream.

Colour 1 kg/2¹/₄ lb sugarpaste pink and use it to cover the cake, following the instructions on page 62, then place on a 30 cm/12 inch cake board. If liked, spray pink colouring around the sides of the cake, and leave to dry.

Colour the remaining sugarpaste light brown. Roll out thinly on a surface dusted with icing sugar and, using the template (*see* page 250), cut out the lamp shape. Dust with gold lustre powder and lift onto the cake. When you are happy with the positioning, lift up a few edges and brush a little cold boiled water underneath to stick the lamp to the cake.

Colour a small amount of royal icing light brown and, using a fine writing nozzle, pipe the details on the lamp.

Colour one third of the royal icing blue. Using a medium writing nozzle, pipe the curlicque design around the cake, plus the dots on the lamp as shown. Attach the ribbon frill around the base of the cake (*see* page 64 if you prefer to make the frill from sugarpaste).

Colour the remaining royal icing purple and, using a star nozzle, pipe shells around the base of the cake. Use the last bit in a small paper piping bag (*see* page 58) to pipe the purple dots on the lamp. Lightly brush gold lustre powder on the piping around the lamp to finish.

PRETTY PRINCESS CAKE

Serves 8–12

For the cake base:

1 x 18 cm/7 inch, round rich
chocolate cake (*see* page 27)

To decorate:

¹/₄ batch chocolate buttercream
1.1 kg/2 lb 8 oz ready-to-roll
sugarpaste
brown, cream, flesh, chestnut, pink
and black paste food colourings
1 Walnut Whip
icing sugar, for dusting
4 silver or pearl dragees
6 candles

Trim the top of the cake flat if it has peaked and spread the buttercream over the top and sides. Colour 600 g/1 lb 5 oz sugarpaste brown and use to cover the cake (*see* page 62). Trim (reserving the offcuts) and place on a 25 cm/10 inch, square cake board. Remove the walnut from the Walnut Whip, trim the bottom edge inwards and chill to avoid a sticky mess!

Colour 165 g/5¹/₂ oz of the sugarpaste cream, 100 g/3¹/₂ oz flesh toned, 40 g/1¹/₂ oz chestnut brown and 250 g/9 oz pink. Roll out 25 g/1 oz of the cream sugarpaste on a board or surface dusted with icing sugar, then cut out hearts and stick to the cake with a little cold boiled water. Roll half the remaining cream sugarpaste into a ball, flatten, roll out and quickly wrap around the Walnut Whip, covering it. Place it in the centre of the cake for the body and press the pearl dragees down the front. Take a ball of the flesh sugarpaste, model the head, creating features with bits of pink and brown, and stick on top of the body with cold boiled water. Using the remaining cream and flesh sugarpastes, model the rest of the figure as shown, starting with the legs, then the skirt, sleeves and arms. Use the chestnut sugarpaste for the hair and paint on the eyes with black food colouring.

Using the pink sugarpaste, roll out a strip to fit around the base of the cake and press into place. Use the rest to make a bow (*see* page 63) and press into place. Model a tiny pair of wings with any pink offcuts and place on the board. Press six candles into balls of the brown sugarpaste offcuts and place around the board to finish.

VINTAGE STYLE CUPCAKES

✿

Makes 24

For the cakes:

2 batches vanilla cupcakes
(*see* page 33)

To decorate:

125 g/4 oz ready-to-roll sugarpaste
2 batches vanilla buttercream
pink paste food colouring
selection of pearls and small jewels

Roll the sugarpaste until flexible, then take a pea-size ball and roll into a cone shape. Take another ball and flatten out into a petal shape. Wrap the petal round the cone and continue to add petals to make an open rose (*see* page 63). Trim the base and leave to dry in an egg box lined with crumpled foil for 2 hours to firm. Make three roses.

Trim the tops of the cakes flat if they have peaked. Colour the buttercream a delicate pale pink then place half in a large piping bag fitted with a large star nozzle. Pipe the buttercream onto the cakes in large swirls. Refill the bag and continue piping onto all the cakes.

Place the cupcakes on a large tray or flat serving platter in the shape of a dress, then place the roses in a belt arrangement with the pearls and jewels, as shown.

TIERED PRINCESS BIRTHDAY CAKE

꧁꧂

Serves 20

For the cake base:

1 x 15 cm/6 inch, round almond
Madeira cake (*see* page 28)
1 x 23 cm/9 inch, round almond
Madeira cake
6 tbsp apricot glaze

To decorate:

1.8 kg/4 lb ready-to-roll sugarpaste
blue, purple and pink paste food
colourings
15 cm/6 inch, round cake card
icing sugar, for dusting
small quantity blue royal icing

Trim the tops of the cakes level if they have peaked, then brush the apricot glaze over the cakes. Colour 1.4 kg/3 lb sugarpaste blue. Roll out two thirds on a board dusted with icing sugar and use to cover the larger cake (*see* page 62). Trim the bottom neatly and transfer the cake to a board or plate. Cover the smaller cake in the same way with blue sugarpaste and lift it onto the cake card. Lift the smaller cake on top of the larger one.

Colour half the remaining sugarpaste purple and half deep pink. Roll out the purple and, using a small, sharp knife, cut out diamonds the same size as the depth of the smaller cake. Dampen the diamonds and press them around the sides of the cake so they are just touching. Using the templates on page 253 cut out four fairy castle shapes from the purple sugarpaste. Roll out the pink sugarpaste and use the templates, cut out four slippers and one crown. Dampen the castle and slipper shapes and press them alternately around the sides of the larger cake. Dampen the crown shape and press onto the centre of the top of the smaller cake. Cut small triangles from the pink sugarpaste, dampen and press around the top edge of the cake. Roll the remaining pink sugarpaste into pea-size balls, dampen and press around the base of the smaller cake.

Spoon the blue royal icing into a small piping bag fitted with a star nozzle and pipe tiny rosettes between the pink triangles, and shells between the fairy castles and the slippers.

OVER THE RAINBOW CUPCAKES

Makes 12

For the cakes:

1 batch vanilla cupcake mixture
(*see* page 33)

To decorate:

red, yellow, green, pink and blue
paste food colourings
flat, thin toffee strips or bought
rainbow strip sweet
caster sugar
150 ml/¹/₄ pint whipping cream

Make up a batch of cupcake mixture (*see* page 33) and divide it between three bowls. Colour one batch red, one yellow and one green.

Line a muffin tray with paper cases and place a layer of green cake mixture in the base of each case. Spoon a layer of yellow mixture on top, then top each case with a layer of red mixture. Bake following the instructions on page 33 until the cakes are well risen and springy to the touch. Cool for a few minutes, then turn out onto a wire rack to cool.

If you are not using bought rainbow strip sweets, cut the strips of toffee into 8 cm/3¹/₄ inch lengths. Carefully paint on red stripes, leave to dry for a few minutes, then paint on yellow, green, pink and blue stripes, allowing the colouring to dry in between. Sprinkle the strips with caster sugar on both sides.

Whip the cream until stiff and place in a piping bag fitted with a plain nozzle. Pipe two blobs onto each cake, then carefully bend the bought rainbow strip sweet or toffee strip over and press into the cream to secure. Serve the cakes within 30 minutes, as the toffee will start to soften.

SHIP AHOY CAKE

❦

Serves 14–18

For the cake base:

1 x 30 x 25 x 5 cm/12 x 10 x 2 inch,
all-in-one quick-mix slab cake
(*see* page 31)

To decorate:

¹/₂ batch chocolate buttercream
1.4 kg/3 lb ready-to-roll sugarpaste
brown and blue paste food
colourings
icing sugar, for dusting
¹/₄ batch royal icing (*see* page 50)
wooden skewers

Cut the cake into three oblongs as shown on page 247 and cut the pieces following the diagram. Spread the pieces with buttercream and assemble to a boat shape as shown. Spread the remaining buttercream over the top and sides of the boat and place on a cake board. Colour 900 g/2 lb sugarpaste brown, 50 g/2 oz dark brown and leave the remainder white. Roll out 125 g/ 4 oz white sugarpaste thinly on a surface dusted with icing sugar. Cut out three large squares about 8 cm/3 ¹/₄ inches, and two smaller squares about 5 cm/2 inches and make a hole at the base and top of each square. Cut out a small and a large triangular pennant shape. Cover a rolling pin with clingfilm and place the sails over to make them curve. Leave to dry for 4 hours until firm.

Roll out the brown sugarpaste and use to cover the boat (*see* page 62). Trim and place on a board. Mark a wood effect on the top and sides of the boat using a round-bladed knife. Roll brown trimmings into a long, thin sausage and press this round the top of the boat to make a border. Roll small brown squares and a round for portholes. Decorate these and the prow with darker brown sugarpaste, as shown. Roll out a small white sugarpaste window and stick on, then lightly paint with blue food colouring. Spread half the royal icing on the board around the cake. Roll the remaining white sugarpaste thinly, place on the icing and pinch together to represent waves. Dab with blue food colouring. Roll a scrap of white sugarpaste into an oblong banner, place on the waves and paint on 'Happy Birthday' or another message of your choice with blue food colouring. Thread the sails onto the skewers and place in position. Colour a little royal icing brown and pipe on a ladder and window frame as shown.

LOVESTRUCK TIERED CAKE

༄

Serves 20

For the cake base:

1 x 20 cm/8 inch Madeira cake
(*see* page 28)
1 x 15 cm/6 inch Madeira cake

To decorate:

1.75 kg/3¹/₂ lb ready-to-roll
sugarpaste
pink and red paste food colourings
icing sugar, for dusting
¹/₂ batch vanilla buttercream
edible silver balls

Reserve 225 g/8 oz sugarpaste. Divide the remaining sugarpaste into 575 g/1¹/₄ lb and 450 g/1 lb batches. Knead the largest batch until soft, add pink paste colouring, then roll out on a surface dusted with icing sugar to a circle large enough to cover the large cake. Spread the cake with buttercream, then place the sugarpaste over the cake, smooth down over the top and sides and flatten with an icing tool or your palms. Trim the edges, then repeat to cover the smaller cake with the 450 g/ 1 lb white sugarpaste. Place the smaller cake on a 15 cm/6 inch, thin, round cake board and stack the smaller cake on top of the large one.

Colour 50 g/2 oz of the remaining sugarpaste deep pink and 75 g/3 oz red. Roll the pink sugarpaste out thickly and cut out a large heart shape. Leave to harden for 4 hours on nonstick baking parchment.

Roll out the red sugarpaste thinly and cut out a strip 2 cm/³/₄ inch wide. Dampen the underside of the red strip and press round the base of the white cake, pinching the sugarpaste into pleats at intervals as shown. Using a small heart cutter or the pattern on page 252, cut out a small red heart and place at the front of the cake. Roll out the white sugarpaste and stamp out 30 small hearts with a cutter or follow the pattern as above. Dampen the underside of each heart and press round the base of the pink cake to make a border. Press silver balls onto the white cake and press the pink heart into the centre of the top white cake to finish.

Hobbies & Interests

❦

Whether it be photography, dancing, football, trainspotting or even shopping, most children have at least a couple of hobbies or interests to their name. Celebrating these with a themed cake will be much appreciated and will encourage them to keep it up. Fans of the great outdoors will be charmed by the Camping Fun Cake, and budding rugby players will love the Rugby Ball Cupcakes, whilst the Disco Diva Cake would fit in perfectly at any teenage disco.

TEDDIES IN TUTUS CUPCAKES

❦

Makes 12

For the cakes:

1 batch vanilla cupcakes
(*see* page 33)

To decorate:

225 g/8 oz ready-to-roll sugarpaste
beige, pink and dark brown paste
food colourings
icing sugar, for dusting
^{1}/$_2$ batch royal icing (*see* page 50)
1 batch vanilla buttercream
tiny edible seed pearls

Colour 175 g/6 oz sugarpaste beige and 50 g/2 oz pink. Roll out the beige sugarpaste thickly on a board or a surface dusted with icing sugar. Dust a small teddy embossing mould lightly with icing sugar and flick away the excess with a soft paintbrush. Press the beige sugarpaste into the mould and press out the teddy shape. If you don't have a mould, shape the bears by hand following the pattern on page 255. Make 12 bears and leave to dry for 2 hours on nonstick baking parchment.

Colour three quarters of the royal icing bright pink and place in a paper piping bag fitted with a medium plain nozzle. Pipe on the tops for the tutus, tiaras and leggings. Use the pink sugarpaste to make ruffled frills (*see* page 64) for the tutu skirts and stick in place. Colour the remaining royal icing brown and place in a paper icing bag fitted with a small plain nozzle. Pipe on the bears' faces and leave to dry for 1 hour.

Colour the buttercream pale pink with a little pink food colouring and place in a large piping bag fitted with a star nozzle. Pipe a frilly swirl on top of each cupcake. Place a dancing bear on each cake and then sprinkle the buttercream with tiny edible pearls.

CUPCAKE CRAZY CAKE

❧

Serves 40

For the cake base:

1 x 23 cm/9 inch chocolate cake
(*see* page 27)
1 x 18 cm/7 inch Madeira cake
(*see* page 28)
1 large bought giant cupcake

To decorate:

1 1/4 batches vanilla buttercream
1.8 kg/4 lb ready-to-roll
sugarpaste
pink and brown paste food
colourings
icing sugar, for dusting
coloured sprinkles
1 glacé cherry
thin angelica or liquorice strip
(optional)
gold lustre powder

Cut the tops of the cakes flat if they have peaked. Spread the tops and sides with buttercream and coat the cupcake lightly with buttercream. Colour 1.25 kg/2 1/2 lb sugarpaste pink and 250 g/12 oz dark brown. Divide the pink sugarpaste into 700 g/1 1/2 lb and 450 g/1 lb batches. Colour the larger batch a darker shade of pink and use to cover the larger cake (*see* page 62). Cover the smaller cake with the lighter pink sugarpaste. Roll 50 g/2 oz white sugarpaste into a strip and wrap round the sides of the cupcake.

Place the larger cake on a 15 cm/6 inch, thin, round cake board, and stack the cakes as shown. Colour the remaining buttercream pink and spread over the top of the cupcake, then scatter sprinkles over and top with the glacé cherry (adding a thin strip of angelica or liquorice for the 'stalk', if liked).

Colour white sugarpaste scraps pink to create a marbled effect. Roll into 3 long, thin, strips then coil round into 3 circles. Push a cocktail stick into each circle and leave to dry on nonstick baking parchment for 2 hours until firm. Add a little extra pink colouring to the scraps to make deep pink, then roll into strips along with the brown sugarpaste, dampen the underside of each with a little cold boiled water and press onto the larger cake as shown. Roll the pink sugarpaste scraps into a thin strip, flatten and press round the base. Roll out scraps and cut out white, pink and brown large and small discs and decorate as shown. Roll the remaining sugarpaste into 18 large and 8 small balls in each colour and position as shown. Brush gold lustre powder over some of the strips and balls. Push the lollipops into the cake before serving.

HAPPY ENGINE CAKE

⊂෴෴⊃

Serves 14–18

For the cake base:

1 x 20 cm/8 inch, square
chocolate cake (see page 27)
1 bought chocolate Swiss roll
1 bought mini Swiss roll

To decorate:

1¹/₂ batches vanilla buttercream
blue, red, yellow and black paste
food colourings
25 g/1 oz ready-to-roll red
sugarpaste
icing sugar, for dusting
15 g/¹/₂ oz ready-to-roll black
sugarpaste
2 bought mini meringues

Cut the cake in half, then cut one half into two squares. Place one square on top of the other, then stack the squares on top of the oblong piece. Cut a curve round the front part of the oblong. Spread the pieces lightly with buttercream and stick in position. Cut the Swiss roll to size if needed, then place on top of the oblong and stick down with buttercream. Cut the mini Swiss roll in half and shape into a chimney funnel and stick in place.

Divide the remaining buttercream into five batches and colour them light blue, dark blue, red, yellow and black.

Roll the red sugarpaste on a surface dusted with icing sugar into a round large enough to cover the front of the engine. Roll the black sugarpaste into a thin sausage between your palms. Cut strips to make a smiley mouth and two eyes as shown and press onto the red sugarpaste. Press the red disc onto the front of the engine.

Place the light blue buttercream in a piping bag fitted with a small star nozzle and pipe stars on to cover the body of the engine. Pipe three wheels on each side of the engine with the blue icing. Clean the bag and refill it with dark blue buttercream and pipe stars on the back of the engine as shown. Clean the bag and refill with black buttercream and fill in the design as shown. Repeat with the red buttercream. Clean the bag and fill with the yellow buttercream and pipe a border of stars round the engine parts as shown. To finish, place small meringues in the chimney funnel as shown, for smoke.

FOOTBALL FANATIC CAKE

Serves 10–12

For the cake base:

20 cm/8 inch, round all-in-one quick-mix sponge (see page 30)

To decorate:

1/4 batch vanilla buttercream
750 g/1 lb 10 oz ready-to-roll sugarpaste
black paste food colouring
icing sugar, for dusting
red ribbon trim (or ribbons of your team colours)

Trim the top of the cake flat if it has peaked and spread the buttercream over the top and sides. Use 650 g/1 lb 7 oz sugarpaste to cover the cake following the instructions on page 62 and place on a 25 cm/10 inch cake board or plate.

Press the edge of a ruler or the back of a long knife across the top of the cake and then at two diagonals to make the indented pattern markings.

Colour the remaining sugarpaste (and any trimmings) black, roll out thinly on a surface dusted with icing sugar and cut out one hexagon and six half hexagons. Stick these in place on the top of the cake with a little cold boiled water. Arrange the ribbon around the base to finish.

TEA PARTY CAKE

❧

Serves 20

For the cake base:

1 x 23 cm/9 inch, square rich
chocolate cake (*see* page 27)
1 x all-in-one quick-mix sponge
cake baked in a 900 ml/1¹/₂ pint
pudding basin (*see* page 32)

To decorate:

1 batch vanilla buttercream
875 g/1³/₄ lb ready-to-roll chocolate
sugarpaste
icing sugar, for dusting
700 g/1¹/₂ lb ready-to-roll white
sugarpaste
fancy paper napkins
¹/₄ batch royal icing (*see* page 50)
green paste food colouring
bought iced piped flowers, 1 rose
and 3 daisies
thin pink and brown satin
ribbon trim

Cut the top of the square cake flat if it has peaked, then spread with two thirds of the buttercream. Roll out the chocolate sugarpaste on a surface dusted with icing sugar and use to cover the cake (*see* page 62).

Carve the pudding basin cake into a round ball shape with a sharp knife. Spread with the remaining buttercream. Roll out half the white sugarpaste to a circle large enough to completely enclose the ball and use to cover

(*see* page 62). Place the ball on the square cake with the join underneath. Model a teapot lid and stick in place with a little cold boiled water.

Roll thick sausages of white sugarpaste and model into a handle and teapot spout. Leave these to dry and harden on nonstick baking parchment for 3 hours until firm. Cover the outside of a small upturned plastic carton or teacup with clingfilm. Roll some white sugarpaste into a small circle and mould over the cup. Repeat with a small upturned saucer covered in clingfilm. Model a handle for the teacup and leave to dry as above. When firm enough, remove the cup and saucer from the moulded sugarpaste.

Roll a small square of sugarpaste and place on the cake with a fancy napkin on top. Cut a border from a matching napkin and stick round the teacup with a dab of royal icing. Stick the teapot handle, spout and teacup handle in place with a little royal icing. Colour the remaining royal icing pale green and place in a paper icing bag fitted with a leaf nozzle. Pipe leaves as shown and add the iced flowers. Attach the ribbon round the base to finish.

MY CAMERA CAKE

❧

Serves 18

For the cake base:

1 x 20 cm/8 inch, round
Madeira cake (*see* page 28)
1 x 16 cm/6 inch, square
Madeira cake

To decorate:

$^1/_2$ batch vanilla buttercream
700 g/1$^1/_2$ lb ready-to-roll
white sugarpaste
turquoise and pink paste
food colourings
icing sugar, for dusting
350 g/12 oz ready-to-roll black
sugarpaste

Trim the top of the round cake flat if it has peaked and spread lightly with buttercream. Colour 575 g/1$^1/_4$ lb white sugarpaste turquoise. Roll out on a surface dusted with icing sugar to a circle large enough to cover the cake. Lift over the cake, smooth over and trim the edges. Roll the trimmings into a thin strip and press round the base of the cake.

Cut the square cake in half and, following the diagram on page 246, cut one half into a cylinder shape and one half into a camera shape.

Lightly coat the camera pieces with buttercream. Roll 25 g/1 oz of the white sugarpaste out to a disc wide enough to cover the end of the lens and press into place. Roll out a quarter of the black sugarpaste to a strip wide enough to wrap round the lens. Smooth into place and mark on a square pattern with a knife. Roll out half the remaining black sugarpaste and cover the body of the camera, press into place, then stand on top of the cake and place the lens in front of it.

Roll the remaining black sugarpaste out into a long, thin strip about 30 cm/ 12 inches long and 5 cm/2 inches wide. Colour the remaining white sugarpaste pink and roll into two thin strips about 2 cm/$^3/_4$ inch wide. Stick the strips on either side of the black strap with a little cold boiled water. Mark ridges onto the strap with a knife and drape the strap in position in front of the camera.

CARNIVAL CUPCAKES

Makes 12

For the cakes:

1 batch chocolate cupcakes
(*see* page 33)

To decorate:

1 batch cream cheese frosting
(*see* page 44)
pink and purple paste
food colourings
350 g/12 oz ready-to-roll
sugarpaste
icing sugar, for dusting
1 tbsp royal icing (*see* page 50)
or a small tube
small edible silver balls

Trim the tops of the cakes flat if they have peaked slightly. Colour the frosting deep pink and place in a large piping bag fitted with a star nozzle.

Colour half of the sugarpaste pink and half purple. Model the pink sugarpaste into six small carnival masks using a mould or by hand, then roll out the scraps thinly on a surface dusted with icing sugar and stamp out 18 tiny stars using a star cutter. Leave to dry out on nonstick baking parchment for 2 hours. Repeat with the purple sugarpaste. When firm enough to handle, stick the pink stars onto the purple masks and the purple stars onto the pink masks as shown, using a little royal icing to secure them.

Pipe the pink frosting onto the cakes in large swirls, then place the masks in the frosting as shown. Sprinkle over edible silver balls to finish.

CAMPING FUN CAKE

☙❧

Serves 20

For the cake:

1 x 23 cm/9 inch, square
chocolate cake
(see page 27)
1 x 13 cm/5 inch, square
chocolate cake

To decorate:

2 batches vanilla buttercream
green, orange, grey, red, blue,
brown and turquoise paste
food colourings
700 g/1½ lb ready-to-roll
sugarpaste
icing sugar, for dusting
chocolate drops
mini marshmallows

Colour half the buttercream pale green and smooth over the top and sides of the large cake with a palette knife. Place the cake on a cake board. Cut the smaller cake in half and stack one half on top of the other, sandwiching with buttercream. Cut away two sides to form a sloping roof for the tent.

Colour 450 g/1 lb sugarpaste orange, 75 g/3 oz grey, 50 g/2 oz red, 25 g/1 oz blue, 50 g/2 oz dark green and 25 g/1 oz brown. Roll out the orange sugarpaste on a surface dusted with icing sugar and use to cover the tent (see page 62), re-roll the scraps and cut out tent flaps and trims and stick in place with a little cold boiled water. Roll the orange scraps into short lengths for logs. Place a pile by the tent, then pile up more to make the fire. Make a ring of chocolate drops round the fire. Roll the grey sugarpaste into small balls and make two lines across the cake as shown. Colour half of the remaining buttercream light blue and spread between these grey pebbles to make a river, flicking up with a small palette knife. Press the dark green sugarpaste through a garlic press to make grass and arrange as shown.

Model the red sugarpaste into a cube and top with white sugarpaste, then make a white lid for the cool bag. Roll the blue sugarpaste into a sausage and cut to make the cans. Place a white disc on each can and place in the cool bag. Mould the brown sugarpaste into a chimney and axe handle, position as shown and make a grey blade for the axe. Paint the logs with brown food colouring, add red scraps for flames, then attach two mini marshmallows to cocktail sticks and place on the fire. Colour the remaining buttercream turquoise and use a star border to pipe around the cake base.

FASHION FIEND SHOE CAKE

࿊

Serves 20

For the cake base:

1 x 20 cm/8 inch, square Madeira
cake (see page 28)
1 bought trifle sponge square
1 bought mini Swiss roll

To decorate:

1/2 batch vanilla buttercream
1.3 kg/3 lb ready-to-roll sugarpaste
icing sugar, for dusting
pink and black paste food
colourings

Trim the top of the cake if it has peaked and cut the cake in half horizontally. Spread the buttercream over one half, then sandwich the layers back together. Spread the top and sides of the cake with buttercream. Roll out 700 g/1½ lb sugarpaste on a surface dusted with icing sugar and use to cover the cake (see page 62). Trim the edges neatly, then place on a cake board. Gather up the trimmings and colour half the remaining sugarpaste pink and half black.

Cut the trifle sponge into a triangular shape and spread with buttercream. Roll out the black sugarpaste thinly and cover the triangle neatly. Repeat with the mini Swiss roll, stand it upright, cut away a slope from the top and press the base out to represent a shoe heel. Roll a black sole shape from black sugarpaste and leave this to dry for 2 hours, draped over the side of a small upturned pudding basin lined with clingfilm, to make a curved shape. Roll out the remaining black sugarpaste and cut into random curved shapes and stick to the sides of the cake with a little cold boiled water.

Roll the pink sugarpaste into 52 small pink balls and press round the base of the cake. Roll the remaining pink sugarpaste out thinly and cut out a curved shape for the centre of the cake as shown, dampen lightly and stick into place. Roll out the pink trimmings and decorate the triangular shoe front and the top of the curved sole shape. Decorate the pink shoe front with small black balls of sugarpaste and position the shoe front on the pink sugarpaste. Dampen the top of the heel section, stick the back of the sole to this and carefully position the other end of the sole behind the shoe front.

STACKED SUITCASES CAKE

❦

Serves 20

For the cake:

To make these deep cakes, use
enough mixture to make
2 x 20 cm/8 inch Madeira cakes and
divide between 1 x 15 cm/6 inch
square tin and 1 x 20 cm/8 inch
square tin
(*see* page 28)

To decorate:

1 batch vanilla buttercream
1.5 kg/3 lb 3 oz ready-to-roll
sugarpaste
icing sugar, for dusting
ivory paste food colouring
gold lustre powder
edible icing pen (optional)

Trim the tops of the cakes flat if they have peaked and trim off one side of each cake to make them slightly oblong. Spread the buttercream over the top and sides of both cakes. Using 1.1 kg/2 lb 5 oz sugarpaste, cover the cakes following the instructions on page 62 and stack them up on a 25 cm/10 inch, round cake board. Press a ruler or the back of a knife a couple of times around the sides of each cake to mark where the suitcase would open.

Colour 250 g/9 oz sugarpaste ivory and, using three quarters of it, roll out long sausages to fit around the tops and bases of the cakes. Attach these with a little cold boiled water.

Roll out pieces of white and the leftover ivory sugarpaste on a surface dusted with icing sugar and cut out the lock, handle and strap details as shown and attach them with a little cold boiled water. A plastic drinking straw is a good tool to make the holes in the straps.

Roll out any leftover white sugarpaste very thinly and cut out luggage labels. Attach them with a little water and, when dry, paint details with a little gold lustre powder mixed with a little water – you can even write a name and address with an edible icing pen, if wished.

CATWALK CUPCAKES

⟨◦⟩

Makes 12

For the cakes:

1 batch chocolate cupcakes
(*see* page 33)

To decorate:

$^1/_2$ batch flower paste
(*see* page 48)
hot pink and black paste
food colourings
tiny edible silver seed pearls
1 batch vanilla buttercream

Divide the flower paste in half and colour one half hot pink and the rest black. Model six high-heeled shoes from the pink flower paste and six from the black, pressing tiny silver seed pearls into the sides of the shoes before the paste hardens. Leave the shoes on nonstick baking parchment for 2 hours to dry and become hard.

Trim the tops of the cupcakes if they have peaked. Reserve 2 tablespoons of the buttercream and colour this black. Colour the rest of the buttercream hot pink.

Spoon the pink buttercream into a large piping bag fitted with a star nozzle and pipe large swirls over the tops of the cupcakes, starting at the outside of each one and working towards the centre. Scatter tiny silver seed pearls over the top of each.

Stand a shoe on top of each cupcake, pressing it down gently into the buttercream. Using the frosting left in the bag, pipe a small rosette of pink buttercream on the front of each pink shoe. Spoon the black buttercream into a small piping bag fitted with a star nozzle and pipe rosettes on the front of the black shoes.

SUNSHINE RAILWAY CAKE

❧

Serves 12–14

For the cake:

1 x 20 cm/8 inch, round chocolate
cake (*see* page 27)
1 mini chocolate Swiss roll
2 bought cake bars

To decorate:

$^1/_2$ batch vanilla buttercream
1.75 kg/3$^1/_2$ lb ready-to-roll
sugarpaste
blue, green, orange, yellow, red,
turquoise, brown, grey and black
paste food colourings
icing sugar, for dusting
black bootlace liquorice strips
small candle
edible silver balls

Cut the cake in half, spread 1 half with buttercream and sandwich together. Spread the top and sides thinly with buttercream, using the remainder to coat the mini Swiss roll and cake bars. Colour 225 g/8 oz sugarpaste light blue, 350 g/12 oz light green, 125 g/4 oz dark green, 125 g/4 oz orange, 50 g/2 oz yellow, 50g/2 oz red, 125 g/4 oz turquoise, 125 g/4 oz brown, 125 g/4 oz grey, 25 g/1 oz black and leave the rest white. Cover the cake top with rolled light blue sugarpaste and the sides with light green. Place on a large board, half-covered with the remaining green sugarpaste as shown. Roll the brown sugarpaste into 6 cm/2$^1/_2$ inch railway sleepers and the grey paste into two rail tracks and attach both as shown. Model the dark green sugarpaste into trees and white sugarpaste into trunks and stick onto the sides of the cake.

Cover the mini Swiss roll with turquoise sugarpaste. Cut cake bars to make 2 carriages, a funnel and cabin for the engine. Cover the funnel with black and blue sugarpastes and the cabin with blue sugarpaste. Cover the carriages with trimmings. Thickly roll the orange and yellow sugarpastes and cut a number 2 and a sunshine. Leave to dry on nonstick baking parchment until firm. Cut out carriage roofs and stick in place. Assemble the train pieces on the track. Make wheels from red sugarpaste. Cut the liquorice and stick to the wheels and carriage roofs. Decorate the carriages, engine and sunshine as shown. Make and decorate a small sugarpaste cake as shown. Roll white sugarpaste into clouds and a strip for a message. Stamp out white daisies with daisy stamps and attach with a silver ball in each. Paint the track and cake sides with green colouring. Attach the number 2 and sunshine to finish.

OFF TO SEE THE WORLD CAKE

Serves 16

For the cake base:

1 x 20 cm/8 inch, round lemon
Madeira cake (*see* page 28)
6 tbsp apricot glaze

To decorate:

1.1 kg/2^{1}/$_{2}$ lb ready-to-roll
sugarpaste
dark blue and leaf green paste
food colourings
icing sugar, for dusting
candles

Trim the top of the cake if it has peaked, then brush the apricot glaze over the top and sides of the cake.

Colour 900 g/2 lb of the sugarpaste dark blue, then roll it out on a board dusted with icing sugar to a round large enough to cover the top and sides of the cake. Using both hands, carefully lift over the cake and smooth down. Trim the bottom edge neatly, then transfer the cake to a board or plate.

Colour the remaining sugarpaste leaf green and roll it out to about 5 mm/^{1}/$_{4}$ inch thick.

Trace the map of the world template on page 254 onto nonstick baking parchment and cut round the different continents with scissors. Place the cut-outs on the rolled-out green sugarpaste and cut around each piece. Dampen the undersides of the cut-outs by brushing with a little cold boiled water and press gently into position of the top of the cake. Add candles to finish.

PRETTY HANDBAG CAKE

❧

Serves 12–16

For the cake base:

1 x 25 cm/10 inch, round
Madeira cake
(*see* page 28)

To decorate:

200 g/7 oz flower paste
(*see* page 48)
icing sugar, for dusting
brown and pink paste food colourings
1 1/2 batches vanilla buttercream
700 g/1 1/2 lb ready-to-roll sugarpaste
1/4 batch royal icing (*see* page 50)
gold lustre powder

Roll out the flower paste on a surface dusted with icing sugar and cut out two 2 x 23 cm/1 x 9 inch strips and four 2.5 x 5 cm/1 x 2 inch strips. Loop the shorter strips in half as shown and secure with a little cold boiled water. Add a tiny ball of white to each for the rivets. Do the same with the ends of the longer strips and then arrange them as shown, hanging over a bottle or rolling pin to dry. With the offcuts, model the tassel, then colour a little light brown to make the zip and tassel top.

Cut the cake in half across the middle and sandwich the halves together with half the buttercream. Stand the cake up on the cut edge and trim all round to make a smooth bag shape. Cover with the rest of the buttercream.

Colour 700 g/1 1/2 lb sugarpaste pink then roll out to a piece large enough to cover the cake. Lift this carefully over the cake and smooth down the top and sides. Press an indentation where the zip will fit. Trim round the base and place on a large plate.

Roll out the remaining white sugarpaste into long sausages to fit all round the base of the cake and two strips over the top. Attach these and the rest of the decorations with dots of royal icing.

Make tiny sausages from the scraps of light brown flower paste and tuck them into the handles to look like links, then paint them with gold lustre powder mixed with a little water to finish.

RUGBY BALL CUPCAKES

❧

Makes 12

For the cakes:

1 batch chocolate cupcakes
(*see* page 33)

To decorate:

125 g/4 oz ready-to-roll
sugarpaste
brown and green paste
food colourings
1 batch vanilla buttercream

Colour 75 g/3 oz sugarpaste dark brown and leave the remainder white. Roll the brown sugarpaste into 12 small balls, then shape each ball into an oval. Roll the white sugarpaste into a thin sausage between your palms, then place thin strips onto the top of each rugby ball to represent the laces as shown.

Trim the tops of the cakes flat if they have peaked. Colour the buttercream bright green, then place the buttercream in a paper piping bag fitted with a no 2 straight nozzle. Press the nozzle of the piping bag onto the top of a cupcake and pipe out a small green dot. Pull the bag away to make a point then continue piping all over the top of each cake, carefully filling in all the spaces to represent grass.

Place a rugby ball in the centre of each cake to finish.

DISCO DIVA CAKE

[✦]

Serves 40

For the cake base:

1 x 20 cm/8 inch, round
chocolate cake (see page 27)
1 x 15 cm/6 inch, round
chocolate cake

To decorate:

1½ batches vanilla buttercream
1.8 kg/4 lb ready-to roll sugarpaste
pink and brown paste food colourings
icing sugar, for dusting
44 brown and 44 white chocolate-
coated ball sweets (Maltesers)
floristry wires

Cut the tops of both cakes level if they have peaked, then cut each in half and spread one half with a little buttercream. Sandwich the cakes back together, then spread the remaining buttercream thinly over the top and sides. Colour 900 g/2 lb sugarpaste pink. Cover the larger cake with

700 g/1½ lb white sugarpaste (see page 62), and repeat with the smaller cake, using 450 g/1 lb pink sugarpaste to cover. Place the larger cake on a thin, 15 cm/6 inch cake board, then stack the small cake on top.

Reserve 125 g/4 oz pink sugarpaste. Colour half of the remaining pink sugarpaste a darker pink and the remaining 225 g/8 oz white sugarpaste brown. Roll out both pink sugarpastes thinly, cut into strips 2.5 cm/1 inch wide and stick to the sides of the larger cake with a little cold boiled water. Roll the reserved pink sugarpaste into a long strip 4 cm/1½ inches wide, dampen and press round the cake as shown. Press the sweets round the base of each cake as shown. Mould the trimmings into a bow (see page 63) and attach. Roll out the remainders and stamp out 15 small pink stars and 1 brown star with a cutter, and cut out the letters 'DIVA' in brown, using cutters or template on page 251. Thread wires into the stars and leave the stars and 'DIVA' letters to dry flat on nonstick baking parchment for 2 hours until firm.

Re-roll the trimmings and cut out large and small discs in pink, darker pink and brown, and stick to the sides of the cake with a little cold boiled water. Stand the letters on top of the cake, pushing some of the stars on wires in behind them for support. Position the remaining stars on wires as shown.

BABY BLUE CAR CAKE

⊂◯◯⊃

Serves 10–12

For the cake base:

20 cm/8 inch, round Madeira cake
(see page 28)
1 bought Madeira cake bar

To decorate:

3/4 batch vanilla buttercream
1.3 kg/2 lb 14 oz ready-to-roll
sugarpaste
cream and blue paste
food colourings
icing sugar, for dusting
floristry wire (optional)

Trim the top of the cake flat if it has peaked and spread two thirds of the buttercream over the top and sides. Colour 650 g/1 lb 7 oz of the sugarpaste cream and use to cover the cake (see page 62). Trim, then place the cake on a 25 cm/10 inch cake board and cover the edges of the board with the trimmings.

Reserving 100 g/3¹/₂ oz for the details on the car, colour the rest of the sugarpaste bright blue. Roll out 175 g/6 oz of it on a surface dusted with icing sugar and, using the template on page 255, cut out 14 little cars. Mark the door detail on each and stick round the sides of the cake with a little cold boiled water. Press two tiny balls of white onto the wheels.

Carve the shape of the car body from the Madeira cake bar (chill the cake first, see page 60), then spread with the remaining buttercream. Roll out 200 g/7 oz blue sugarpaste and use it to smoothly cover the car cake. To raise the car off the 'ground', place it on a thick slab of 150 g/5 oz white sugarpaste, slightly smaller than the car base, on the top of the main cake. Roll out the remaining white sugarpaste and cut out windows, lights and a radiator and four wheels. Attach these with a little cold boiled water.

Roll the remaining blue sugarpaste into small balls and press round the base of the cake to finish. If liked, add a few balls of blue and white sugarpastes pushed onto curled floristry wire pressed into the cake. Remove these before serving.

CRICKET CRAZY CAKE

⸙

Serves 10–12

For the cake base:

1 x 20 cm/8 inch, round
Madeira cake
(*see* page 28)

To decorate:

1.1 kg/2 lb 6 oz ready-to-roll
sugarpaste
black, brown, green, pink, red and
tan paste food colourings
icing sugar, for dusting
1 batch vanilla buttercream
small amount royal icing
(*see* page 50)
small tube writing icing
green ribbon trim

Colour 100 g/3½ oz sugarpaste black, roll out on a surface dusted with icing sugar and cut out enough 2 cm/¾ inch squares for your message. Leave to dry on nonstick baking parchment. Colour 75 g/3 oz sugarpaste brown and model the trophy as shown using bits of white to make the labels. Leave to dry on nonstick baking parchment until firm.

Trim the top of the cake flat if it has peaked and cover with buttercream. Colour 700 g/1½ lb sugarpaste green and use to cover the cake (*see* page 62). Trim, then place the cake on a 25 cm/10 inch cake board. Cover the edges of the board with the trimmings.

Using 175 g/6 oz white sugarpaste, make the cricketer – take half, roll into a sausage about 15 cm/6 inches long, flatten, trim, fold in half and hang over the side of the cake, attaching with a little cold boiled water. Use the rest to make the body, arms and feet and attach them with a little water. Colour 40 g/1½ oz sugarpaste pink and make the hands and head from small balls, pressing features into them with a knife or modelling tool. Attach the head with a cocktail stick. Colour the remaining sugarpaste red and tan to make a ball, bat, stumps and hair, attaching them all with a little cold boiled water. With black paste colouring mixed with a little water, paint the trophy label and features on the face. Paint a little pink colouring on his cheeks and nails. With royal icing and a small writing tube, pipe markings on the cricket ball and letters on the black tiles. Stick these and the trophy onto the cake with dots of royal icing. Trim with a green ribbon around the board.

TRUCK DRIVER CAKE

Serves 8–12

For the cake base:

1 bought mini cake bar
20 cm/8 inch, square Madeira cake
(*see* page 28)
8 tbsp apricot glaze

To decorate:

1.3 kg/2 lb 13 oz ready-to-roll
sugarpaste
red, black, orange and green paste
food colourings
icing sugar, for dusting
silver lustre powder
small amount royal icing
(*see* page 50)
50 g/2 oz fudge chunks

Chill the cake bar in the freezer. Colour 25 g/1 oz sugarpaste red, then roll out thickly on a surface dusted with icing sugar and cut out two road signs. Press a damp cocktail stick into the side. Repeat with 25 g/1 oz white sugarpaste. Leave to dry.

Trim the top of the cake flat if it has peaked, then brush most of the apricot glaze over the cake. Cover the cake with 750 g/1 lb 10 oz white sugarpaste (*see* page 62). Trim and place on a 22 cm/9 inch plate or board.

Colour 200 g/7 oz sugarpaste black, 200 g/7 oz orange and 150 g/5 oz pale green. For the road, roll out 100 g/3$\frac{1}{2}$ oz black, cut out a strip to fit across the cake and attach with a little cold boiled water. Use 25 g/1 oz of the orange sugarpaste to model two traffic cones with a small strip of white sugarpaste around each. For the truck, brush the mini cake bar with the remaining apricot glaze, roll out half the remaining orange sugarpaste and cover. Model the orange cab as shown, adding black details. Stand the truck on a small block of black sugarpaste on the cake and stick on wheels made from flattened paste balls, brushing the centres with silver lustre powder mixed with a little water.

Using royal icing, pipe details on the signs, a line down the centre and sides of the road plus dots on top of the lorry. Press on chopped fudge chunks. Roll out the green sugarpaste and cut circles using a fluted pastry cutter, cut in half and stick round the base. Press on the road signs and cones to finish.

JOLLY CLOWN CAKE

⚬❀⚬

Serves 20–24

For the cake base:

1 x 25 cm/10 inch all-in-one quick-mix sponge made in 1 x 20 cm/8 inch, round tin and 1 x 20 cm/8 inch, square tin (*see* page 30)

To decorate:

225 g/8 oz desiccated coconut
orange liquid food colouring
3 batches vanilla buttercream
various coloured sweets and jellies

Put 50 g/2 oz coconut in a bowl and, while stirring, add drops of orange food colouring until the coconut is sufficiently coloured.

Cover the round cake with one third of the buttercream and position it towards the bottom of a large board.

Following the template on page 245, cut up the square cake and cover each piece with most of the remaining buttercream.

Scatter the white coconut on a sheet of nonstick baking parchment and dip the pieces into it, assembling them on the board as shown. Repeat with the orange coconut and the hairpieces, then position them and scatter orange coconut across the top of the head to join up the hair. Use up any leftover buttercream and coconut to tidy up any holes.

Press sweets and jellies onto the cake to make the face and decorate the bow tie and hat.

HEELS & FLOWERS CUPCAKES

✑

Makes 12

For the cakes:

1 batch vanilla cupcakes
(*see* page 33)
2 tbsp apricot glaze

To decorate:

875 g/1³/₄ lb ready-to-roll sugarpaste
pink, green, yellow and purple paste
food colourings
icing sugar, for dusting
edible pearls and tiny coloured balls

Colour 225 g/8 oz of the sugarpaste pink, 225 g/8 oz lime green, 225 g/ 8 oz yellow and 125 g/4 oz purple.

Trim the cupcakes to give them a rounded shape and brush the apricot glaze over. Roll out the pink sugarpaste thinly on a board or surface dusted with icing sugar. Using a round cutter, stamp out four circles 6 cm/2¹/₂ inches wide. Repeat with the green and yellow sugarpastes, and re-roll the scraps.

Dust the inside of an embossing pattern mould lightly with icing sugar and flick away the excess with a soft paintbrush. Press the circle of pink sugarpaste into the mould, pressing around the pattern, then lift it out carefully and drape the paste over the cupcake. Press the sugarpaste into position, being careful not to touch the design.

Press the plain green and yellow discs onto the remaining 8 cakes. Using an embossing mould and daisy stamps, cut out yellow and pink petals and decorate the pink cakes. Stick the pieces in place with a little cold boiled water. Using shoe moulds, green strips and small pink stars decorate the yellow cakes. Stamp out pink daisies, purple daisy centres and an embossed pink flower to decorate the green cakes. Stamp out tiny purple stars and press them onto the cakes. To finish, press coloured and pearl balls into the centres of the daisies.

FLYING PILOT CAKE

✺

Serves 12–14

For the cake base:

1 x 20 cm/8 inch, round lemon
Madeira cake (*see* page 28)

To decorate:

1/4 batch lemon buttercream
1.5 kg/3 1/3 lb ready-to-roll
sugarpaste
blue, red, orange, black, brown
and flesh toned paste
food colourings
icing sugar, for dusting
6 medium and 10 mini
marshmallows
1 mini Swiss roll
blue trim

Trim the top of the cake flat if it has peaked and spread the buttercream
over the top and sides. Colour 700 g/1 1/2 lb sugarpaste blue. Use to cover
the cake as per the instructions on page 62. Trim, then place the cake
on a 25 cm/10 inch cake board and cover the edges of the board with
blue trimmings.

Roll out 275 g/10 oz white sugarpaste thinly. Cut out cloud shapes,
dampen lightly with cold boiled water and press onto the top and sides.
Roll out thin scraps and wrap around 10 small and 6 medium-size
marshmallows, for the fluffy clouds, smoothing over the joins. Place on
top of the cake.

Colour 225 g/8 oz of the sugarpaste red, 25 g/1 oz orange, 15 g/1/2 oz
black, 15 g/1/2 oz brown and 50 g/2 oz for the skin. Roll out a little red paste,
cut out the wings and fins of the plane and leave to dry on nonstick baking
parchment for 2 hours. Make a small hollow in a mini Swiss roll, then roll out
the remaining red paste to an oval large enough to cover it. Smooth over,
keeping the joins underneath, and place in the middle of the clouds. Model
the pilot's head, body and arms with the skin-coloured sugarpaste and
place the body in the cockpit. Roll out some orange sugarpaste thinly and
make the jacket, propeller and wing trims. Stick on the jacket, make brown
hair for the head and mark on the face. Secure the head onto the body with
a cocktail stick. Roll, cut out and attach the finishing details, rest the wings
on the clouds and attach the fins at the back. Add the blue trim to finish.

CAKE CUTTING GUIDES & TEMPLATES

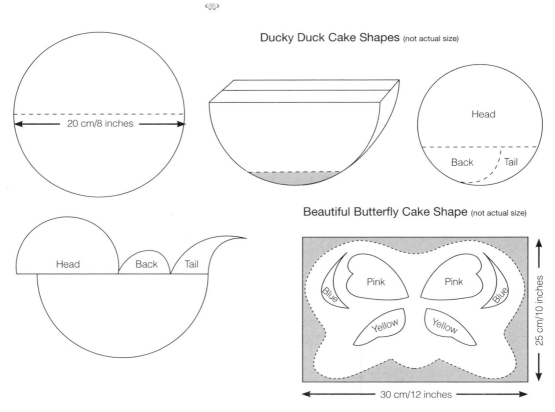

Ducky Duck Cake Shapes (not actual size)

20 cm/8 inches

Head

Back   Tail

Head   Back   Tail

Beautiful Butterfly Cake Shape (not actual size)

Blue   Pink   Pink   Blue

Yellow   Yellow

25 cm/10 inches

30 cm/12 inches

Jolly Clown Cake Shapes (not actual size)

Tie Left

Tie Right

Hair
Right

Hat

Hair
Left

Hat
bobble

Tie
mid

20 cm/8 inches

20 cm/8 inches

Smiling Crocodile Cake Shape (not actual size)

Front
Foot

Front
Foot

Body

Tail

Back
Foot

Back
Foot

25 cm/10 inches

30 cm/12 inches

Fuzzy Bear Cake Shape

(not actual size)

Ear

Ear

Foot

Foot

Snout

Arm

Arm

Leg

Leg

18 cm/7 inches

20 cm/8 inches

20 cm/8 inches

Happy Engine
Cake Shapes (not actual size)

My Camera Cake Shapes (not actual size)

16 cm/6 inches

16 cm/6 inches

Camera

Lens

Ponies in their Stables Cake Shapes

(not actual size)

20 cm/8 inches

20 cm/8 inches

Ship Ahoy
Cake Shapes

(not actual size)

25 cm/10 inches

30 cm/12 inches

Bird's
Eye
View

Farmyard Friends Cow Template

Finished Cow

Farmyard Friends Horse Template

Finished Horse

Farmyard Friends Pig Template

Finished Pig

Farmyard Friends Sheep Template

Finished Sheep

Farmyard Friends Chicken Template

Finished Chicken

Here are suggested shapes to cut out for your farmyard friends, along with how to arrange them into the finished designs.

Cake Cutting Guides & Templates.

Genie Lamp Template

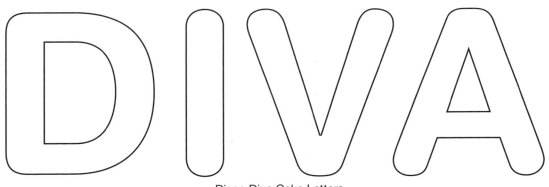

Disco Diva Cake Letters
Templates

Magic Garden Cake Butterfly Template

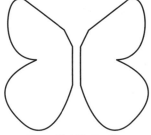

Beautiful Butterfly
Cupcake Template

Starbright Fireworks Cupcakes
Star Template

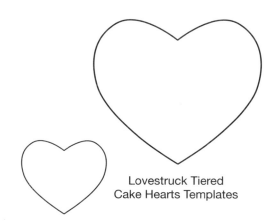

Lovestruck Tiered
Cake Hearts Templates

Under the Sea Cake Starfish Template

Buzzy Bee Cupcakes Flower Template

Sleeping Angel
Cake Star Template

Tiered Princess Birthday
Cake Crown Template

Tiered Princess Birthday
Cake Slipper Template

Tiered Princess Birthday
Cake Castle Template

Cake Cutting Guides & Templates

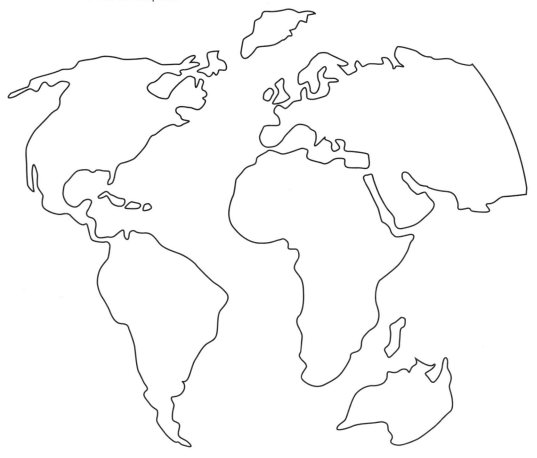

Baby Blue Car Cake Template

Patchwork Bears Christening Cake Template

Teddies in Tutus Cupcakes Template/ Guide

Carnival Cupcakes Mask and Star Templates/Guides

INDEX

꧁꧂

Kids' Party Cakes